101 TIPS FOR GRADUATES

REVISED EDITION

A Code of Conduct for
**Success and Happiness in
Your Professional Life**

SUSAN MOREM

Ferguson
An imprint of Infobase Publishing

101 Tips for Graduates: A Code of Conduct for Success and Happiness in
Your Professional Life, Revised Edition

Ferguson
An imprint of Infobase Publishing
132 West 31st Street
New York NY 10001

Library of Congress Cataloging-in-Publication Data

Morem, Susan.
  101 tips for graduates a code of conduct for success and happiness in your professional life
/ Susan Morem. — Rev. ed.
      p. cm.
  Includes bibliographical references and index.
  ISBN-13: 978-0-8160-8225-4 (hardcover : alk. paper)
  ISBN-10: 0-8160-8225-1 (hardcover : alk. paper) 1. Success in business. 2. Performance. 3.
Employees—Attitudes. 4. Self-management (Psychology) 5. College graduates--Life skills
guides. 6. Young adults—Life skills guides. I. Title. II. Title: One hundred one tips for gradu-
ates. III. Title: One hundred and one tips for graduates.
  HF5386.M754 2010
  650.1--dc22
                              2009038100

Ferguson books are available at special discounts when purchased in bulk quantities for
businesses, associations, institutions, or sales promotions. Please call our Special Sales
Department in New York at (212) 967-8800 or (800) 322-8755.

You can find Ferguson on the World Wide Web at http://www.fergpubco.com

Text design and composition by Mary Susan Ryan-Flynn
Cover printed by Art Print Company, Taylor, PA
Book printed and bound by Maple Press, York, PA
Date printed: February, 2010
Printed in the United States of America

10 9 8 7 6 5 4 3 2 1

This book is printed on acid-free paper.

TABLE OF CONTENTS

COMMUNICATION SKILLS
Communicate Effectively Through Your Image, Listening, Speaking, and Writing

LEADERSHIP SKILLS
Become a Leader

DEMONSTRATE A POSITIVE ATTITUDE
Make Your Life a Little Easier

AREAS OF DISTINCTION
Rise Above the Ordinary and
Live an Extraordinary Life

Acknowledgments

This book is the result of the contributions made by many people. To those of you who responded to my request for input, thank you for taking the time to respond and for sharing your personal stories and sage advice. Your contribution is appreciated more than you know. This book was written for and is dedicated to anyone who is transitioning from one stage of life to another, to all past, present, and future graduates, and to my three daughters who inspired me to write it.

Introduction

I've been fortunate to have the opportunity to speak with hundreds of high school and college students over the last few years, and every time I do, I am inspired. I have three daughters of my own and I've seen firsthand how competitive their world has become. Students must work hard to achieve academic success. They face fierce competition both in gaining admission into the college of their choice and in finding a job in their chosen profession.

Today, high school and college students live in a time of rapid change and enormous advancement. It is not uncommon for young adults to own a personal computer, automobile, television, cell phone, iPod, unlimited articles of clothing, and too many downloaded songs to count. Most have had more disposable income than generations before, and although they enjoy many privileges, they also face some of life's darkest moments and harshest realities.

When I received a tearful call from my daughter, who was just two months away from graduating college, I was alarmed. She was convinced there were *no* jobs available and that she would not be able to work after graduation as she had planned. One of her professors had emphasized in class that day how awful it was "out there"—that it has never been so bad as it is today.

As a mother, I wanted to console my daughter. As someone who has made a career out of helping people find work and succeed, I tried to understand this professor's motive and felt compelled to speak out. I am well aware of the business climate and the challenges that grads and others are experiencing, however, I see no point in creating a feeling of hopelessness and fear, especially in our young adults just starting out. There *are* jobs to be found—one must dig a little deeper and become more resourceful to find them. It may take a little longer to get a career on track today, but even in difficult times, new opportunities will surface.

When I wrote the first edition of *101 Tips for Graduates*, there were endless possibilities for new grads and few worried about a successful career in their chosen profession. Today, finding—and keeping—a job is a major concern for most. They are graduating at a time when unemployment is on the rise: Some have seen parents lose jobs and homes; others have friends and relatives out of work for extended periods of time.

Realizing that the first edition of this book was not fully addressing the needs of grads today, I knew I needed to update it, and I set out to find the most pressing issues to address. Since the first edition was released, technology has dramatically changed both the way we find jobs and connect with others; therefore, technology is much more prevalent in this edition. Other new tips adddress employers' expectations and playing to win the game of office politics. Also covered is the value of internships and how to find one; dealing with job loss, and managing money, a big challenge for most. In addition there are tips on creative ways to find work, stay employed in a slugglish economy and what it takes to succeed as an entreprenuer.

This (revised) edition reflects the new realities grads face and many other changes that have taken place over the last few years. While some of the tips remain the same, over 20 new tips have been written and many more updated and enhanced. Although I've addressed many of the grim realities grads may face, the hopeful tone for a bright future remains the same. Every generation has its struggles and this one is no exception. We complained when we felt they had too much too easily; now they, too, will pay their dues. It's time for this generation of new grads to step up and demonstrate their skills, abilities, and character.

I remain motivated by young adults because *they* are still motivated. I see possibilities for them because *they* see possibilities. I am optimistic about their future because *they* are optimistic, at least for now—at the start of their careers. Unfortunately, as time passes, I've seen too many people replace optimism with pessimism and either limit or give up on themselves. That is why I feel so strongly about the need to reach out to them at this pivotal time in their lives.

I don't ever want my daughters to give up on their dreams, and I don't want the bright and talented young adults who have inspired me to lose their inspiration. In an attempt to prevent new graduates from becoming a future generation of grumpy old men and women who age with regret, I want to do what I can to help prepare them for what lies ahead. When I immersed myself in a quest to find out how prepared young adults are to enter the real world after graduation, I discovered that high school and college graduates are more equipped to live and succeed on their own than their predecessors were as little as a decade ago. Graduates today know they must excel, and most expect to do well. However, I also found that many young adults have unrealistic expectations and are unprepared for what lies ahead.

The number of young adults pursing higher education is on the rise, and many students participate in meaningful internships or related work experience prior to graduation. While this is encouraging, a clear understanding of the dynamics of corporate life seems to be missing from most students' knowledge, according to Rock Anderson, Director of Recruiting Services and Diversity for Siemens Corporation. This includes understanding the politics of corporate life and the importance of seeking and gaining mentorship.

Parents are focused on managing their own busy lives, school counselors and teachers are working at maximum capacity, and employers haven't the time to train the recent graduate in need of continuing education. Through her work with employers and teens, Renee Ward, founder of Teens4hire.org, has found that the majority of young adults have very little knowledge about the basic rules of the workplace. When high school students were asked how many times it is acceptable to be late for work before it becomes a problem for an employer, the majority said eight or nine times. When asked if it is appropriate to leave the workplace without asking to handle a personal emergency, most said yes.

In the real world, arriving late for work is *never* acceptable, nor is leaving unannounced, despite the reason.

After graduation, students are expected to become responsible young adults who move smoothly into their work and home communities, but many still feel and act like children. They may have advanced degrees, a fancy resume, and answers to tough interview questions, but some lack the confidence to look an interviewer in the eye or the common sense to turn off their cell phone during a meeting.

Life as an adult is much different from life as a student. In school, if you do enough to get by, you'll pass. The more you study and the harder you work, the better the grade you'll receive. Although standards for graduation have changed over the years, the objective has remained the same: to meet or exceed the minimum requirements to receive a passing grade.

From kindergarten to graduation, academic and personal success is measured by a report card. In elementary school, equal emphasis is placed on the skills we learn and the way we behave. As we progress, we are expected to understand the code of conduct and behave appropriately. Once the conduct portion of the report card is removed, we are graded solely on our knowledge. Students gain merit solely through their academic achievements.

After years of grading, ranking, and assessing, report cards disappear. Recent graduates, who for the most part have identified themselves through their academic success, are thrust into the mainstream, receiving little or no feedback along the way. At some point, the question, "How am I doing?" requires an answer.

Paychecks and pay raises replace report cards and become the only tangible measure of success. However, neither guarantees the personal satisfaction of a job well done or a balanced and meaningful life.

Graduates rightly assume that more lies ahead for them than working and collecting a paycheck, but when dreams begin to fade and goals seem unattainable, no degree can provide the solution. Grade point average and class rank do not guarantee a life of health, wealth, or successful relationships.

The more complex life becomes, the more difficult it is to evaluate our progress. When faced with mounting responsibilities, it's easy to lose sight of what's important. If we thrive in our careers, we consider ourselves successful. Money and power can be addicting. The praise and respect we receive through our achievements sustain us and provide the personal acknowledgement we crave.

Once we've made the grade, we persevere; we focus on our work while neglecting ourselves and our relationships. It may take years to realize the impact of our neglect, and by the time we do, it may be too late to change the damage that's been done.

School report cards may vanish, but the grading continues; *we are evaluated throughout our entire lives.* The grading system becomes more complex, and we often lack the information we need to do well.

In the real world, we are graded on our *skills*: work skills, communication skills, leadership skills, and social skills. We also are graded on our *behavior*: We're expected to practice self-discipline, work well with others, and have a positive attitude.

There are many unspoken expectations in life, and they come in the form of an unwritten code of conduct. The astute catch on by observing, while others quickly fall behind. Meeting the minimum requirements of this code may be enough for some, but for those who seek an *extraordinary* life, doing enough to get by simply isn't enough.

Earning a degree is an accomplishment, and one to be proud of, but it does not prepare anyone for all that lies ahead, nor does it increase the odds of living a successful, meaningful, or happy life.

Every family, every home, every school, and every community has a code of conduct. As graduates move away from their roots and become members of the real world, they are presented with a new code: the code of conduct *for life.*

Everyone is expected to abide by this code, and anyone can follow it. Those who do will have an advantage, and those who do not will suffer the consequences. Until now, this code has only been *implied.* Now that it's expressed, you can keep it and refer to it anytime you need to.

There are seven sections in this book. Each section represents a different set of skills to master. While some people might emphasize the significance of one section over another, each section and every tip is of equal importance.

The 101 tips in this book came from an initial list of over 200 tips. To make sure I selected the most important tips, I solicited input from people of all walks of life, and they enthusiastically responded.

My request for advice for new graduates struck a chord with people who have genuine concerns about young adults and their ability to make it on their own. Many were happy to share their own tips, words of wisdom, and lessons learned.

I received responses from business executives, entrepreneurs, and employees from a variety of industries. Ideas were sent in from stay-at-home parents, teachers, writers, lawyers, doctors, musicians, and young adults themselves. Responses came from near and far and from all parts of the world. I am deeply touched by the number of people who took time to reply to my request.

Their responses were thoughtful, insightful, and candid. You will find portions of some of the comments I received in a special quotes section in the back of this book.

You can use this book in a variety of ways. Read it from cover to cover, or start reading the section, or tip, that interests you most. It's your book and your life. After reading each tip in its entirety, you can reinforce the concept by glancing through the tip titles.

This book is written for graduates starting out in life, but it serves as a valuable tool for *anyone*. Some books are meant to be read and enjoyed; others are intended to be read and applied. This book is a little of both. I hope you enjoy what you read and that you live your life differently as a result. My life changed from writing this book, and I know yours can change from reading it.

—Susan Morem

If you have a tip, a personal story to share, or advice you'd like to pass along to be included in a future edition of this book, please send your tips to: tips@tipsforgrads.com.

Work Skills

Find a Job and Achieve Career Success

TIP # I

**It's no longer about the grades you make;
it's whether or not you make the grade.**

Congratulations graduate! The time has come for you to say good-bye to your life as a student and hello to your life as an adult. As an adult, you don't have teachers to answer to, tests to study for, or grades to make. Your year isn't divided into quarters or semesters, and, unless you go back to school, you don't have to look at a report card *ever* again.

Welcome to the real world! In the real world, you'll find that success isn't measured with an A or a B; success is about learning, then living, your new ABCs.

Real world ABCs: Your code of conduct for life.

A **is for Adult.** You're an adult now for the rest of your life. As an adult, people expect you to *look, act,* and *dress* professionally and appropriately. It *does* matter what people think of you now. Maintaining your individuality is great—and encouraged. But a certain amount of conformity and maturity in appearance and behavior is expected.

B **is for Better.** Be better than you need to be. You are a work in progress—become a student of life. Be someone for whom good isn't good enough. Look for new ways of doing things, and don't be afraid of change. Strive to improve yourself professionally and personally every single day.

C **is for Control.** Take control of your life; don't let life control you. Decide what you want. Don't be wishy-washy. Life is not a dress rehearsal; every decision you make will either move you toward your goals or push you away from them. Make good decisions. As comedian Tim Allen once said, "If you don't make decisions in life, life will make decisions for you."

D **is for Dream.** Dare to *dream*. Dare to dream the *impossible* dream. If you dream it, you can create it; it depends on what you're *willing* to do. Don't listen to people who try to destroy your dreams. Most likely, someone tried to spoil theirs and probably succeeded. If you don't think dreams are possible, ask anyone whose impossible dreams came true. They'll tell you dreams really do come true.

E **is for Enthusiasm.** Enthusiasm matters a great deal. Enthusiasm is contagious. Infect the people you work with; create a more pleasurable, meaningful work environment. If you aren't enthusiastic about what you're doing, consider doing something else. Life is too short to curb your enthusiasm.

F **is for Failure.** When you fail in school, you are *held* back; when you fail in life, you are *set* back. Failure is temporary and is nothing to be embarrassed about. Some of the greatest victories are a result of the worst defeats. Everyone faces personal struggles, failures, and moments of truth. Be a student of your own failure. There's no shame in failing; the shame is in not trying.

G **is for Give.** Be known as a giver, not a taker. Make a difference in someone's life; pay a compliment, do something nice, and volunteer. When you give to simply give, with no strings attached, you always end up getting more back. Try it and see for yourself.

H is for Happy. If you can wake up every day and be happy with yourself, your relationships, and your job, you are living life at its best. I know it isn't easy; there's always something to gripe about or problems that get in the way. Abraham Lincoln once said most people are about as happy as they make their minds up to be. Don't complain; forget about your problems. Make your mind up to be happy.

I is for Invest. Invest in your future *now*. Just because you're making money doesn't mean you have to spend it all. Learn from the millions of people who wish they had *invested* their money rather than thrown it away. Don't spend *more* than you earn; spend less. Stay out of debt and *invest in yourself.*

J is for Joyfulness. Find joy and meaning in everything you do. Find joy making others joyful; make your day by making someone else's day. Call the store clerk, the driver, or the receptionist by name, and ask about his or her day. Then watch the response you receive. Reach out to others and make a personal connection; then feel and see joyfulness at its best.

K is for Knowledge. You may be done with your formal education, but some of your best lessons are yet to be learned. Become a *lifelong* learner; be a student of *life*. I heard this saying years ago: *The more you know, the more you know you don't know.* The older I get, the more I understand it. Know that you don't yet know all you need to know. Seek knowledge and learn something new every chance you get.

L is for Listen. There is a reason we all have two ears and only one mouth. Use yours proportionately. Listening is more than hearing. You are responsible for getting what someone's telling you, so listen carefully.

M is for **Mistake**. Make mistakes; make *lots* of *new* mistakes. It's the best way for you to learn. Don't be afraid—*everyone makes mistakes*. Let your mistakes get you down. Take some time to grieve over, not *gloss* over, what you learned from your mistake. Then get back up, and strive to never repeat the same mistake.

N is for **No**. Know how to say no. Say no to overindulgence, say no to risky behavior, say no to your bad habits, and say no to the toxic people you meet. Know when and how to say no and *mean* it.

O is for **Opportunity**. Opportunity sometimes knocks very quietly. If you listen, you will hear when opportunity knocks at your door. Pay attention to everything you see and hear. Take risks, seize opportunities, and create your own good fortune.

P is for **Patience**. Like Rome, your career won't be built in a day. Everyone starts somewhere, and everything takes time. Although it may be difficult to understand now, you really will enjoy and appreciate what you have much more if you have to work for it and toward it. Patience really *is* a virtue. Be patient. The best is yet to come.

Q is for **Quality**. Put a stamp of quality on *everything* you do. Seek quality relationships, buy quality clothes, eat quality food, get a quality job, be a quality person, turn in quality work, and think quality thoughts. Remember, it's not quantity you want; it's quality. Live a quality life.

R is for **Reputation**. Your permanent record, for the rest of your life, begins *now*. Think about what kind of person you want to be known as in your personal and professional life. A gossip? A backbiter? Someone who will step on others to get where he or she wants to be? Think of your reputation as your little shadow, because it will follow you *wherever* you go. Take care to cultivate a reputation that you can live with for the rest of your life.

S is for **Success.** Success isn't measured by the title you have, the money you make, or the value of your possessions. Success is what you make of your *life.* If you compare yourself to others, you will always fall short. Compare yourself to *your* goals and desires; you have everything you need to succeed.

T is for **Thankful.** Be thankful; appreciate the opportunity to work, and do your best, regardless of the position. No job is beneath you. Any job that's legal is honorable and probably pays you more in a month than people in many parts of the world make in a year. Be thankful for your health, your family, and all the goodness you see every day.

U is for **Understanding people.** Understand that people matter; *all* people. Always remember the people who helped you. Always try to help others. Treat *everyone* with respect, regardless of status or position. As you mature, you will come to realize that it's not who you *know* but who you *are.*

V is for **Values.** Identify your values; know what's important to you in life, and never compromise the things you value most. Take a stand for what you believe. If you *stand* for nothing, you'll *fall* for everything.

W is for **Willing.** Be willing to stay late, come in early, skip going out for lunch, or whatever it takes to get the job done well and on time. Most important, be willing to start at the bottom and work your way up; everyone has to start somewhere.

X is for "X"traordinary. Some things happen for no reason at all, with no warning and no explanation. You can think you've got the world in the palm of your hand, but when something unexpected happens, you learn you do not. Never become so smug that you think you're infallible. You are not. Live your life and go for your dreams, but never take your health, your family, your country, your job, or *anything* for granted.

Y is for You. You are enough. Don't focus on those who have more than you; help out those who have less. Don't feel bad for what you *don't* get to do; be glad for what you get. Don't live your life regretfully; envision a bright future ahead.

Z is for Zoom. Get ready, get set... zoom! Enjoy the ride of your life. There's a wide-open road ahead of you now; follow the road to your dreams.

TIP # 2
Your first job is finding a job.

If you aren't working, technically you are unemployed, but theoretically, you do have a job; your job is to find a job. Whether you realize it or not, you are now self-employed; you've got a job to do, but there's no time clock you need to punch or supervisor you must report to. You're free to begin and end your day as early or as late as you choose and are responsible for setting your goals and tracking your progress. You can put as much or as little effort into your job search as you want, because the only person you have to answer to is yourself. Your success (or lack of it) is up to you, and if things don't go well, there's no one to blame but yourself.

Think of your job search as one of your first entrepreneurial experiences. You are about to begin an adventure in which you'll experience good days and bad days, highs and lows, and ups and downs. Your moods are likely to fluctuate, and your feelings of exuberance, empowerment, and excitement will probably be intertwined with feelings of rejection, loneliness, and, at times, desperation. You will fail before you succeed, and there will be times you'll feel like giving up. But you won't give up. You know you need a job to live the life you choose, so you'll reassure yourself that what you are experiencing is normal; considering that the length of the average job search spans months, not weeks, you will remind yourself that finding a job takes time. It won't take long before your enthusiasm to find a job returns and you are inspired once again to pursue your dreams.

Anything worth having in life is worth pursuing, and to have a job you'll look forward to each day, you'll need to work hard to find it. The secret to a successful job search is to take it seriously and treat it like a job by devoting a significant amount of time to it each day.

You'll need to create a work area devoted to your job search "business." Your ideal office should include a desk, chair, telephone, answering machine, fax machine, printer, planning calendar, computer, and Internet connection. If you don't have all of the equipment you need, find a resource to use; don't be shy about asking family and friends or using the school resource center. You will be most effective when you are organized and prepared. Make sure you have plenty of working pens and pencils, pads of paper, file folders, copies of your resume, and letters of reference on hand at all times.

Because you are your own boss, you can work whatever hours you want, but since you need to connect with potential employers, you'd be wise to work during regular business hours. Go to bed at a reasonable hour and set your alarm clock to wake you in the morning. When your workday begins, turn off the television, stereo, and instant messaging, and minimize your time spent on the phone or in person with friends during business hours.

During your temporary job search career, work on developing new skills and good work habits. Whether you have meetings scheduled for the day or not, get out of your pajamas in the morning and get dressed for work. It will be much easier for you to take yourself and your business seriously and will improve your chances of sounding professional over the phone if you look and feel as though you are a professional businessperson.

There are many ways to go about finding a job; use a variety of resources. Don't hesitate to call a company you want to work for to request an informational interview. Every day, you should generate new leads for yourself and make new contacts. Tell everyone you know you are looking for work, but never rely on anyone else to get you a job; it's *your* job to find work and no one can do it for you.

When you find yourself waiting for the phone to ring, pick it up and make a call, then another and another. While you never want to become a pest to anyone, you must pursue the job you want and set yourself apart from others who are vying for the same position.

When you treat looking for a job like a job, before you know it, you will have a real job to go to every day. And if you work hard at getting the job you *want*, chances are you'll land a job you really *like*. It's worth the extra effort.

TIP # 3
Add a dose of realism to your optimism; know the realities of a job search.

Kim left a voice message that caught my attention. She was frustrated with her lack of progress in her search for a job and was reaching out to me for guidance. She said she started out optimistically just three months prior after reading my book, *How to Get a Job and Keep It*. She was doing the things I suggested, but was feeling sad and confused because as she put it, *no one* was hiring. The next day I returned her call.

At first, she didn't realize who I was, but when I reminded her that she left me a message about her struggle with her job search, she became ecstatic. She repeatedly told me how surprised she was that I actually called her back. I told her I do not typically offer personal advice over the phone, but because she reached out to me in such a personal (and desperate) way, I knew I had to respond.

After asking her a few questions about her situation, I assured her that three months into a job search is NOT considered a long time, especially during a recession. When she told me she was sending out a lot of resumes and couldn't understand why no one was responding, I told her that sending out resumes is not the most effective way to connect with prospective employers.

She was determined to find a job in television production and frustrated because she couldn't get anyone to talk with her. I reminded her that it is a difficult time to be pursuing such a position and that many networks and stations were cutting back, not adding to their workforce.

It never is my intention to discourage someone. Kim had many things going for her, but the one thing that was getting in her way was that she, like many others, was unrealistic about the arduous task of finding a job. Sometimes we are so focused on what we want that we lose perspective on what's realistic. Keep the realities in mind.

Reality # 1. The average job search (in a healthy economy) is several months, sometimes longer. If you are looking for work during a more sluggish economy, don't be too discouraged when things move slowly. There *are* jobs and new opportunities out there although finding one can take much longer than you want or expect. Rarely does the hiring process move as quickly as you'd like. Many companies are cutting back, leaving human resource and other departments understaffed and overworked. It can take weeks, sometimes months, for an offer to be made. Do what you can to help move things along, but don't become too discouraged when it takes some time.

Reality # 2. No matter how sure you are about a potential offer coming your way, keep searching and applying for other positions until you are certain you have a job. Kelly was sure she was going to be offered the marketing position for which she had been interviewing. After three interviews and being told what a great fit she was and how impressed they were with her, she was confident the job was hers. When they told her they were doing a few more interviews with others, just to be fair, she still thought she would get the job, but the offer never came.

Kelly was not only disappointed, she was mad. She couldn't understand why they led her on to believe she was the perfect fit, and then hired someone else. Although she was angry at those who led her to believe the job was hers, she was also mad at herself. She had been so sure the job was hers that she stopped pursuing other prospects and lost momentum in her job search.

If you've had a few interviews with an organization and they are interested in you, *don't stop looking for other opportunities* until you have accepted an offer.

Reality # 3. Sending out your resume is fine, but if that is all you are doing, don't expect your phone to ring off the hook. The content of your resume and your approach to distributing it is paramount to your success. The more targeted the selection of companies and the more tailored your cover letter and resume, the better.

Consider your resume a work in progress. You must continually tweak and update your resume to reflect your most recent accomplishments and current skills. You can gauge the effectiveness of your resume based on the number of responses you receive and the number of interviews it generates. However, even the most perfected resume is not enough. You still need to network, contact companies, and do all you can to generate interest and leads.

Reality # 4. Narrowing your job search to a specific position or industry is ideal but will limit the opportunities you find. Kim knew what she wanted and was focusing on finding a job in television. Upon realizing that there had been a hiring freeze, she expanded her search into other areas. Even when you know exactly what you want to do, if it is a struggling industry with little growth, think about ways you can transfer your skills to other industries and positions.

Reality # 5. Be leery of any job that seems too good to be true, because it probably is. You are likely to stumble upon postings that promise huge earnings, the chance to be in business for yourself, and more. Many will turn out to be scams. Checking out a company's Web site may not be enough; it's also a good idea to check with the Better Business Bureau. If someone is promising you a get-rich scheme, pressuring you to make a decision, requesting payment or personal information, beware and be very cautious.

Reality # 6. No one cares about what *you* need. It is important to offer employers what *they* are looking for. I know you have bills to pay and a vision to fulfill, but you won't go very far if you appear desperate or are only concerned about what *you* want.

Reality # 7. Do not rely on job boards to find a job. Not all openings are posted. Look for and create your own opportunities. A speaker series I attended had been sponsored by the newspaper in my area for years. When I learned that the series was based in Tampa and had parted ways with the newspaper, I wondered who was going to manage the details in the Twin Cities where I live. I was a fan of the program and sensed I could help. At first when I thought about contacting the company, I hesitated. I didn't know if they were hiring and assumed others would be contacting them too. I reminded myself to practice what I preach and to take the risk. I sent an e-mail introducing myself, then picked up the phone and made a call. To my surprise and delight I heard back from someone within a couple of weeks, and guess what? They were grateful that I reached out to them and very interested in talking with me. They did need help and were considering *looking* for someone to work with them in my area.

At a time when there was a recession and millions of people losing jobs, I discovered and went after a unique opportunity. It wasn't advertised and I didn't know if they were hiring, but I perceived a need that I could fulfill. As a result I've been doing some work with the series and it has evolved into a mutually beneficial partnership.

Reality # 8. The more personal your approach, the better off you will be. Dealing with people directly is *always* preferable. It really is true that who you know and who you connect with matters. It is estimated that 85 percent of jobs come through networking with other people. Do whatever you can to connect with someone in the field or company you want to work with. Ask people you know who they know. Seek out Web sites of companies you'd like to work for and contact them directly. And, if an office number is available, use it.

Pick up the phone and make a call. Then make another and then one more. And, just when you are ready to call it a day, make one more call. Finding a job requires many connections and lots of effort. Anyone can send a resume, but few people pick up the phone to make that call.

Kim had the courage to pick up the phone and call me, something few people do. I suggested she use the same approach to help move her job search along. If there is a company you want to work for, a person you'd like to talk to, call. The worst that can happen is that someone will be unavailable or say no.

The amount of time it takes to find a job will vary from person to person. Be optimistic, but be realistic: The more time you devote to your search, the more activity you will generate. Finding a job takes time and effort. When you fully immerse yourself in the process, you will have momentum, and although it may take some time, you *will* see results.

TIP # 4

Practice makes perfect; rehearse before you interview.

Few things are as nerve-wracking as a job interview. You know your words will be scrutinized and your demeanor evaluated. You want to be yourself, but it's not easy when you feel as though you're trying to be someone else. You're going to be on stage in one of the most important performances of your life, so it's natural to feel a little jittery, but rehearsing will help ease your nerves.

Think of yourself as the lead actor in a play. You are playing a job seeker. Since you have the starring role, you'll need to do what any actor would do to prepare: Do plenty of research to understand the premise of the story, change your appearance to convincingly portray the character you are playing, and rehearse, rehearse, rehearse.

You'll need an understanding of the setting of each scene and the characteristics of the character you will play. To prepare for a role, some actors will gain or lose weight, cut or color their hair, grow a beard, or shave a mustache, all in an attempt to look and feel authentic.

The storyline. You are looking for a dream job. The job market is competitive and you're a little apprehensive. You know how important each interview is and want to determine what you need to do to feel better about your interviews and get the results you desire.

Research. You need to research the industry and company prior to every interview. You'll enhance your performance when you are knowledgeable about the company you are interviewing with. An understanding of the company's background, mission and purpose, products and services, corporate culture, headquarters and locations, and its competition is essential. When possible, speak directly with employees of the company to gain an understanding of what it is like to work there. Your preparation will be obvious to the interviewer; you will talk in specifics rather than generalities, and you will respond to and ask questions with ease.

Background of script. Although every interview will differ, some aspects will be quite similar. You'll be asked questions, and your answers will determine how well you do. You need to have several responses prepared and memorized in advance so you are not caught off guard. You should tailor your responses to each question and industry. You need to know what's on your resume because you may be asked to talk about it, and you must be prepared to tell your story briefly when you are asked to talk about yourself. This story is not intended to be a detailed life history but a summary of what you're all about. Practice telling your story, because it must be relayed in a minute or less.

You need to identify your strengths and weaknesses and reasons for both, what makes you unique, and the reason you want to work for the company you are interviewing with. You must be prepared to talk about your outside interests, experiences, goals, and plans for the future.

The setting. Most interviews will take place in an office setting, but a few will be conducted over the phone, in a boardroom, at a restaurant, or in other public places. Whenever possible, become familiar with the setting of your interview ahead of time. A trial run ensures you will be able to find the place when you need to, and you will be able to visualize the interview during your rehearsal. Know how to conduct yourself and eliminate distractions when on the phone, and brush up on your table manners before you hit the restaurant scene.

Wardrobe. You need to look like a polished, professional, and successful business person, so business attire is a must. Whether you are male or female, a conservative business suit will be your best choice. Pay attention to detail; make sure the suit fits and is clean and well pressed and that your shoes are shined.

Hair and makeup. Hair should be freshly cut and styled, clean and combed. Women should wear subtle makeup, and men should be clean-shaven.

Accessories. Few accessories are necessary. Men and women should wear a small to medium watch and no more than one ring on each hand. Men should remove all earrings; women can wear small earrings, but no more than one per ear. Any additional accessories should be kept to a minimum.

Props. A small to medium briefcase in good condition, a professional-looking pen in working condition, a pad of paper, and copies of resumes. If you take your cell phone to the interview, be sure to turn it off. The risk of having it ring in the middle of a scene (or interview) is too high.

Body movement, expression, and posture. Your goal is to play someone confident, assertive, and comfortable with him or herself and others. You can accomplish this by standing and sitting tall, your shoulders back and your head held high and straightforward. Offer your hand for a handshake and shake briefly and firmly. Walk slowly and deliberately, keep your hands out of your pockets, and don't fidget or play with your hair, rings, or pen. Keep your eyes on the person you are speaking with, glancing away only occasionally. Vary your facial expressions; smile, raise your eyebrows, tilt your head, nod in agreement, and do everything you can to appear interested in the person and conversation.

Vocal intonation. Speak at a moderate pace with vocal variety and inflection. Avoid being loud or too quiet. A mid-lower tone will help convey confidence. Practice making statements sound like statements, not questions. In other words, avoid lifting your voice, as you do when you're asking a question, *unless* you're asking a question.

Practice and rehearsal schedule. Hold as many practice sessions as possible, and keep practicing until you are sure you have the look, moves, and script mastered. Practice your lines by yourself and with others. You should have at least one dress rehearsal and get a friend to videotape it. I highly recommend you view and review your video several times, both with and without sound. When you watch it without sound, you'll focus on the message you send nonverbally. Watching your own performance is the best way to critique and, ultimately, improve it.

TIP # 5

Get in the driver's seat.

Ruth used to drive everywhere. She drove cross-country for her vacations and drove over 2,000 miles to her son's wedding. Her fear of flying kept her on the ground, driving everywhere she went. When her health problems prohibited her from driving long distances, she sought professional help to overcome her fear of flying. She learned how to cope with her fear and came to realize her fear of *losing control* had been controlling her.

The need to control and the fear of losing control can do funny things to people. Many people say the best way to conquer a fear is by facing it. Yet fear can be overpowering, and sometimes it's easier to give in to our fears than it is to take control of our lives.

Don't let your fear of failure, rejection, embarrassment, or *any* fear paralyze you. Take control of yourself, your life, and your career. Everyone has fears, and you must identify and face yours. Where did the fear originate? Is it *helping* you or holding you back? Are you willing to do whatever it takes to control the fear you have?

You can drive your life or let it drive you; you can be either a driver or a passenger of life. You can go where you want or let others take you where they think you ought to be.

Don't depend on others for your happiness or success. You're on your own now, and it's up to you to take your life in the direction you choose. It's not easy making decisions when you're insecure and afraid of making a mistake. Trust yourself. *No one* knows what's better for you than *you* do.

If you can't find a job, create one. If you want more knowledge, seek it. You can accomplish anything you set your mind to. Only you can determine the course of your life.

Steps to a successful road trip through life:

Get in the driver's seat. Take control of your life and career.

Ignite your imagination. Dare to dream. Imagine anything is possible.

Determine your course. Make a plan. You won't end up where you want to be if you don't create a road map to help you get there.

Watch for signs along the way. Pay attention to the people you meet and the obstacles you encounter; there is a reason they will surface. You can learn something from everyone you meet and everything that happens.

Proceed with caution. This is your life; handle it with care. Never become so focused on driving that you bypass opportunities or overlook the most important people in your life.

You are about to embark on the trip of your life. Many people discover that the journey is much more exciting than the destination—enjoy your journey!

TIP # 6

Your resume will *not* get you hired.

I was talking with a couple of recent grads about their job search. Jennifer was working relentlessly at finding a job. She'd been attending career fairs and responding to openings she found through her college career center. Even though she was on her second round of interviews with one company and the third round with another, she continued her job hunting activity.

Dan had attended a career fair or two, but wasn't concerned about finding a job because as he put it, "I've been sending out resumes and posting them online." In his opinion, that was enough; he felt he was looking for work by having his resume "out there."

I followed up with both of them a few months later. Jennifer had accepted one of two job offers she received and was already working. Dan was still looking for work. He blamed his lack of progress on the poor economy.

There is a lot of emphasis on creating a resume. You want to make sure your resume represents you well, but even the best resumes can only do so much. Having your resume "out there" isn't a bad idea, but it's somewhat like playing the lottery; you might hit the jackpot, but the odds are against you. Consider your resume the "bait"; you have to do more than post it if you want anyone to "bite."

The most common mistake job seekers make is posting their resume and doing nothing else. Posting resumes is one of the laziest and most useless things a grad can do at a job board, according to Steven Rothberg, president and founder of CollegeRecruiter. com. CollegeRecruiter is the leading job board for internships, entry-level jobs, and other career opportunities. Few employers have the time to search resume banks, especially for entry-level employees. It is much more efficient for employers to post a job opening and wait for candidates to apply.

Creating a resume is essential, but only one of many important steps you must take in looking for a job. You may spend hours perfecting your resume, but an employer will only spend seconds looking it over. Do not rush through the process of putting it together. Make sure it is concisely written and easy to scan.

Your resume will *not* get you hired, but an effective resume *will* get you an interview and your foot in the door of a company.

Always include a cover letter with your resume. Some employers won't even look at a resume unless it is accompanied by a cover letter. A well-written cover letter enables you to set yourself apart from others and serves as an introduction. Your goal is to write a letter that will interest an employer enough to want more information. A cover letter should accompany every resume you send out.

Don't rely on a one-size-fits-all resume and cover letter. Make every cover letter you send as personalized as possible. Make an effort to find out who is doing the hiring and use that person's name. Tailor both your cover letter and resume for that particular position. Almost all postings will include requirements and preferences along with jargon or buzz words; parrot those back in your cover letter and resume so they can easily and quickly see that you're highly qualified.

Check and double check your documents. Nothing stands out more than a typo or misspelled word. Don't assume if you are using spell check that there are no errors. If you want to increase your chances of keeping your resume out of the garbage, take the time, multiple times, to proofread your resume and cover letter before sending.

Add the right words. Using the right words is important when your resume is being sent electronically. When an employer receives numerous resumes, he or she is looking for the most efficient ways to screen them. In order to speed up the process, employers will scan for key phrases and words relevant to the position. The goal is to eliminate candidates' resumes that don't meet the criteria and narrow down the selection to those who do. Using their buzz words will help ensure that when they keyword search their internal resume database, your resume will come up at the top of the pile.

Determine the best format. The layout and design of a resume is important. However, what looks good when you print it from your computer will look differently when submitted electronically. Most job boards require resumes in text. Some employers will specify the required format; others will not. Some will accept a resume attachment; others prefer it included in the body of an e-mail. You will need to have multiple versions of your resume available so that you are able to print, scan, post online, and submit through e-mail.

TIP # 7
Maximize your job search and your time online.

Whether you've already started looking for work or are about to begin, the Internet is one of your greatest job-search tools. You are not limited to conducting your search during business hours; you can look for jobs online and post your resume for others to find you anytime of the day or night. Yet with so many benefits, finding a job on the Internet is no simple task. You can spend hours upon hours searching, yet make little progress.

In order to maximize your time, you must be prepared and know what you are searching for in order to sift through the many things the Internet has to offer job seekers. The following tips will help you get started:

Identify the industry and type of position you are seeking. The clearer you are about what you are looking for the better. You will find it much easier to navigate your online job search if you have some idea about the type of work you are seeking. If you are unsure, you can still be open to other types of work and change your course along the way. However, if you are able to zero in on a particular profession, you will be more focused and able to use smaller, niche sites more tailored to your needs.

Focus on a small number of sites. You don't need to be on every job site to find what you are looking for. Many employers post the same positions on multiple sites to help them reach different audiences. Almost all major job boards share some of the jobs posted to it with other job boards. Doing so helps ensure they have something for every candidate who runs a search at their sites. Start by registering at the three of the biggest general job boards such as Monster, Careerbuilder, and HotJobs.

Identify a few niche sites. Niche sites tend to have a much lower profile than many of the larger, advertised sites. Niche sites post jobs at all levels and are targeted to specific industries, occupations, and audiences. Employers who use niche boards do not always use general job boards to fill the same positions, preferring niche sites because the quality of the candidates there is generally higher. Be sure to register at a few sites that target your desired occupational niche.

Register with college job boards. If you are looking for an internship or entry-level job, you will find more of what you are looking for on a college job board such as CollegeRecruiter.com than on a typical general job board. An employer who wants to hire an intern or recent graduate is far more likely to reach out to and hear from students and recent graduates if they use a college job board. In addition, the articles, blogs, videos, and other content on these sites will be geared to students and recent graduates

Post your resume and respond to advertised jobs. Once you have chosen the sites and are registered on them, post your resume and begin applying to jobs you are interested in and qualified for.

Use a job search aggregator. Job search aggregators, such as Indeed.com, enable you to find job listings that have been posted on thousands of company career pages, Web sites, classified ads, job sites (both large and small), and more in one easy to use database.

Check out Craigslist. Craigslist is not like other job sites nor is it used only for finding a job. It contains all types of classified listings, is easy and free to use, and does contain many job postings as a result.

Use keywords. Using the right keywords will help you filter through jobs to find those most closely matched to the type of work you are seeking. You can use keywords to narrow your search to a specific location, a particular company, full- or part-time work. If you are not finding what you want or are unable to come up with keywords, select from the keyword options available on most sites. Most importantly, consider all of the possible keywords that an employer might use for the type of position you are seeking and then use them when searching.

Run multiple searches. It is not uncommon for an employer to post ads for account executives, for example, without using the word "sales" in the ad at all. Candidates who search for sales positions might search using the word "sales" and not consider the likelihood that an employer posted an ad for a sales person but didn't use the word "sales" in it. The best approach in overcoming this is to run multiple searches using multiple keywords.

Set up job match alerts. Set up alerts for positions of interest to you to be received by e-mail, RSS feed, or even text messaging. Once you have alerts set on your selected sites your work is done (on those sites), and you can move on to other tasks.

Stay current. Check dates to make sure the ads you are responding to are current. It is futile to spend time applying for a position that may already be filled.

Build online profiles. Post a complete, comprehensive profile and a professional looking photo on a few select and professional social networking sites, such as LinkedIn.com. Use keywords in your profile to make it easy for others to find you. Expand your connections by connecting with people working in your target industries and organizations, among others with which you want to connect.

Grow your network. There are many ways to utilize and expand your connections with others. Don't simply announce you are looking for work or ask for help. You must find ways to offer value to others too. Respond to inquiries of others; pass along information that might be of interest; send a link to an article related to that person's industry. Be a person who gives— and adds value to your relationships.

Create a spreadsheet. Keep track of everything related to your job search activities. Note the employer, position, date of application, and anything else that is relevant. You can create your own system or may find it beneficial to purchase an inexpensive system designed to help you manage your search. Employers use systems to help them track candidates through the application process and you can do the same. Sites such as JibberJobber.com put the same types of tools employers use in your hands. Employers post the same positions on multiple sites to help them reach different audiences. The only way to know if you're looking at the same job is to keep track of them.

Customize your documents. Review the requirements and preferences in the job posting. Note the jargon and buzz words used and include them in your e-mail introduction, cover letter and resume. Using their language is one way to help ensure that when they keyword search their internal resume database that your resume will come up, hopefully at the top of the pile.

Contact companies directly. Some companies never post available positions anyplace other than on their own Web site. Research and identify companies you'd like to work for by visiting the company Web site, search for possible job opportunities, and submit your resume.

Do your homework. When you do have an interview or opportunity to talk with someone, be prepared by doing plenty of research on the company, industry trends, and by researching information about the person you are interviewing with.

Utilize free resources. The Internet is filled with valuable resources that will aid you in your job search. You will find a wealth of information offered on blogs, Web sites, articles, podcasts, videos, and webinars offering career and job search advice, resume and cover letter writing tips, interviewing tips, and much more.

Vary your activities. Too many job candidates spend the majority of their time on the job boards, yet only about 12 percent of people are hired from them, according to Steve Rothberg, president of CollegeRecruiter.com. That means that 88 percent are not finding jobs that way. Rothberg says the entire job board process should take you no more than one day. Do more than check out job sites and job boards. Be sure you are connecting with others and utilizing a variety of other tactics to aid you in your job search and maximize your efforts.

Watch out for scams. Unfortunately there are people who will take advantage of free job boards and unsuspecting job seekers. Businesses often post frivolous job listings designed to lure job seekers to pyramid schemes, buy-ins, or other low-grade work opportunities. Those who pursue these opportunities online waste their time and end up demoralized and frustrated. Be prepared to encounter these types of job postings. If you become suspicious or get lured in, do not hesitate to walk away.

Legitimate employers do not require payment or financial information from you. Do not freely divulge your credit card or bank account information, transfer money, or provide your social security or driver's license number to a potential employer. Be suspicious of anyone asking for personal information and always check out the ads and employers you connect with to ensure their validity.

TIP # 8

Go to work every day as if it were the first day of your job.

It's the day you begin your first real job. Finally, the moment you've been preparing for has arrived. The excitement you feel, combined with your desire to learn and do well, will make your first day one of your best. You'll wake up extra early and give yourself plenty of time to get ready. You'll select one of your nicer outfits to wear in your effort to make a really good impression and will leave a few minutes early to assure you arrive on time.

You'll smile at the people you see, offer to help others, and ask lots of questions to make sure you do everything right. You'll be excited to share the details of your day with your family and friends and decide you like the way it feels to be a part of the real world. You'll be excited the day you receive your first paycheck, which will be a substantial increase from what you've made in the past.

I hope the exhilaration you feel at the start of your career will last, but, sadly, over time, some people lose the excitement they once held for their work. The joy they felt toward their job diminishes, and their desire to learn and do well is replaced by their desire to simply get through the day.

Imagine this: You no longer feel the need to make a good impression, so you stay in bed until the last possible moment you can. You rush to get ready for work, and you bypass the nicer outfit for the dreary one that reflects your dull mood. You don't really care that you've arrived a few minutes late, and you don't bother acknowledging the people you see. You watch the clock as the time slowly passes each day, and by the time you arrive home you're too tired to talk about your day and don't have much to say anyway.

I sincerely hope you will never experience job burn-out, but unfortunately, many people do. Some people become overwhelmed by their responsibilities; others lose their gusto and no longer try. Sometimes physical problems lead to burn-out, but more often than not, it's the *attitude problems* that do.

As you get more comfortable in your environment, the excitement of the first day will decrease, and the pressures of life will increase. Not everyone will burn out; you can and should enjoy the work you do throughout your entire career. Never forget how hard you worked to get the job you have or the excitement you felt on your very first day. When you go to work every day as if it were your first day on the job, your days will be brighter. As a result, you will shine brightly too.

TIP # 9

If you are looking, but not finding a job, consider other options.

I remember the various periods in my life when I was looking for a job. It was not only hard work, but it was emotionally taxing too. While finding work was essential for my basic survival and ability to pay the bills, not finding what I wanted went beyond the financial implications.

When in search of a job and starting a career, most of us are looking for more than a paycheck. Upon meeting someone new, one of the first questions asked is "What do you do?" The answer to that question informs others about us. When we aren't "doing" anything or working at a job we feel is beneath us, it affects our sense of self.

Everyone has their own career path—and story to go along with it. Few people create and follow an exact plan. A slight detour off the course you thought you'd be on isn't detrimental and can even be the push you need to move in a new direction.

Betsy was thrilled when she received her teaching degree. Her entire focus in college and her internships was to prepare her for a teaching position. The problem was that she was looking for work at a time when schools were cutting back and few were hiring. She was determined to find a teaching job, but her parents were pressuring her to take *any* job; they wanted her to start working and earning money. Betsy defined herself as a teacher. She couldn't imagine doing anything other than teaching nor did she have a clue about what else she was qualified to do. But she did have options. If you've been looking but aren't finding a job, you have options too.

Consider an alternative career. I realize this is tough to do when you've devoted much of your time in school preparing for a specific occupation, but if you are looking for work in a field that is not growing and not hiring, it is in your best interest to consider other options. It doesn't mean you wasted your time in school; all knowledge is worthwhile. The skills and knowledge you gain doing something else will be beneficial too. Accepting a job in a different field may lead to an entirely new career you choose to stay in or could be something you do until you are able to find a job in the career of your choice.

Consider positions that may lead to something better. If you've exhausted all avenues in your pursuit of your "ideal" job, consider other positions that may lead to what you are looking for, even those you think are beneath you. Many people take positions they feel are less than ideal but which may be a stepping stone to something better. You are better off working, being productive, and gaining experience than sitting at home waiting for that "perfect" job that may never surface.

Think about furthering your education. When you aren't finding what you want, sometimes going back to school may be the answer. An advanced degree or new skill set may be just what you need to help you get your foot in the door to a better job. Once you start looking, you will find a wide array of programs and courses available.

Reevaluate your resume and interviewing skills. Has your resume been working for you? If not, it's time to view your resume with a critical eye. Ask others to do the same. It might be time to make some changes. If you are not getting interviews or being asked back for second—or third—interviews, you may need to improve your interviewing techniques. Practice and preparation is the key to successful interviewing.

Change your timing. If you are having trouble reaching someone, determine the best time to call. You may have to learn by trial and error or ask someone to help you out. You might prefer to make calls mid morning, but if the person you need to reach is in meetings by then, you're out of luck. When you call at different times, you'll increase your chances of making a connection.

Years ago, I tried and tried to reach the busy CEO of a company but was having difficulty getting through to him. One night I had worked late and although it was after business hours and I was sure he had gone home, I decided to call him one more time. I was shocked when he answered his phone, and he was impressed I was calling as late as I was. He rarely answered his phone and was very selective in the calls he took, but since he was the only one working that night, he answered. Change your pattern of calling to increase your chances of reaching someone.

In addition, changing the time of your interviews may benefit you. The results of a survey developed by Accountemps, a temporary staffing service, suggest job seekers schedule early morning interviews in order to have an advantage in the hiring process. More than two-thirds of the financial officers of accounting firms polled said the most productive time for meeting with applicants is between 9:00 A.M. and 11:00 A.M.

Request informational interviews. The best way to get answers to your questions about breaking into a field or a company is by talking with those who know. The tables are turned in an informational interview; *you* are the one doing the interviewing. It's easy to do when you know someone but doable even when you don't. Most people will be willing to give you 15 or 20 minutes to ask a few questions, and if they don't have the time they might be able to refer you to someone else. Informational interviews are great in person, but they can be equally effective over the phone or through e-mail.

Find an internship. An internship is a viable option and a great way to gain experience. You might even be able to find an internship that pays, but many do not. If you can afford to put off earning a salary during the duration of an internship, it may be just what you need to boost your confidence and give you the experience you need to restart your search in a few months.

Take on temporary assignments. When you want to work but aren't able to find a permanent job, consider temporary work. In some instances, temporary work will lead to permanent employment. Even when it doesn't, you will be gaining valuable experience, be exposed to new industries, and expand your network.

Start your own business. If you have an idea that solves a problem or fulfills a need, perhaps you have the foundation for a business. You can still keep looking for a "real" job while testing the waters with your idea. Many businesses are started this way. If you've ever thought about starting your own business, this might just be the perfect time.

Seek out freelance or contract work. Freelancing offers you flexibility and some control over your schedule. You have to put yourself out there to obtain freelance jobs, but it can be worthwhile. It's a win for companies too; a company contracts work when they need it and don't have to commit to full-time employment or benefits. The need for freelancers is expanding and is evident by the growing number of Web sites connecting freelancers with employers. Freelancing does have drawbacks; you never know how busy you will be and therefore have no guaranteed income. However, it may be something to consider for getting you through until you find a full-time position.

Consider a part-time job. Working one, two, or more part-time jobs is the solution for some and may be easier to find than the full-time position you want. You will be earning money, developing new skills, and feel better than if you had nothing to do. Although it may not be your first choice, it is an option to consider.

Change locations. If you are sitting at home on your computer day after day, sometimes a change in environment can provide a fresh perspective. Go to a coffee shop, a book store, the library. A change in scenery and the chance to utilize other resources might be just what you need. In addition, if you've only been looking for work in one city, consider expanding your search to include a broader area or another city.

Talk with others. Being unemployed and spending a lot of time alone can make you feel disconnected from others. Make and keep dates to meet with friends and other contacts; consider attending a job or other support group. Talk about what you are doing and seek input from others. It can be difficult to feel energized without any input from other people. Talking with others will help you put things in perspective and, hopefully, generate a few new ideas.

Reenergize your job search. If it's been awhile since you began looking for work, you may have gotten yourself into a rut. A job search requires you to be resourceful. If the things you have been doing aren't generating results; it's time to change your job search tactics. Remember, finding a job *is* a job; are you devoting enough time to your search? Do more than wait to see what's posted on job boards; ask yourself what more you could be doing. Most people look at the same job boards on the most popular sites. Dig deeper to find smaller, more targeted niche sites. Seek out and contact both large and small companies you'd like to work for; request informational interviews; revaluate and make changes to your resume. Do whatever you can to give yourself a new perspective and reenergize your job search.

TIP # 10
There's nothing more disruptive than being interrupted.

You arrive at work a little early to catch up on some of your work that's been piling up. As your coworkers begin to arrive and stop to say hello, you feel your momentum begin to slow. Your phone rings, your computer dings, and a coworker asks you for help. It's still early in the day, yet you feel yourself growing tense.

There's nothing more disruptive than being interrupted. Constant interruptions, no matter how brief, can interfere with your thought process and ability to complete a project on time. Some interruptions are inevitable and you'll never be able to avoid them entirely, but you can take steps to reduce the number of needless interruptions you have.

Just as others interrupting you is disruptive, so is you interrupting others. Think twice before you interrupt someone else; become more aware of your tendency to disrupt someone, and know the difference between an interruption that is self-serving or due to a critical matter.

An interruption is *preventable* when:

- You ask a question or ask for information you could answer or obtain yourself, respectively.
- You want something irrelevant to the person you are interrupting.
- The issue can wait until later.
- It's unimportant.

An interruption is *unpreventable* when:

- Your boss, supervisor, or other authority says it is.
- It's life threatening.
- There's a medical emergency.
- There's a family emergency.
- You're dealing with a work-related crisis.
- You risk losing a customer and need to resolve a customer-related predicament.
- The matter is time sensitive and vitally important to the person or company.

Prevent other disruptions:

- Hang a "Do not disturb" or other sign on your door, wall, or desk.
- Alert others: Tell people you will be unavailable in your outgoing voice mail greeting, in person, or by using the out of office reply on your e-mail.
- Leave your office; find another place to do your work.

- Tell the interrupter you can't talk now, and then offer to set a time to meet later.

- When someone approaches, stand up.

- When someone interrupts you, ask, "What can I do for you?"

- When someone asks you to do something, ask, "When do you need to have this done?"

- Remove all extra chairs near your desk.

- When someone interrupts you, be honest. Say something like, "I'm really busy now. Is this something that can wait until later?" or "I'm on a deadline. Can you come back at three o'clock?"

- Turn off the ringer on your phone.

- Leave an informative outgoing voice mail message and e-mail response; if you are working on a deadline and won't be returning calls that day, let others know.

- Turn off the sound on your computer.

- Reserve time to get your work done.

- Establish set hours for interruptions; let others know when interruptions are interfering with your ability to do your work.

Avoid disrupting others:

- A phone call is an interruption to someone; don't make a call unless you have a valid reason.

- When you call, be brief. Ask if you are calling at a good time. If so, state the reason for your call, stick to your purpose, and hang up.

- Be resourceful: If you're looking for information or seeking an answer to a question, try to find what you're looking for yourself.

- Take a break if you need one, but don't bother someone else because you are bored or need a break.

- If you want to talk about your weekend, happy hour, or last night's football game, do it when you share a break with someone or after work.

- If you are upset or feel the need to complain, call a friend. Better yet, let it go and get back to work—you're interrupting yourself.

- If the issue can wait until later, don't interrupt someone now.

- If it's all about you, you're the only one involved, so it's not worth bothering someone else.

TIP # 11

Your employer is watching you

Don worked hard at building his own successful sales agency. With only a handful of employees, he viewed each one as an extended member of his family. Due to his extensive travel, each of his employees had a key to the office, enabling them to come and go as they pleased. He didn't bother creating a policy manual nor did he ever question the loyalty of his employees. He didn't have the interest or the time to keep a close watch on their activities as he was more interested in generating sales and profit for the company.

It wasn't until the day his computer system crashed that he discovered how naïve he had been. Upon hiring a specialist to help him with his computers, he discovered that one of his employees had logged on to the corporation's system over the weekend and onto an Internet porn site. Upon further investigation he learned that this same employee had been job searching and spending large amounts of time online during his work day.

Although this employee apologized and claimed his friends were the ones who logged onto the porn site, he lost his job as a result. And Don began monitoring all of his employees and company computers.

Many employees feel justified using their work computer for both business and personal purposes. Some assume it is the norm and, therefore, allowed. Others know it is wrong, but sneak and do it anyway. Just because you have access to the Internet, do not assume it is a free ticket to any destination. The loss in productivity and the cost to companies is staggering. Studies have found profits increase when companies monitor computer and Internet use.

If you are using a company computer or any other company owned equipment, your employer has the right to monitor that equipment. Some companies will block access to certain programs or Web sites to reduce the potential abuse of spending work time on personal matters.

It isn't only computers that are monitored. Video cameras are installed in many workplaces; some are visible, others are not. A company will often have video cameras for safety reasons, but increasingly these cameras are used to monitor employees and prevent theft.

If you drive a company vehicle, it may be equipped with Global Positioning System (GPS) tracking technology to track your whereabouts and prevent you from using it for your personal transportation.

As technology use continues to expand, so do the capabilities of tracking and monitoring. While most companies will be up front about their surveillance, some are not. Don't assume no one is watching just because you haven't been informed. It may be too late if you find out after you have been caught; inappropriate and excessive use of equipment could cost you your job.

The following are some of the most common types of electronic surveillance and monitoring:

Internet activity. All Internet surfing, sites visited, search engine keywords, and length of time spent on sites are recorded by your computer. Keep in mind that messages you post online may bear the electronic signature (IP address) of your organization. There is really no such thing as anonymous Internet usage.

E-mail. All e-mails sent through your employer's e-mail system are most likely logged and archived (even if you delete them). For legal reasons, e-mails are often kept in storage for up to seven years. The rule of thumb is to never write anything via e-mail at work that you would not want your boss to read, including e-mails sent from work on your personal e-mail account. This includes internal company correspondence, e-mails sent to other companies and customers, deleted e-mails, and correspondence from other e-mail accounts.

Instant messages. Instant messages are usually logged at work. Your company's IT department will have more important things to do than to monitor your computer usage all day and are probably not reading every word you type. However, they do have that capability and may check up on you from time to time, so always assume you are being monitored.

Telephone and cell phone. Voice mail and text messages; outgoing and incoming calls are logged in by your company phone system.

It is important to be informed about company policy, but policy or no policy, it is wise to limit personal use of company property. This doesn't give you permission to use your equipment during the course of the day. Even though your company may not be able to monitor or track the number of calls or text messages you send on your own phone, limit your use. Your coworkers and supervisor will see that you are distracted and it is likely your productivity will suffer. When you are at work your focus should be on your job.

You may be wondering how you will manage to keep in touch with everyone or tend to personal tasks. The truth is it isn't always easy to do and will be challenging. When you are working full time, little time is left each day and you may find it difficult to get everything done. However, with proper planning and good time management, you will find a healthy balance. Some organizations do allow a small amount of time for employees to use the Internet for personal purposes; know what the policy is at your company.

Knowing you are being monitored is important, but even more essential is that you monitor yourself. Avoid the temptation to check e-mail and missed calls frequently throughout the day. Turn off your phone when you are working and check your calls when on a break.

Being focused and present at work is crucial. When you find yourself straying, remind yourself that you are being paid to work. Even when you think you can get by with it, think twice: You never know for sure if or when your employer may be watching you.

TIP # 12
You are a product; market yourself.

You're spending the weekend at your friend's cabin. You stop at the store in the small town nearby to pick up a frozen pizza, snacks, and a box of cereal. You're unfamiliar with some of the brands you see, and there are so many choices you're having a difficult time deciding which products to buy.

You finally select a pizza and some munchies but get stuck in the cereal aisle. You see several brands of corn flakes and aren't sure which brand to choose. The brand you usually buy is the most expensive; the least expensive is in a cellophane bag and is a generic brand you've never heard of.

Which cereal will you buy? If advertising and marketing departments are doing their job, you'll either buy the brand you're most familiar with or the one in the package you find most visually appealing.

Packaging is important; there's a reason you wrap the gifts you give with expensive wrap and fancy bows. You could just use a paper bag or cardboard box, but you probably don't. Why? Because when you give a wrapped gift, it is evident you took the time to prepare. In addition, a nicely wrapped gift is much more enticing than one that is not. There is a mystique and feeling of anticipation about what's hidden behind the fancy trappings.

You are a gift; you're smart, motivated, capable, and ambitious. But not everyone knows this about you, and you can't go around telling people how great you are. If you want to know how to get others to notice your gifts, the answer could be in your packaging.

When Jay Lipe, author of *The Marketing Toolkit for Growing Businesses,* began to think of himself as a product while looking for a job, he distinguished himself from other interviewees. His marketing strategy was a result of his unique packaging (how he dressed and acted), positioning, pricing (his salary), and even the copy (words) he used to describe himself. As a result, every time he received a callback from a company, he knew the company was interested in the unique skills he had successfully marketed.

When he called a woman in the real estate business to request an informational interview, he had no ulterior motive; he simply wanted to learn more about the real estate industry. One week after meeting the woman, she called and offered him a job. He hadn't sought a job, but because she knew he was available she chose the product (him) she felt most comfortable with. Jay's effective marketing and research campaign worked; he had better results from his informational interviews than he did from job interviews!

There's a reason you receive trial-sized samples and a reason ads and commercials are shown repeatedly: *Consumers buy products they are familiar with.*

There's a reason companies invest time and money developing the packaging of a product: *Consumers buy products that are visually appealing.*

There's a reason companies conduct research: *Consumers respond to products that have been marketed effectively to fill a need.*

Steps to creating a marketing plan:

Step 1: Know your target market. Use resource centers, the library, and the Internet to learn more about job and industry trends or to find detailed information about a company. Read industry publications, trade journals, company brochures, and annual reports of the companies you are interested in. *Become as knowledgeable as you can about your market.*

Step 2: Research your consumer. Interview the people you will be *marketing* to. Ask for informational interviews. *Become as knowledgeable as you can about your consumer.*

Step 3: Distinguish yourself. Set yourself apart from your competition. Know what your unique skills and talents are. If you don't know what they are, talk with others who know you and trust you and ask for input. Evaluate your experiences and identify the successes you've had and the lessons you've learned. No matter how insignificant you think something is, it may be the one thing that distinguishes you from others. *Become as knowledgeable as you can about your uniqueness.*

Step 4: Create an attractive package. Your packaging should be based on what your consumer will buy. Keep this in mind when deciding what to wear and determining the manner in which you will behave. *Become as knowledgeable as you can about your consumers' expectations.*

Step 5: Launch a marketing campaign. Use your creativity to come up with multiple methods of marketing. Determine the important selling points and right words; then make phone calls, send mail or e-mail, use the Internet, attend networking events, join a job or other support group, request meetings and informational interviews, and use any other method you can think of. *Become as knowledgeable as you can about the most effective ways to market yourself.*

Step 6: Become a familiar brand name. Keep your name in front of people. Do what you can to stay connected to your consumers. Remember special occasions, call to say hello, or check in occasionally to offer an update on your status. Send thank you notes, a brief e-mail, or a related article you've read. Never become a nuisance, but always look for a reason to keep in touch with your contacts. *Become as knowledgeable as you can about ways to become a familiar brand name.*

TIP # 13
You're never too old for an internship.

Not finding a job? Thinking about changing careers? Unsure about what you want to do? Consider an internship. If you've already had an internship or two, try another. While the majority of internship programs are geared to high school and college students, you don't need to be a student or participate in a formal program to benefit from interning. An internship provides you with invaluable experience beyond the classroom. It can give you the added confidence and knowledge you may need to interview more effectively, make valuable contacts, and, ultimately, find a job.

When Lauren was a freshman in college she inquired about an internship posted in her college career center and was told that she couldn't apply for the position until her senior year. She didn't want to wait that long so she contacted the company directly and, as a result, got the job.

Over the years she contacted more companies she wanted to work for, rather than waiting and hoping for an opportunity to be posted. Her strategy worked; she completed 15 internships during her four years of college. Lauren is now referred to as the "Internship queen" and has made a business out of helping others find and get the most out of their internships, too.

There is no limit to the number of internships you can participate in. It is up to you to go after the ones you want and make the most of each one you have. Internships can be brief or last many months. You will benefit whether your internship is in your home town, another state, or abroad. You can work for a high-profile corporation or a smaller, privately owned business. You'll find internships that pay a good salary, some that pay nothing, and internship programs that require *you* to pay for the experience.

Some internship experiences are better than others. Brooke had high hopes for her summer internship, but the description she received about the job was nothing like the work she ended up doing. Her boss was disorganized and unprepared; he made and broke promises, came to work late, and some days, didn't show up at all. She spent most of her summer helping *him* figure out what *he* wanted to do.

Brooke completed the internship and although she felt it was a waste of time, it really wasn't. Every experience teaches you something of value even if it's discovering what *doesn't* work or what you *don't* want to do. Internships expose you to a variety of people and personalities in the workplace. Some jobs—and some bosses—are better than others. You need to learn to deal with, and get along with, both the good and the bad.

Ben was just a week into his first internship when I talked with him. "It's a little disappointing," he told me. "My boss is never around and I don't have enough work to keep me busy so I spend most of my time watching videos on You Tube." I informed Ben that even though his boss wasn't present it didn't mean he wasn't observing Ben's performance. I also strongly suggested he not only stop watching videos at work, but that he find ways to make the most out of his internship.

The key to a successful internship is in your commitment and desire to get the most out of it. The more assertive and proactive you are the better. If you are left floundering, speak up. Ask for more work, offer to help others, and be the one to take the initiative.

Lauren's first internship was with FOX. She wanted to meet and talk with as many executives as she could while she was there. With her supervisor's approval, she sent an e-mail to a number of the top executives. She introduced herself and requested a brief meeting with each. Most met with her. She got the chance to ask questions, and even more importantly, make connections that have proven valuable over the years.

You don't have to settle for the one or two internship experiences you've had. If you feel you'd benefit from additional internship experience, go for it. An internship allows you to sample different industries and companies and will aid in the decision-making process when deciding what type of work you want to do. In addition, the contacts you make are an asset; you can tap into the knowledge of others and expand your connections, which could lead to future opportunities.

After graduation, Matt had been looking for a marketing job for more than five months with no success. He ended up interning for a few months with a company he hoped might eventually hire him. Although he wanted a full-time job, he decided he was better off doing *something* even though it was short term. The break from job hunting was a welcome relief, and the internship gave his confidence a boost.

A survey conducted by the National Association of Colleges and Employers found that more than three-quarters of employers say they would prefer to hire college graduates who have relevant work experience, although nearly 20 percent said they look for any type of work experience, relevant or not. When an internship works well for both parties and full-time positions are available, it can lead to permanent employment. More than one-third of the employers surveyed said the new college graduates they hired in the past year came from internship programs.

Returnships are another form of the typical internship. One of the most publicized returnship programs was with Sara Lee Corporation. Sarah Lee's chairman and chief executive officer Brenda Barnes had taken a seven-year break after resigning as president of PepsiCo North America to spend more time with her children. She was able to reenter the workforce and as a result, wanted to help others who took a break during their career to do the same. Thus she created a returnship program with the intent of helping women get back into the workforce. Other companies are creating their own version of such a program.

Whether you do an internship, a returnship, or some other variation, there is much to be gained. It's never too late and you're never too old!

TIP # 14
Do it now, not later; don't become a procrastinator.

When you were in school and given an assignment, did you typically begin working on it right away or wait until you were closer to the deadline to begin? If you had a tendency to wait and often found yourself cramming at the last minute to get an assignment done on time, you are not alone. Many people procrastinate, although some people struggle with procrastination more than others.

When given a choice, most people prefer to do the things they enjoy rather than those they do not. When you are faced with the daunting task of doing something unpleasant, it is easier to put it off than it is to do it. When the consequences of not doing something are worse than the consequences of doing it, however, you're more likely to get it done. Necessity can be a big motivator.

If you know you should look for a job, begin a project, or confront someone about a problem, but doing so is difficult or makes you feel uneasy, you might be tempted to avoid it. Most of the things we put off eventually have to be done, and the anxiety we create as a result of procrastinating can be equal to or worse than the negative feelings we were trying to avoid.

The most common reason for procrastination is perfectionism. We tell ourselves that if we can't do it right, or *perfectly*, we'll put it off until we can. One of the more unusual reasons I've heard for procrastination comes from Mark Goulston, author of *Get Out Of Your Own Way*. His theory is that people procrastinate when they are lonely. We may not want to do something if we become isolated as a result. Therefore, enlisting the support of others or doing the dreaded task with someone else is often the solution. A procrastinator can become an activator when around others. That's why people have jogging buddies, study groups, and collaborators.

Take a good look at the things you tend to procrastinate about. Identify the reasons you put off a particular task, and then try to come up with solutions to help you overcome procrastination.

For example, if you are postponing a project because it requires a large amount of time, blocking off time to do it will ensure you have the time you need to get it done. If you lack the information or resources you need, gathering what you'll need ahead of time will make it easier for you to do the task.

When faced with a large project, breaking it down into smaller tasks makes it less intimidating and more manageable. Being held accountable can be a motivator; announcing what you intend to do to friends, family, or coworkers might help, especially if they will be checking on your progress.

In addition to discovering the reasons you avoid certain tasks, determine what motivates you and reward yourself for doing something you didn't want to do. Although some people work better under the pressure of a deadline, doing so often creates additional stress for you and others.

When hurrying to meet a deadline, you leave little time to deal with unexpected problems and may become careless as you rush to finish. People have different work styles. If you tend to put your work off but share responsibilities with someone who prefers to get everything done ahead of time, you might find it challenging to work together.

When you have something you need to do, make a plan to meet the deadline. If you are overcommitted, speak up; it's better to address your concerns up front than to disappoint those who are counting on you to get something done.

Do it now, not later. Don't become a procrastinator. When you do, others will learn they can count on you. More important, you will be able to count on yourself.

TIP # 15
Make yourself memorable.

I was in Sydney, Australia, participating in a panel discussion. The panel was made up of American and Australian business owners, managers, and heads of human resource departments. We were answering questions from college seniors participating in an internship program.

The students expressed varying concerns about the hiring process. They were seeking special nuggets of information to help them get their foot in the door and land the job they wanted. Many were surprised at the simplicity of the advice they heard, which was unanimous. Everyone on the panel agreed that, when hiring, they look for more than qualifications and experience in a candidate; the people who make an *emotional* connection make a much better impression.

One of the panelists ran an advertising agency. He told about an e-mail he received from a young woman interested in working with his agency. She was young and didn't have much experience, but her creative and personalized approach intrigued him enough to meet with her. She came to the meeting so well prepared it was evident she had spent time learning about his agency and the firm's clients. Her conviction made his decision to hire her easy. There were other, more *qualified* candidates, but none who were as *memorable* as this one.

An employer lists desired qualifications for many reasons. Sometimes it *is* all that matters. But more often than not it is more about desired characteristics than exact criteria to be met. If credentials were all that mattered, making hiring decisions based on a resume would be the norm, but it isn't.

Derek works for a performance improvement company. When he was interviewing for the position of account executive, the competition and the process were tough. As part of his research he sent an e-mail out to everyone he knew asking for help in connecting with anyone who worked for or was familiar with the company. After every conversation he had, he asked who else he should talk with to better understand the company culture and he always got more referrals. He made it to the last stage of the interview process, which was a full day of interviews, including one with the president of the company.

In preparation for the final phase he spoke with 21 people who either worked for or used to work for the company in a variety of positions. This gave him tremendous insight into the organization as he prepared for the final interview process.

He wrote and dropped off his thank you notes the next day. But he wanted to do something more creative as a follow-up and came up with a plan. He recalled an old Harley Davidson ad from the 1980s: It was a picture of a biker's arm with a Harley tattoo and a caption that read, "When was the last time you felt this strongly about anything?"

That night, he did 100 arm curls to pump up his arms, and had his wife draw a tattoo of the company logo on his arm. She photographed it, inserted the same caption, and printed off three copies. He put each picture in an 8x10 frame and delivered one to the president, senior vice president of sales and marketing, and the area vice president the next day.

Forty-five minutes after dropping off the photos he received a phone call and was offered the job. They told him it was the most creative follow-up they had ever seen. He later learned that he was competing against three other candidates who were more qualified than he was, yet he was the one who got the job.

It's been five years, but they are still talking about what he did to this day. Derek managed to make a most memorable impression!

He is convinced that people think too logically when pursuing a job, assuming the best and most qualified candidate always gets the offer. He and numerous others are proof that there are other important factors to be considered.

Derek wanted the connection with the decision makers to be an *emotional* connection. Whether you are looking for a job, establishing a relationship with a potential client, or meeting someone for the first time, if you want a meaningful connection, make an emotional connection. Put in the extra effort by thinking in terms of what that person needs or wants and what you have to offer. Following up and staying in touch with your contacts from time to time will not only help you stay connected, it will help people *feel* connected and make them more likely to remember you.

How are *you* connecting with the various influencers and decision makers you meet with? Are you doing enough to get by or seeking creative ways to connect? If you want people to remember you, *make yourself memorable!*

TIP # 16
There is life after a layoff.

Aaron graduated with honors. He secured an internship and then was offered a job with the firm of his choice. He was fulfilling his dream of working on Wall Street and living in New York City. Three months into his training, the program was cancelled. Aaron was out of a job and living his biggest nightmare.

Aaron did everything right, yet through no fault of his own he was unemployed. However, he is not alone; he is just one of many whose dreams and hopes have been dashed.

Being laid off is devastating no matter what the reason. We can rationalize the reasons, but being let go from a job hurts. At first the pain comes from the feeling of rejection and disappointment; the loss of something that was a part of you. Even the most confident people feel a blow to their self-esteem.

Once the reality hits, fear and anxiety can set in. Being ousted from the security of a job creates uncertainty about the future. Although losing a job is upsetting, putting it in perspective is important.

Should you find yourself suddenly out of a job, consider the following:

Don't panic. Your world may feel as if it has been turned upside down, but sit down and take a deep breath. Everyone has career disappointments and setbacks; it is part of what creates character. Do what you can to stay calm and rational. Control your impulses; this isn't the time to seek revenge or make irrational decisions. Chances are that years from now you will look back on this experience and be able to see how it contributed to the direction of your future. You will get through this.

Don't personalize your layoff. When decisions are made due to downsizing, restructuring, or other economic reasons, it isn't about you. It's about company direction and the bottom line. Although it may be difficult not to take it personally, it's important to remind yourself that the decision wasn't personal. It is very difficult for the person who has to let you go and for others who are left behind. A layoff affects everyone.

Leave on a good note. Your last day on the job is just as important as the first. Your employment is ending, but your connection to those you worked with can be long lasting. Always do what you can to leave on a positive note with your reputation intact. Finish all of your work, leave any and all essential information, and make yourself available to answer questions once you are gone. If you have an exit interview, use it to your advantage, not to vent or complain. Ask questions about your performance that will help you in the future and thank the interviewer for the employment opportunity and taking the time to meet with you.

Talk about your feelings. You need to process what's happened and you don't have to make sense of this on your own. Talking with others can be therapeutic. Talk to your family and friends about your feelings. Consider attending a job-loss support group. It's always helpful to talk with others who've been through a similar situation.

Focus on your accomplishments. The loss of a job can cause even the most confident people a hit to their self-esteem. Be sure to remind yourself of the successes you've had. Focus on your strengths and accomplishments.

Give yourself some time. Give yourself a little time to grieve the loss, to accept what's happened, and to gather your thoughts before moving into the next phase of your life.

Don't be embarrassed. Years ago being let go might have been something to be embarrassed about. The stigma that used to be attached to being "fired" is gone; layoffs are a part of the ongoing economic struggles and restructuring of businesses that has become commonplace. There is no need to be embarrassed or cover up the real reason you are seeking work. If you are laid off because of something you did, you can still find a way to talk about it without shame as long as you own up to your part in it. There are a number of reasons a job doesn't work out.

Spread the word. If you didn't get to say good-bye to your coworkers, customers, or vendors, get in touch with as many as you can. Let them know you are gone and how to get in touch with you. Stay connected to as many people as possible and let them know you are back in the job market. You never know who might help make the connection to your next job opportunity.

Don't badmouth the company. No matter how betrayed you feel or how bad a decision you think the layoff was, avoid belittling and badmouthing the company or people in it. Complaining will reflect poorly on you and keep you stuck in the past.

Get a handle on your finances. If you are able to file for unemployment do not delay. It will help to have money coming in and enable you to get a better grasp on your finances once you know what you have coming and for how long. It is wise to curtail any unnecessary spending and cut back where you can.

Get busy. Update your resume and spread the word; reach out to your business contacts and friends. Let others know you are in the job market again. Start searching to see what's out there and preparing for your job search.

Consider the alternatives. If you aren't sure what you want to do or are having trouble finding something, consider your options. Is this a good time to go back to school, learn a new skill, move into a different field, or start your own business? Is working part time, temp jobs, or freelancing an option?

Focus on your accomplishments. Your ability to bounce back after a layoff is an asset and will be respected by others. When you are networking and interviewing for jobs, don't dwell on the layoff. Focus on your accomplishments, the things you learned, and what you have to offer.

Most people will tell you that they are better off as a result of their layoff although it takes time to view it that way. For some it is the push they need to move onto another career or pursue dreams that have been on hold.

I hope you are able to decide when to leave a job rather than having that decision made for you. But if you do end up getting the dreaded pink slip, you will get through it. *There is life after a layoff.*

Communication Skills

Communicate Effectively Through Your Image, Listening, Speaking, and Writing

TIP # 17
Your image speaks volumes about you.

You probably already know that image is important, but do you know just how important it is when applying for a job or establishing yourself as a credible business person? Have you thought about your image and what it communicates to others? Do you know what image you need to project as you transform yourself from a professional student to an employable professional? Your image is the first thing people see when they meet or greet you. Your image is who you are to others. Your image will influence how people view you and respond to you. Your image is one of your most valuable career tools. Do you know what your image says about you?

The way you look sends a message. Without uttering a word you communicate how you feel about yourself and others. If you don't care enough to pay attention to your appearance, people will draw their own conclusions and may think you don't care about anything. Chances are others won't pay much attention to you. If you don't look as though you take yourself or your career seriously, no one will take you seriously either. If you look like you are still in school, you won't look as though you are ready for the business world, and you will reduce your chances of a job offer or promotion.

You're competing with others who match your knowledge and ability; you can differentiate yourself by the way you look and act. If you look successful, you'll increase your chances of becoming successful. Take some time to craft an image that will help you achieve your objectives. Consider your image your most valuable career tool.

If you haven't done so yet, it may be time for you to do an image makeover. You might not feel you can afford to buy new clothes, but you can't afford not to. You don't need to purchase an entirely new wardrobe, but you do need to have at least one good suit to wear to interviews and a few additional pieces to mix and match. You don't want to wear the same outfit every day or show up at the second or third interview looking as though you never change your clothes.

As you create your professional image, consider the nature of the industry you will be working in when deciding how formally or informally you will dress. Even casual workplaces have guidelines; what's considered appropriate casual wear for work is much different from the casual attire you've been accustomed to.

You don't need to purchase an entirely new wardrobe for work; a few basic pieces are all you need to get started. No one will notice when you are wearing the same pair of dark slacks you wore the day before as long as you change the shirt, jacket, or accessories you wear with them.

Purchase the best quality, work-appropriate clothing you can afford. You're better off owning fewer articles of *quality* clothing than a large quantity of poor quality. When you shop for clothes to wear to work, avoid trendy styles. It's important to look up to date, but you don't need to wear all the latest fashions. Classic clothing will be a better investment, and you will be able to wear your clothes longer if you buy items that don't go out of style quickly.

Watch for sales and special discounts, and you should never have to pay full price for your business clothes. Check out second-hand stores, eBay and other online resources. If you need help with your shopping and deciding what the best look is for work, ask a salesclerk, mentor, or trusted friend. Stay away from clothing that is too tight, too loose, too short, too long, too youthful, or provocative. Looking sexy will not help you look professional; it does the opposite. You don't want your body to be the focus of attention, and it will be if you emphasize it.

Your hair, makeup, hands, nails, shoes, briefcase, and accessories also play an important role in your image. Long hair and nails, high heels, clunky shoes, gaudy jewelry, and trendy styles all diminish your efforts to appear more professional. People are likely to respond negatively to visible tattoos and face or body piercings, so do what you can to cover up.

When your image reflects your confidence, ability, ambition, and desire to succeed, it will be obvious to others. You won't have to work as hard to convince others of your intentions because they will be apparent.

If you look like a student, you'll be treated like a student. If you look like you're stuck in the past, you'll miss out on future opportunities. But if you look successful, you'll increase your chances of becoming successful. Never, ever, underestimate the power of your image.

TIP # 18
Turn off your cell phone.

I was speaking to a group of mothers and daughters and I was ready to bring my talk to a close. The moment I waited for had arrived; I surprised my mother by asking her to join me onstage. I turned toward her and started to read the poem I wrote about mothers and daughters. I could see tears filling the rims of my mother's eyes, and I felt a lump in the back of my throat. The room remained still, and the moment was heavy with richness, until it was abruptly interrupted by a ringing cell phone.

Everyone's attention shifted from the stage to the audience. People began chattering and snickering, and more than a few women pulled out a purse to glance at their phone. By the time the excitement from the disturbance subsided, the poem I spent hours writing and the mood I worked so hard to create had evaporated. And although I tried, I never got it back.

It only takes one person, one phone, and one second, to alter the tone of a meaningful experience, while overshadowing the memory of a pivotal moment or important event. Sadly, my experience is not unique; cell phones have been responsible for disrupting funerals, weddings, and meetings, and can be heard ringing in places of worship, hospitals, classrooms, restaurants, and more. Even though announcements to "turn off your cell phone" are made and signs displayed, people bring their phones and either refuse or forget to turn them off.

If you think turning the sound off is equivalent to turning your phone off, think again. A phone that is vibrating can be just as disruptive as a ringing phone. When making a call would be disruptive you may think sending a text is the solution, but if you are in a meeting or a public place it can be both rude and annoying to others. I've been in movie theatres and Broadway plays and witnessed people around me texting during the show. I didn't *hear* anything, but the bright light was just as disturbing and distracting.

I have to remind my daughters that it is rude when they are out to dinner with *me* to be texting *others*. I am amazed at how often I see people out somewhere; two or more people together, yet not connected to each other as they text or talk with others on the phone.

Do you have difficulty turning off your phone for a few hours or when out with friends? Do you wake up during the night to check for messages? Texting can be addicting. If you are used to texting friends and family throughout the day it may be a difficult habit to break. For some, breaking the addiction is a serious problem requiring professional help.

Bring a cell phone to a job interview and it can prove disastrous; 86 percent of employers said they would automatically reject an otherwise qualified candidate who accepted a phone call during an interview, according to a Vault.com poll.

When you have a job, frequent use of the phone for personal reasons will not only interfere with your productivity, it could cost you your job. Before making any assumptions about using your phone, find out what the company policy is for personal phone use.

Appropriate cell phone use is largely common sense, but that knowledge is seldom enough to resist the temptation to answer a call or send a quick text. Following are a few reminders about basic cell phone etiquette:

- Even if your company permits personal cell phone use, limit your time on the phone.

- If you must keep your phone on during work hours, turn the ringer off and let calls go to voice mail.

- Check messages during break time and do it away from your desk.

- Speak quietly and do not use the speakerphone when in a public place; no one wants to hear your entire conversation.

- Save personal conversations for private locations.

- Avoid the temptation to check for messages, text, or e-mail when with others. If you are waiting for an important call or message, tell the people you are with ahead of time.

● Think twice about the ringtone and ringback tone you select. Some songs may be inappropriate in a business setting and offensive to others.

● Avoid engaging in lengthy conversations in public places and avoid talking on your phone in a public restroom.

● Practice safe driving and never text while driving.

Don't let your cell phone distract you or be a distraction to others. Be present with people; every interaction will be more meaningful as a result.

TIP # 19
Give yourself a voice over.

My daughter, Samantha, was eight years old and excited to share the events of her day. She was laughing and interrupting herself as she tried to get through the story she attempted to tell, and we were laughing along with her. When we realized how many times she kept using the word *okay*, listening to her tell the story became even funnier.

When I brought it to her attention and suggested she stop saying *okay* she agreed by saying, "Okay, I will." Every time I stopped her, she'd pause for a moment to collect her thoughts, and begin again. "Okay," she'd say, and then she'd laugh. "Okay, okay," and it happened again and again. The harder she tried, the more obvious it became; she wasn't okay without saying *okay*.

Samantha said *okay* when she needed some time to collect her thoughts. Instead of pausing in silence to think what to say next, she passed the time by saying *okay*. The next story she told, I counted 17 times she said *okay*. If you think reading this is frustrating, imagine listening to it!

Speech patterns are hard to break. When you are used to saying *um*, *ah*, or *okay*, you may not even realize you are saying those things. But other people do. When you use speech fillers repeatedly, other people can't help but notice. The problem is that it often becomes the *only* thing noticed, and the meaningful things you say get overlooked.

I remember a substitute teacher I had in high school. Her problem communicating her thoughts was so profound that I've never forgotten it. Her opening comments went something like this: "Um, today, um, I, um, need to, um, work with you, um, on the um, um, chapter, um, on um, um." I don't remember anything else about the class, the teacher, or that day, but I do remember my impression and surprise at the number of *um*'s she said. I remember many of the students trying to hold back their laughter. For some, it was funny. For others, it was distracting and interfered with their ability to listen and understand what she was trying to say. For many, it was a source of irritation; her overuse of the word *um* made people feel uncomfortable. As I think about it now, I wonder if it might have been one of her first days teaching. She must have been nervous or terribly unprepared.

Being prepared is important. There will be times, however, when you are not as prepared as you'd like to be or caught off guard when you're asked a question. Whenever you're asked a question or having a conversation, you need time to process your thoughts and prepare your response.

No one wants to look dumb or seem unprepared, so when the pressure is on, we end up speaking when we have nothing to say. *Um*, *ah*, *er* are the *noises*, not the *words*, we mutter as we collect our thoughts and search for more effective words to say. Silence isn't as bad as you think. A pause here and there can be a welcome relief.

Become aware of the jargon you use and the manner in which you speak. The way you talk may be the norm around your friends but might sound abnormal around other people. When negative speech patterns are brought to your attention, you can replace them with different words or, if you'd prefer, with silent pauses.

Listen to people of *all* ages, and notice their manner of speech. What makes children *sound* like children? What makes teenagers *sound* like teens? Which teachers are easier to listen to, and which ones make you squirm or seethe? Do their statements sound like statements? Does their pitch go up or down? Do some people sound too squeaky or speak in monotone? Which styles of speech do you find most pleasing, and which styles are most frequently used?

Pay attention to your manner of speech, and make sure you communicate your thoughts to others clearly, concisely, and professionally. As you increase your awareness of speech patterns, be sure your statements sound like statements; you don't want to sound as if you are asking a question when you're not. *When you feel strongly about something, say it with confidence and sound as though you mean what you say.* "**I feel strongly about this.**" You're not seeking approval and you're not asking permission; you are making a *declaration*. Once you say it, *stop talking*.

When the tone of your voice goes *up* at the end of a sentence, instead of *down*, you undermine your intent and cause confusion for your listener. Instead of *making a declaration*, you *sound* as though you're *asking a question*.

When you make a statement that sounds like a question, you *sound unsure* of yourself, as if you need permission to feel the way you do. "I feel strongly? about this?" As a result of your "uptalk" (which comes from the higher tone at the end of your words and/ or sentence), and your *lack of confidence* in your words (which comes from less emphasis on certain words), your listener interprets your statement this way: "I *think* I feel strongly, but I'm not really sure. Do *you* think it's *okay* if I do?"

There are other ways in which we undermine the intent of our conversations. Sometimes we use repetitive words or words that don't belong in a sentence at all. If you are asked why *you* are the best person for a job, be sure to answer clearly and concisely. Imagine an interviewer hearing this response:

"Well, I don't know, I mean, I think? I'd be really good? You know what I mean? Whatever, I really think? I'm really qualified? Like, this would be a cool place to work and everything? I work really hard, I catch on really fast, and like, I've got really good references and whatnot."

Give yourself a voice over:

Get a clue. Pay attention to the way professional business people talk and sound.

Lower your pitch. The higher your pitch, the less appealing and more insecure you sound.

Turn up or down the volume. Speak up to be heard, but never so loudly you disturb other people.

Slow down. Take time to express your thoughts; slow down so people can understand you.

Watch your tone. If you say you are not upset but you sound irritated, your listener will assume you are irritated. The way you *sound* will overshadow the words you *say*.

Vary your inflection. You will sound more interesting when you do.

Emphasize the right words. Place emphasis where it belongs. If you have a point to make, emphasize your point.

Use proper grammar. "Ya ain't gunna go nowhere when ya dunno nothin bout grammah."

Enunciate. Speak clearly; avoid garbled speech and mumbling.

Get rid of speech fillers. Minimize your use of the *ums*, *ahs*, *ers*, and *okays* that take up space in your speech.

TIP # 20

Manage your image on the Internet.

I've spent the vast part of my career reinforcing the importance of one's image. When all else is equal, image is often the determining factor in selecting one job candidate over another or in deciding who to promote. What you wear to an interview or an important meeting matters. Fair or not, you will, at times, be judged solely by your image. It is imperative you craft an image that reflects the best of who you are both in person and on the Internet.

Whether you are seeking employment or a new place to rent, chances are that employer and landlord will conduct a search in order to learn more about you. Details about you are widely accessible and available to anyone interested enough to investigate. If you wanted to learn more about someone, you'd probably do a search on the Internet. When an employer wants to gather information about a potential job candidate, he or she will use the Internet. As long as you monitor your image online you have little to be concerned about. However, if you have been careless with your Internet use, beware: It can come back to haunt you.

Do you have any idea what people will find if they do a search on you? It is imperative you know what your Internet image is and ensure it's appropriate. It isn't difficult to find out and is something worth taking the time to do. The best way to find out is by doing your own research (or search). Put your name in several search engines such as Google, Bing, and Yahoo to see for yourself what others will see when they do the same.

When you search, it is often helpful to include a geographic identifier, such as your state; this is especially important if you have a common name. Search engines can find especially personal information about you primarily from tagged images, social media sites, and public databases. View the information from the eyes of an employer. You might be surprised by what comes up, but hopefully you won't. Sometimes it's the most embarrassing moments and personal details that are captured in search engine results. Once information is on the Internet it can be difficult to remove, but it is not impossible. Do what you can to get rid of any and all inappropriate content. Fairly simple things you can do are to request Web sites to remove links to unfavorable content (although this can be a gamble) and for you to remove tags of yourself in images. There are additional ways to hide unflattering information online, but you may need to enlist the help of others.

Use the Internet wisely and think carefully before posting any comments or pictures from this point forward. Even once you are employed your employer may conduct random searches as a way to keep tabs on you. Think twice before posting pictures or comments for everyone to see, and if you aren't sure about posting something, you are better off erring on the side of caution. When using social networking sites, opt for strict privacy controls and avoid posting public comments unless you are fine with any and everyone viewing them.

Eliminating anything you feel is a negative reflection of you is one way to improve your Internet image; adding appropriate and positive content is another. Creating your own online profiles, writing a blog or launching your own Web site enables you to further control the content. In addition you are able to showcase your writing, creativity, and other accomplishments.

Be sure to monitor and maintain your online image on a regular basis. Conduct monthly searches on yourself to see if any new (or disparaging) information pops up. In addition, consider setting up search engine alerts, utilizing blog search engines, and whatever else you can do to stay informed and in control of your online image.

TIP # 21
Watch your tone when you're on the phone.

Meeting with someone in person is advantageous. Talking with someone face to face is the most personal and direct way to communicate. Seize opportunities to conduct interviews in person, meet clients in their offices, or discuss problems personally with other people. But when distance makes it too difficult or time constraints limit your options, the next best thing to a personal conversation is to talk over the phone. You might be more comfortable communicating by e-mail, but e-mail can too easily be misconstrued and tends to feel impersonal. Since it's most efficient to take care of matters as they arise, using the phone is often the most practical option.

Many of your initial conversations will occur over the phone. The person on the other end cannot see you, but you *will* be making an impression about yourself by your manner and the way you sound. Your ability to skillfully use the phone is crucial to your overall success. Learn to use it proficiently, and the phone will become one of your most valuable business tools.

It can be difficult reaching people directly and might take several calls before you speak with the person you want. You can always leave a message, but there's no guarantee it will be returned. Don't give up when you fail to reach someone, and don't avoid using the phone. The more you use it, the more comfortable and efficient you'll become.

When you know how to use the telephone effectively, you increase your comfort level, save time, and are better able to keep in touch with others. You may be thinking you already know how to use the telephone, but the *way* you use it is about to change. Your friends may not care how you sound on the phone, but when you call a potential employer or important client, it matters to the person on the other end. Your manner and tone will either help or hurt you, determining the way others respond to you. Every time you have a conversation with someone by phone, you validate, improve, or diminish the impression that person has about you.

A phone conversation is similar to any other type of conversation. If you had a face-to-face meeting with someone and the person you were with was working on the computer, glancing through mail, or carrying on another conversation instead of looking at you, how would you feel?

It's tempting to continue to work while you talk on the phone because you feel you are being more productive, but you are not accomplishing as much as you think. You're more likely to miss what you need to hear and overlook something you need to do. Ineffective communication can be costly. If you do not listen attentively to the person who is talking, your risk of misunderstanding increases dramatically. It's impossible to take notes while you're doing other things, and doing too many things at once leads to sloppy work and costly errors.

Although the person on the other end of the phone cannot see you, you are not as invisible as you think. Sound becomes amplified through the phone; if you are typing, chewing, or whispering, you *will* be heard. Act as you would if you were having a face-to-face conversation when you are on the phone.

- If you wouldn't walk in to someone's office and start talking without first making sure it was a good time, don't do it over the phone; always ask if it's a good time.

- If you wouldn't eat your lunch, clip your nails, or use the computer while talking with someone sitting across from you at your desk, don't do it during a telephone conversation.

- If you wouldn't have another conversation or answer your phone at the same time you were talking with someone else, don't do it when you're on the phone.

The person on the other end can't see you and cannot know if you are busy, in a hurry, or in a good mood or bad. You may be frustrated because your printer jammed, but if you *sound* frustrated, the person on the other end might think you are frustrated with him or her. Remember, they can *hear*, but they cannot *see*, so they'll fill in the blanks, right or wrong.

Put forth the extra effort to sound relaxed and cheerful when you're on the phone.

- *Smile* and you will put a smile in your voice; you will *sound* happy.

- *Stand* and you will become energized; you will *sound* energized.

- *Sit up* and you will think more clearly; you will *sound* focused.

- *Pay attention* and you will be attentive; you will *sound* interested.

Keep a mirror by your phone as a reminder that the person on the other end cannot see you, but your manner and tone can be heard over the phone!

From the moment you start sending out resumes, be prepared to receive calls on your phone. Your interview begins the *second* you, your voice mail, or anyone else answers your phone.

The people you call will respond favorably when you pay attention to the following:

Always have a specific purpose for your call. Don't bother someone who's working on a critical deadline for an unimportant reason.

Identify yourself. State your first and last name and company name, even when you think your voice will be recognized.

State the specific reason for your call at the *beginning* of the conversation. This helps you stay focused and helps the person you called determine the relevance of your call.

Ask if it is a convenient time to talk. Determine the best time to talk; it may be a convenient time for you but might not be for the other person.

Keep your conversation brief. Focus on your main objective, and say good-bye when you accomplish what you intended; don't waste time—yours or anyone else's.

Leave an informative message. Speak *clearly, s-l-o-w-l-y,* and *repeat your name and number*, both at the beginning and end of your message. There's nothing more frustrating than having to replay a message over and over in an attempt to understand it or capture the phone number to call back.

Request a specific response. Tell the person what you expect. If you need a response, tell the person *what* you need and *when* you need it.

The people calling you will respond favorably when you pay attention to the following:

Answer your phone promptly. Always answer your phone and set your voice mail to pick up by the third ring.

Keep your voice mail greeting brief. State your first and last name and your company's name, as well as when the caller can expect a return call; if you won't be calling back as soon as you can, don't say you will.

Maintain a current voice mail greeting. Hearing you say "Happy Holidays" is nice around the holidays but irritating soon after. Informing callers you are on vacation long after you're back is a disservice.

If you change your greeting daily, *change it daily*. It's pointless to hear about your schedule for September when it's the third week of October. The *silent* message of an outdated greeting suggests you are overwhelmed and too busy to change it or too careless to remember.

Give the person on the other end your full attention. Anything you do has the probability of being heard. If you can't stop typing, writing, or talking with someone else, admit it isn't a good time to talk.

Additional ways to make a good impression over the phone:

- When you place someone on hold, use the hold button; don't put your hand over the receiver or put the phone down and leave it.

- Limit the time you keep someone on hold; check back after 30 seconds and thank them for holding.

- Return calls promptly, ideally within one business day.

- Eliminate background noise and distractions; turn down the sound on your computer, music playing, or other interferences.

- Don't eat, chew gum, or smoke while on the phone.

- Listen attentively; don't interrupt.

- Talk directly into the receiver.

- If you don't have a good reason to make a call, don't make it.

TIP # 22
Apologize; you can't always be right.

Apologize:

I'm sorry.

I apologize.

Please forgive me.

I am sorry I hurt you.

I beg your pardon.

I am so sorry.

Express your regret:

I wish I hadn't said that.

I feel terrible about this.

I regret what I did.

I'd do it differently if I could.

I regret hurting you.

I shouldn't have said that.

Take responsibility for your actions:

I am responsible; it's entirely my fault.

I overreacted.

I didn't pay attention.

I made a poor decision.

I was being defensive.

I wasn't careful enough.

Validate others:

You are right.

You didn't do anything wrong.

This isn't your fault.

You have a right to be upset.

I'd be upset if I were you.

No one expects you to be perfect. Everyone makes mistakes. Admit yours when you make them. It doesn't matter which way you say it, as long as you sincerely mean it.

Apologize when appropriate; you can't always be right.

TIP # 23
Proofread *every* document.

You've spent hours preparing and perfecting your resume. Each time you send it out, you hope it will do its job and you will be called for an interview. When the phone doesn't ring, you wonder why; you know you have ideal qualifications for several of the positions you applied for. When you spoke directly with one of the hiring managers, he told you he'd be moving quickly to set up interviews. You *know* he was interested in you, especially when he asked to see your resume right away. So what are these companies looking for if they're not looking for the most qualified person?

Companies *do* want the most qualified person, but if that person's resume or cover letter has an error, the sloppiness ruins his chances for an interview. A resume or letter that's crumpled, spotted, or stained will *not* represent you well, nor will one with typos or grammatical errors. You might overlook these things, but a potential employer will *not*.

Seventy-six percent of human resource professionals said they would remove an applicant from consideration for a job if they found a typo or grammatical error on a cover letter or resume, a survey conducted by The Society for Human Resource Management revealed.

You've reviewed your resume 100 times. You've read and reread the cover letter you sent. You can't understand why you didn't catch the mistake, but don't be too hard on yourself; it happens all the time.

We're often too close to our own documents and unable to view them objectively. We rush to meet deadlines or finish a project, leaving little time to catch our mistakes. And at times, we are simply careless; we don't bother checking the documents we send.

It pays to proofread your resume and *every* document you create. Typos, grammatical errors, and misspelled words aren't the only problems you'll find. When you write something, you know what you're trying to say, but others do not.

Robert Half, founder of Accountemps, uses the term "resumania" to describe the blunders found in resumes, job applications, and cover letters. The following examples are from Half's resumania file *(and my reaction to each)*:

- I am entirely through in my work; no detail gets by me. *(I can see that.)*

- Computer Illiterate. *(Too bad, because your other qualifications look good.)*

- Thank you for beeting me for an interview. *(I didn't, but you're welcome.)*

- Planned and held up meetings. *(Did you serve time?)*

- Worked party-time as an office assistant. *(Sounds fun.)*

What would your reaction be if you read any of the preceding errors on a resume or cover letter?

One mistake is all it takes to prevent you from getting an interview, and if you make too many mistakes once you *have* a job, you might find yourself looking for another one sooner than you think. Proofread *all* your e-mails, memos, and letters before sending them. Check and double-check your work for accuracy, spelling, and errors. The time you spend up front will save you time and *embarrassment* later on. When you are careless in your work, you create problems for yourself and others. You'll end up working harder, redoing things, and dealing with problems *you* created.

Mistakes are costly; proofreading pays.

- Proofread all documents several times.

- Print the document and then read it.

- Read it out loud.

- Walk away from it for awhile; take a break and then come back to it.

- Sleep on it; come back to it the next day.

- Have someone else read it *to* you.

- Have someone else read it *for* you.

TIP # 24

Emailmatters@work; don't leave a trail of bad e-mail.

Your image is important in person, on the phone, on paper, and electronically. Spend your time at work doing work; don't surf the Internet or e-mail friends and family. There's a good chance your company is monitoring your computer. This means that the trail of e-mails you send or receive, and every Web site you visit, will be followed and found. Don't risk your job or reputation. Follow the basic rules of e-mail etiquette.

A few precautions:

- **Don't hide behind e-mail.** E-mail isn't always the best vehicle for communication. If you use e-mail to avoid phone calls or meetings, be careful. E-mail can be impersonal. Balance your use of e-mail with other channels of communication.

- **Save the address for last.** Do not address an e-mail until you are ready to send it; this will prevent you from accidentally sending it before you are finished.

- **Save your e-mails.** You may want to access the information some time in the future.

- **Think twice before you hit send.** Don't send an e-mail when you are upset. If you are not sure about sending it, don't.

- **Send a hard copy.** When you send something of importance, send a hard copy via mail or personal delivery, too.

To add warmth and make a good impression:

- **Change your e-mail name.** Use a professional screen name. The name you've been using is fine for your friends, but "eyemhot" or "2kool4u" on a resume won't help your job-search image, and it could hurt it.

- **Be discreet with e-mail.** No e-mail is private. If you'd be embarrassed to have anyone else see it, don't send it.

- **Begin and end with a greeting.** If you wouldn't begin a phone call without saying hello or end it without saying good-bye, don't do it in e-mail.

- **Watch your tone.** Don't use all uppercase letters; it's the equivalent of shouting and you'll come on too strong. Don't use all lowercase letters; it's the equivalent of whispering and you'll appear too timid.

- **Proofread before you send.** Check for mistakes, and make sure your message makes sense.

- **Don't send a message you should convey personally instead.** Don't use e-mail because it's easier for you. When it's too personal or sensitive to send in a message, deliver the news by phone or in person.

To ensure your e-mails will be read:

- **Be brief.** The shorter the e-mail, the more likely it will be read.

- **Use the subject line.** If you don't include a subject, it may never get opened.

- **Write an informative subject line.** Your subject line should state the purpose of the e-mail, any deadlines, and action required. Example: *Request for employee nominations due by June 1.*

- **Be concise.** State your purpose for writing up front; then stick to your purpose.

To increase your chances of a prompt response:

- **Inform the recipient when you send an attachment.** Even though it will show up, mention it in your e-mail, or it could be overlooked.

- **Call when sending time-sensitive mail.** Don't depend on e-mail. If you want to be sure something gets read, call and tell the recipient to look for it.

- **Include contact information.** Make it easy for people to contact you. Use a signature with your name, company name, and phone number. Your snail mail address is optional.

- **Be specific. Tell your reader what to do.** If you need a response by Friday at noon, say so. If you are requesting a meeting, specify when you need a response. If you are sending information and don't need a response, tell your reader.

- **Reference previous e-mail.** If you are responding to a previous e-mail, mention it in your subject line.

To send professional-looking e-mail:

- **Use spell-check.** Mistakes reflect poorly on you. Use spell-check, but don't rely on it; some words might get overlooked.

- **Write in complete sentences.** Don't take shortcuts. Sending *Okay* as a reply is unacceptable.

- **Use proper punctuation.** Punctuate your e-mail as you would punctuate any other document.

- **Write out complete words.** Don't abbreviate words; spell them out.

- **Stick with words.** Don't use clip art, smiley faces, or emoticons.

- **Use professional language.** Don't use slang, jargon, or profanity.

- **Create a new document.** Don't continue to reply to an e-mail that's been going back and forth for months. Ideally, you should create a new e-mail every time you write one or at least after the second or third round of sending an e-mail back and forth.

- **Avoid fancy stationery.** If you use stationery, or backgrounds, keep it subtle; avoid anything too colorful or distracting.

Be considerate of others:

- **Don't send jokes or forward chain letters.** We all have plenty of e-mail already; don't add to the overload.

- **Be polite.** Say *please* and *thank you* when making a request or when someone does something nice for you.

- **Don't critique someone's e-mail.** There's no need to point out errors or mistakes you discover in someone else's document.

- **Limit the number of attachments.** Attachments carry viruses; be careful about what you open and send.

- **Inquire about policies.** Some companies don't allow employees to open attachments. Know the policies before you send and receive.

TIP # 25
Say what you mean and mean what you say.

Say what you mean and mean what you say; don't say what you don't mean to say.

When you say it, you should mean it; don't let fear get in your way.

Don't say what you *think* you're *supposed* to say; say what you mean to say.

It's easy to handle the truth; it's the lies that get in the way.

When you say what someone *wants* you to say, you don't say what *you* want to say.

People ask your opinion to hear it; so say what you need to say.

Don't tell me your plans to do it if you won't be following through.

If you make a mistake, admit it; it's okay if I hear it from you.

Once your words leave your mouth, you can't get them back; they travel only one way.

Be careful how you use your words; *say what you mean and mean what you say.*

How clearly do you think you communicate? Most people could improve their communication, yet *think* they communicate effectively. Do you think you say what you mean and mean what you say? See for yourself:

- Do you ever *pad* the truth to avoid hurting someone?

If you do, you'll end up hurting people when they find out. *Padding the truth is equivalent to lying.*

- Do you ever tell people what you think they want to hear?

When people ask you a question, they want to hear what *you* think. When you shade the truth, *you're not telling the truth.*

- Do you ever say yes instead of no or no instead of yes to avoid making someone mad?

If you do, you're likely to get mad at *yourself* when you find yourself doing something you'd rather not. When you say anything other than the truth, *you are telling a lie.*

- Do you ever tell only part of the story?

Maybe you think it is easier for your listener, so you leave out some of the facts. Maybe you want to prevent someone from getting mad or from making yourself look bad. Whatever your reason, when you tell only part of the story, *you are* not *telling the truth.*

- Do you say you'll do something but fail to follow through?

When you say you will do something, others assume you'll do it. Maybe you meant "if time permits"; maybe you meant "you'll try." But if what you meant isn't what you said, *you have told a lie.*

Communication doesn't have to be complicated. Speak the truth. Don't pad it, soften it, or cover it. *Say what you mean and mean what you say!*

TIP # 26

Power up your presentation skills.

My oldest daughter, Stephanie, was selecting her classes for the second semester. When I suggested she take a speech class, she resisted. "I don't like making speeches; I get nervous when I have to talk in front of people. My face turns red and it's embarrassing."

I tried to convince her to take the class and assured her it would help reduce her nervousness, but I couldn't promise her face would never turn red. I did, however, tell her it probably wouldn't turn *as red* as a result of the practice and confidence she'd gain from taking the class. After wavering, Stephanie decided to take the class. And although it took her awhile to tell me, she said that she was glad she did.

Few things generate as much anxiety as speaking in front of other people. Fear of embarrassment is one of the most common reasons. Giving into that fear is a mistake, because few things are as important to your career as your ability to communicate your knowledge, thoughts, and ideas.

You will be asked to present information numerous times throughout your career. At times you will present information in your office in front of only one or two people or in a meeting with three, four, or more. On other occasions you might be asked to present to a very large group. Whether you are responding to an impromptu request or delivering a planned presentation, you'll want to make a powerful presentation.

I've discovered that doing the thing you fear helps rid you of fear. If you fear presentations or speaking to a group (which most people do), you may never eliminate your fear entirely, but I can assure you if you prepare in advance and practice every chance you get, you'll become much more comfortable.

Nervousness has its advantages. You can't ignore the physical symptoms you feel, so do what you can to eliminate them—practice and prepare! Some of your favorite athletes and performers say they get nervous too, often before a performance. It doesn't *stop* them from performing; it *helps* them *get ready* to perform.

Ten steps to help you power up your presentation skills:

1. **Identify your objectives.** Why have you been asked to present? What do you need to accomplish?

2. **Know your topic.** Become an expert; gather as much information as you can about the topic you will be addressing.

3. **Know your audience.** Find out who will be attending, and learn all you can about them; what do they want and need to take away from your presentation?

4. **Develop your message.** Avoid information overload; identify your most important points, and select the information that best supports them. Get rid of the fluff and stick with the most relevant and critical information you have.

5. **Organize your ideas.** An effective presentation has a beginning (*tell them what you plan to tell them*), middle (*tell them what you need to tell them*), and end (*tell them what you've told them*).

6. **Substantiate your message.** The burden of proof is on you. Verify your facts and data, and validate each point you make. Support your message by selecting and including various studies, surveys, statistics, stories, examples, or other relevant information.

7. **Include visual aids.** As you *tell* your audience what you want to tell them, *show* them the information as well. Most people find it difficult to listen attentively for extended periods of time. Visual aids add variety and make your presentation more interesting. However, don't depend entirely on your PowerPoint or other visuals. Always have a back-up plan should you run into problems with equipment.

8. **Prepare in advance.** Practice and preparation are the keys to reducing stress and anxiety. Practice in front of other people, in front of a mirror, or when you're alone in your room or car. Never memorize your talk or read your entire presentation word for word from a piece of paper. Prepare brief notes on numbered note cards instead.

9. **Engage your audience.** Ask for and respond to questions, and always speak directly to your audience. Make eye contact, smile, and stand up straight. Keep your hands *out of* your pockets so you can use them as you speak. When you feel comfortable, your audience will feel comfortable. They *want* you to succeed.

10. **End on time.** If your presentation is supposed to be over at 10:00 A.M., end by then. Unless you've been given permission or have prepared your audience in advance, the *minute* you are scheduled to stop speaking, your audience expects you to **stop**. If you don't, your audience *will*; they will disconnect and stop listening to you.

TIP # 27
Please and *thank you* are powerful words.

You can use them *anytime* you want.

You can use them *anywhere* you want.

You can use them when you *want* something.

You can use them when you *get* something.

You can use them with anyone.

You can share them with everyone.

They will make people *feel* good.

They will make you *look* good.

You will appear nicer when you use them.

They will further your relationships.

They will improve your image.

They will help you gain cooperation.

They will boost morale.

They will humble you.

They will help you.

They cannot be bought.

They cannot be sold.

They never go out of style.

They never get old.

What are they?

They are three very *powerful* words: **Please** and **thank you.** It's
up to you to use them.

TIP # 28
Expand your vocabulary.

Have you ever stalled for time as you struggled to express a
thought or search for the right words to use? Have you ever had
trouble understanding the words you heard others use? The
ability to articulate a thought and communicate it clearly is
important to every aspect of your life. Ineffective communica-

tion leads to breakdowns in communication, misunderstandings, and costly errors. Communication skills are critical to your professional success.

Imagine you're stuck in traffic on your way to an important meeting. You try to call your office, but you can't get through because your cell phone battery is dead. When you finally arrive, you discover your coworker has taken full credit for a project you worked on together. When you look for the spreadsheet you need to prove your involvement, it's nowhere to be found. As you shuffle your papers and look through your folders, you knock over your cup of coffee. The coffee is everywhere: on your pants, on your papers, and on the conference room table and floor. When you access your computer for the spreadsheet you need, it isn't there.

We all have days when everything seems to go wrong and times we deal with more than our fair share of stress. When you're alone in your car, you can respond anyway you choose. If your cell phone goes dead, you can throw it, and you can swear at it; no one cares if you do. But when you are around other people at work and you lose your cool, you'll lose their respect along with it.

When you overreact and use expletives, you draw negative attention to yourself. Your family and friends might put up with your outbursts, but your employers, coworkers, and clients will not.

If you think some swear words are worse than others, you're probably right. In a business environment, however, there are no varying degrees of profanity; swearing is swearing, and is not the best way to express yourself.

The depth and breadth of your vocabulary influences your ability to express yourself effectively. Most successful professionals possess advanced vocabulary skills, yet most recent graduates haven't actively attempted to improve their vocabularies since high school, according to Greg Ragland, vice president of marketing for The Executive Vocabulary Program.

In his workshops, Ragland encourages attendees to reactivate their interest and awareness of new words. He recommends keeping a vocabulary journal, writing down new words and how they are used whenever you hear them. This will help you understand the context in which they are used at work. You will benefit by understanding and using the same words your colleagues use. However, if you have a boss who swears, it doesn't give you permission to do the same.

Don't try to impress people by using big words you can't pronounce or don't understand; you don't want to appear as though you don't know what you're talking about or sound unnatural. If you haven't yet, take some time to evaluate your vocabulary and how expanding it will benefit you. When you expand your vocabulary, you expand your knowledge. Pay attention to new words you *read* and new words you *hear*. People judge you by the words you use.

The next time you are about to let a bad word slip out of your mouth, *stop*. Stop yourself from swearing and offending others. Don't discredit yourself or lose control. Think before you speak and think about the effect your words have on others. Make the commitment to build your vocabulary, your confidence, and your reputation one word at a time.

TIP # 29
Master the art of SMALL TALK.

S **tart a conversation.**
You're not the only one who feels awkward at social events. It's no fun to stand alone while everyone else is

talking and having fun. If you're waiting for someone to start a conversation with you, stop waiting and start talking, and move away from the corner as you do. Get out of your seat and away from the wall. It's easier than you think.

Make people feel comfortable.

If you want people to enjoy talking with you, they need to feel comfortable being around you. If you are at an event and see someone standing or sitting alone, walk over and introduce yourself and invite him or her to sit with you. Shake hands with the people you meet, and introduce them to people they do not know. Make people feel comfortable, and you'll be welcome wherever you go.

Ask questions.

You don't have to tell funny jokes, interesting stories, or say much of anything at all. When you open your mouth, ask an open-ended question and watch the conversation evolve. "How did you get into this line of work?" is open-ended and will help people open up to you. It's better than "Do you like working here?" because someone could give you a yes or no response and the conversation could stop right there.

Lead the conversation.

Lead conversations *away* from sex, politics, religion, income, and personal ailments. Lead the conversation with the safest small talk topics. The weather, sports, current events, industry-related trends or news, hobbies, and movies will get you off to a good start.

L isten attentively.

Be a good listener; pay attention to what's being said, remember names, and look directly at the person talking. Don't let your eyes wander or try to listen in on another conversation. When you listen attentively, you silently let other people know you care.

T ry to keep it positive.

There are plenty of things to complain about. There's turmoil in the world and there's natural disasters. There are diseases with no cure and too few second chances. Relationships are challenging, and work can be a pain, but when you're making small talk, it isn't the time to complain. Small talk is meant to be small; don't waste time trying to solve problems, debate controversial issues, or discuss the woes of the world. Keep it upbeat and positive. It's meant to be kept small.

A ppear interested.

You don't have to talk a lot to be considered interesting. When you appear interested in others, they'll become interested in you. Don't worry about what to say. The conversation shouldn't revolve around *you*. When you get people talking, you take the pressure off, and they will think highly of you.

L ink the conversation.

The best conversations are those that link two people, enabling a bond to be formed. Discovering you have a mutual acquaintance, enjoy the same hobby, share a love of animals, and anything else you find you have in common will put you both on common ground. Even the smallest commonalities can link one person to another. Look for links, and you'll form stronger bonds.

Keep it moving.

Think of a conversation as a game. Imagine an invisible ball being passed back and forth throughout your conversation. You'll have the ball when you start a conversation, but you'll want to quickly pass it to your partner. When you have the ball, it is your turn to talk, but never hold on to the ball too long. The winner of the game is the one who does the best job of giving the ball away. If you monopolize the ball, you'll slow the momentum of the game. The more you practice, the better you will play. Just remember to keep the ball (and the conversation) moving.

TIP # 30
Act confidently—even when you're not; pay attention to your body language.

"Sit still." "Stand up straight." "Look at me when I'm talking to you." You've probably heard these and similar remarks before. They may be irritating to hear at the time, but there's a good reason the adults in your life issue these commands. They want to help you *pay attention* to your body language. Since the day you were born, you've been communicating with your body; your parents knew you were happy when you'd smile and needed no words for reinforcement.

Even as an adult, people can tell when you're happy and when you are not. Everything you do sends a message. You walk fast when you're in a hurry, and you slow down when you're relaxed. You pay attention when you're interested, and you look away when you are not. You stand tall when you feel proud and slump your shoulders when you're down. People who don't know you can tell a lot about you just by looking at you.

Your body language speaks loudly and clearly to others and at times may conflict with your words. When you say something verbally, but communicate something else visually, you confuse people. In an attempt to understand your message, people will look for ways to understand what you are trying to say. They may want to believe your words (your intent) but are influenced more by your actions (your response). We pick up on the visual clues we see, putting our trust in the things we *see* over the things we *hear.*

When your words and your body are in conflict, your *body* will always win.

If you *tell* your friend you don't mind waiting but *become* impatient while you wait, your friend will think you are impatient.

If you *say* you are interested in a job but *look* uninterested during the interview, the interviewer will think you are not interested.

If you *say* you're not nervous but *appear* anxious, people will question your confidence.

Robin, the personnel director of a large retail organization, knows she must be ready psychologically, emotionally, and physically to give her best performance every day. It helps her to think of the workplace as a big theatre. Her customers and coworkers carefully watch every move she makes, and she takes her performance at work just as seriously as she would if she were performing on stage. If she feels awkward or uncomfortable, others pick up on it and feel the same way. For others to have confidence in her, she must have confidence in herself. The more experience and knowledge she has, the more confident she is.

Confidence is built over time. It's not easy to feel confident when you don't know what you're doing, but no one expects you to know everything. If you are asked a question and you don't have the answer, admit you don't know. Don't belittle yourself for not knowing; always speak highly of yourself and focus on the things you do well.

Powerful people *give the impression* they are powerful and know how to command attention. They use their posture, expressions, gestures, and eyes to communicate powerfully and effectively. They weren't born this way; they've worked at and perfected the language their bodies speak.

You don't have to *feel* calm to project coolness or wait years to gain the confidence you seek. Tap into the positive feelings you have when you really are confident as a result of doing something well.

Janie, an avid runner, is confident and secure when she runs but is uncomfortable in most social situations. As she worked on building her confidence when socializing, it helped her to tap into the power she feels when she runs. Try it yourself. The next time you need to boost your confidence, envision yourself doing something that makes you feel sure of yourself; then carry that feeling with you.

The next time you feel unsure of yourself, *act as if* you feel assured. Use your body language to help you. Stand a little taller and hold your head a little higher. Smile when you say hello. Give a nod and acknowledge the people you see. Shake hands firmly, speak assuredly and assertively, and always look directly at the person you are talking to.

When you appear confident, others assume you are confident. No one knows when you're acting; people believe what they see. If you always act confidently, before you know it, you won't need to put on an act. One day you'll realize you've become the confident person you wanted to be. When you do, your overall performance will improve and you'll be performing at your best!

TIP # 31
Listen.

When you hear, you need to listen.

When you listen, you pay attention; when you pay attention, you stop talking.

When you stop talking, you engage; when you engage, you feel connected.

When you feel connected, you invest; when you invest, you see value.

When you see value, you commit; when you commit, you resolve.

When you resolve, you truly focus; when you focus, you can learn.

When you learn, you gain knowledge; when you gain knowledge, you will grow.

When you grow, you will improve; when you improve, you can advance.

When you advance, you develop; when you develop, you mature.

When you mature, you start to notice; when you notice, you can see.

When you can see, you understand; when you understand, you grasp the concept.

When you grasp the concept, you have communication.

When you have communication, you have cooperation.

When you have cooperation, you can achieve anything.

So Listen!

Improve your listening skills by remembering to *stop, look,* and *listen.*

When someone is speaking to you:

STOP what you are doing. Stop talking. Stop to hear what someone's saying.

LOOK at the person speaking to you. Look interested. Look and see a different point of view.

LISTEN and you will learn. Listen and you will understand. Listen and you will hear.

Leadership Skills

Become a Leader

TIP # 32
Play to win the game of office politics.

Amy, who has been out of school for five years, says the one thing she was least prepared for at work and has had trouble adjusting to is the office politics. "The reality is that work isn't always fun" she said. "I was used to support from my parents, teachers, and professors, but it's different at work. People don't care where you came from. They expect you to adapt to the way things are done."

Fitting in to a new environment can be challenging. Every office and every organization has its own set of rules and expectations. The culture of an office or organization may not always be explicit, but complying with it is expected. The more observant you are, the easier it is to understand and fit in to your workplace environment.

From the moment you walk into a building or office of a company, it is the feel and character of that organization that provides clues to the culture inside. From the company mission statement, to its décor, to the music you hear playing in the background, be sure you are paying attention. These are just a few of the clues that can help you understand what the organization is all about.

The corporate culture drives the code of conduct in an organization. It influences the way employees behave, dress, and interact with others. Some offices are more laid back and casual, others more structured and formal. It is easiest when you are working with an organization that matches your personality and style, but if you are adaptable, you should be able to work in a variety of environments. When there is a clash, you are better off acknowledging it and moving on if it isn't the right fit.

Whether you are interviewing and getting to know a company or already working at one, taking time to understand the culture of that organization is essential. Visit the company Web site; the company mission and values are most informative. Talk with and observe people who work there. What is the overall tone? Are employees happy, stressed, upbeat, or fearful? How are people interacting with others?

Learning about the culture will help you understand what is expected and navigate the office politics in that organization. Some companies provide new-hire training classes and company manuals. If you do not receive adequate information, the only way to find out is by asking questions and observing.

Images of backstabbing, conniving coworkers come to mind when people think of office politics. But it doesn't have to be that way. Playing politics is simply playing by the rules. By understanding and then following the rules, your days will run a little smoother and you will increase your chances of achieving your objectives. To help you play and win the game of office politics, consider the following:

Tailor your style of communication. People communicate differently. If you are used to bluntly telling it like it is, you may need to soften your approach to avoid hurting others. If you like to delve into detail, but your boss only wants to hear the bottom line, forgo the details and provide the information he wants to hear. Not everyone communicates like you.

Show your respect. You may feel close to the people you work with, but don't talk to them as you would a friend. No matter how much you think you know or how certain you are that you are right and others wrong, show your respect for others. You are *not* free to say whatever you want, especially to your boss.

Know your place. If you are able to contribute in a positive way, that is great, but know what you can and cannot influence. You don't need to share your opinion about everything. Some battles just aren't worth pursuing and most are out of your hands. There is a time to speak up and a time to shut up. Know the difference.

Don't expect things to be fair. It's bound to happen; the wrong person will get promoted, others will get praise you deserve, and decisions will be made that make no sense. It's just the way it is; you won't agree with every policy or the requests made of you, but if you want to keep the peace and keep your job, you'll have to comply. It helps when you realize that work and life aren't always fair.

Keep your ego in check. No matter how brilliant you think you are, no one likes an egotistical braggart or know-it-all. Instead of trying so hard to make yourself look good, find ways to make others look and feel good. Your humility will be appreciated and benefit you.

Treat people well. Follow the golden rule and treat people as you'd like to be treated. Be kind, courteous, and respectful of others. You will encounter a variety of personalities throughout your career. Some will be easier to work with than others and your patience will be tested. Be nice; nice people do and can finish first.

Avoid the grapevine. Gossip can be destructive. While avoiding it entirely may be impossible, don't be a major contributor to the rumor mill or one to talk badly about others. The less interested you are in the gossip you hear, the better.

Pay your dues. When you accept a job, you accept the responsibility that goes with it. Even the most detailed job description can't predict the additional tasks you may occasionally be asked to do. Your job description may not list housekeeping chores or other tasks you may be asked to do, but you will be expected to do them from time to time. Don't think of these menial tasks as demeaning. Everyone has to pay his or her dues and so do you.

Pitch in. Always leave things as you found them and pitch in when you see something that needs to be done. If you use the copy or fax machine and use the last of the paper in the tray, you have a choice: You can ignore the empty tray, walk away, and let the next person who uses it refill it, or you can fill it yourself. You may not want to bother, but since you were the one who emptied the paper, you should refill it. After all, it made it easier on you to have paper in the tray; why not make it easier for someone else? The brief amount of time it takes to leave things as (or better than) you found them reaps long-lasting benefits. If you fail to pitch in, you'll become an irritation to others who may become resentful of your refusal to contribute or do your share of the work.

Be a team player. Give credit when credit is due; be happy for the success and accomplishments of others. Be helpful, be supportive, and contribute to the good of everyone. Become a valuable member of the team.

Communicate. Don't make assumptions; if you need clarification, ask questions. Be open to the opinions of others and to continuous self improvement. Keep people informed and up to date on important projects and information. If you have an issue with someone, talk to that person about it. The more clearly you communicate, the less room there is for problems and misunderstandings. Do your part to keep the channels of communication open.

Build strong relationships. Your ability to work well with others is essential. The more solid your relationships, the better off you will be. You don't have to be overly chummy inside or outside of work to have good working relationships. Be the kind of person others can confide in and depend on. Be there for others and work at building trust.

Act professionally at all times. The way you dress, the manner in which you act, your sensitivity and attitude toward others, and the things you talk about are all important factors in your ability to blend in with the corporate culture. Inappropriate behavior will make you stand out and could harm your reputation.

TIP # 33

Bring out the best in others.

When Mike enters a room, people notice. When he speaks, people listen. He doesn't have to say much to command attention.

Ann's been referred to as a "people magnet." People surround her. If she won a contest, she'd earn the title "Miss Congeniality."

You probably know people who remind you of Mike or Ann. They are special because they do something special; they bring out the best in others. They both like people and people like them.

If people *like you*, they are more apt to buy from you, hire you, and promote you. People will trust you, confide in you, and help you, but only if they like you. Being likeable has many advantages; how likeable are *you?*

- **Do you like people?** Do you enjoy being around people? Are you the first to say hello or strike up a conversation? Or do you look away, pretending you don't see someone who is there? Are you interested in people and what they have to say?

- **Do you care about other people?** Do you ask people how they are doing and listen to their answers? When you meet someone, do you remember that person when you meet again? Are you able to remember names and the details of previous conversations? When you genuinely like and care about people, you should ask them questions and remember the answers you hear. When you care enough to remember, you show how much you care.

- **Do you make people smile?** When you see someone, do you see a smile? Or do people look away, avoiding contact? Notice the expressions of the people you see; it's likely a reflection of you. If you tend to see a lot of unhappy people, look at *yourself*. Smile often and share your smile with others. When you do, there's a good chance you'll see more smiles smiling back at you.

● **Do you like yourself?** The more comfortable you are with yourself, the more comfortable you will be with others. When you like and accept yourself, it's easier to like and care about other people.

● **Do you bring out the best in people?** What do you look for in people? Do you see good qualities or focus on the bad? Do you criticize, sit in judgment, or offer unsolicited advice? People are hard enough on themselves—they don't need anyone else to remind them of their imperfections. Look for the good in people.

Four steps to a more likeable you:

1. **Acknowledge the people you see.** Smile, make eye contact, and say hello.

2. **Show how much you care.** Be interested in others; ask questions, and then listen to the answers. Listen more than you talk.

3. **Remember people.** Remember and use names. Remember and follow up on prior conversations.

4. **Bring out the best in people.** Look for and point out the good in people through praise, words of encouragement, and sincere compliments.

When you make people feel important, you become important to them. When you make people look good, you look good too. Bring out the best in others; *when you bring out the best in others, you bring out the best in yourself.*

TIP # 34

Under-promise and over-deliver.

You're young and you're working hard to build your career and a good reputation. You seek opportunities to demonstrate your ability, and you want other people to think highly of you. So when your boss asks if you'd like to do the research on meeting sites for the annual conference, you say yes. When she tells you she'd like you to present your findings at a meeting the following Monday morning, you tell her you will as you silently wonder how you'll manage to get it done.

Monday is just a week away and you've got other commitments to honor and deadlines to meet. You have classes almost every evening, and you are attending the wedding of a friend over the weekend. You're not sure how or when you'll get the research done, yet you say nothing. As a result, you stress-out and either do a poor job in your research or apologize for not being able to get it done. Either way, you've undermined your good intentions and disappointed your boss—and yourself.

No matter what excuse you give or how forgiving your boss appears, you both know you failed to deliver; you committed (made a promise) to do something, and you didn't do what you said you would. You took on the project with good intentions. You wanted to please your boss and prove your worth, but instead you let your boss down and diminished your value in her eyes.

Don't be too hard on yourself. Everyone over-commits at one time or another, and you're not likely to lose your job as a result of one mistake. Acknowledge your blunder and learn from your error. The next time you make another promise, be certain you can deliver. If you aren't sure you can get something done, say so. It's easier to work with realistic deadlines than it is to resolve the problems that arise from delays and unmet expectations.

If you try to please everyone, you'll end up pleasing no one. In fact, your desire to please will have the opposite effect; you will end up disappointing people, creating conflict, and damaging your reputation.

A sure way to avoid disappointment is by doing *more* than you promised. If you say you will call someone by the end of the week, don't wait until Friday at 5:00 P.M. (or worse yet, until Monday) to call. Why not plan to get it done in advance? Can you imagine the surprise and delight on the other end of the phone when you call back *earlier* than expected? Every time you exceed expectations and over-deliver, you draw positive attention to yourself and make things easier for others.

Maybe you think you should never say "no" or "I can't" to your boss or turn down an exciting opportunity. "No" doesn't mean "never" and "I can't" doesn't mean "I won't." When you are forthright about what you can and cannot do, people will respect your honesty. When you *meet* expectations, people may not notice; after all, you're just doing your job. But people do notice when you fail to meet expectations and when you *exceed* them.

The next time you make a promise, *under-promise*. Set two dates: the date you promise *someone else* and the date you promise *yourself*. The date you set for yourself should be earlier than the one you give to someone else.

You'll reduce your stress, increase your productivity, and enhance your reputation. Few people manage to consistently over-deliver. Become one of the few who do.

TIP # 35

Lead by example.

When you think of people you consider strong leaders, who comes to mind? Do you think of well-known individuals in high-level leadership positions in business, entertainment, or sports? Do you think of world or political leaders?

Many people look up to those with fame, fortune, or status and assume these things signify a good leader. But sometimes these things create a false sense of leadership. A true leader doesn't thrive or rely on power, control, affluence, or name recognition. Although many successful leaders have these things, plenty of successful leaders do not.

You don't have to be the person in charge to be an effective leader. Natural leaders earn respect as a result of what they *do*, not because of who they are. The best leaders *lead by example*.

Think about the leaders who have been a positive influence in *your* life. Is there a special teacher, family member, neighbor, friend, or other role model who's helped guide you? Think about the people you respect, those you turn to for advice. Is there someone you look up to, enjoy listening to, or someone who enjoys listening to *you*? Is there anyone who motivates you to try harder, be better, or take a risk?

The leaders capable of leading *you* are not necessarily those who are in the spotlight. Be sure you don't overlook the leaders in *your* life—the people who've taken time to talk with you and help you.

There are renowned leaders who do great things and earn the praise and honor they get. There are also leaders we rarely, if ever, read or hear about who deserve but may not ever get the recognition and appreciation they've earned. Some people lead quietly and discreetly. They create and inspire change in others. They don't live spectacular lives. They don't consider themselves to be great leaders and may not even realize they are making a difference. They simply lead by being who they are.

If you think you're too young to lead others, think again. Your actions inform others about who and what is important to you. Your words encourage, or discourage, others. You guide and influence people every day whether you do it intentionally or not. Are you being the kind of leader you want to be?

You determine what you say; you determine what you do. Actions speak louder than words; do your actions speak well of you? When you say you'll do something, *do you do it?*

Your words have more impact than you think—think about the things that you say. If you don't have something nice to say, *don't say it.* If you're afraid you might say something you'll regret, *don't say it.* If it's negative, judgmental, or critical, *don't say it.*

Treat people as you wish to be treated. Strive to be your best and bring out the best in others. Live and lead your life purposefully, carefully, and intentionally, and you will lead others to do the same. Lead by example.

TIP # 36
Be a lifelong learner.

Once you've met the requirements for graduation, your formal education will be complete. You should be proud of yourself and the work you've done. If you're finished with school for now, you can put away your backpack and stop worrying about your grades. You're not a student anymore, but whether you know it or not, in many ways your education has just begun.

Learning is a lifelong process. Many things can't be taught in a classroom, and some of your most valuable life lessons lie ahead of you. You've got a lot of living and learning to do. Continue your education and become a student of life.

As your life changes, so will you. Your learning curve will be highest anytime you do something new or make a major change. When you move away from home or to another city, you will become more independent and responsible. If you are involved in a long-term relationship, marry, or have children, you will learn even more about yourself and others. If you become a student of life, you will learn something new every day.

Continuing your education doesn't mean you have to continue to go to school or take night classes. It is up to you, however, to develop new skills and expand your knowledge. Make sure you keep up with current trends. Take advantage of opportunities to add to your credentials. Consider specializing in a chosen field. Even if you never considered yourself to be a good student or didn't care about learning before, you might be surprised to discover how much you enjoy learning when you're interested in a given subject.

Learn from your mistakes. Some of the lessons you learn will be subtle and accumulative, others immediate and profound. You will learn when you succeed, and you will learn when you fail. Don't be afraid of making a mistake or become embarrassed when you do. Give yourself credit for trying. Everyone makes mistakes. Make mistakes and learn from them. It's one of the most effective ways to learn.

Learn from others. You don't have to learn everything on your own or learn the hard way. There is a wealth of information out there, and more people than you realize are happy to help you. Don't be too proud to ask for help or advice. As long as you ask after you've done some research yourself and aren't taking the easy way out, you will flatter those you ask for advice. Expand your network to learn from others. Join the organizations and associations in your field. Learn from the meetings you attend and learn from the people you meet. The wider your network and the more frequently you talk with others, the more knowledge you will gain.

Learn by acquiring new knowledge and skills. Read professional journals, read books, read the newspaper, stay on top of industry trends, and know public information about your company and its competitors. Never stop acquiring knowledge. The more you know, the more value you bring to everything you do.

Learn by doing. Experience really is the best teacher. Overcoming fear is empowering; face your fears. Stop thinking about what you want to do and start doing something now. Every risk you take will make you stronger, wiser, and teach you something new.

Life is an education; become a student of life. There is much for you to learn about life and from life. The classroom is always open and there is more information than ever before. Commit to your ongoing education. Be a lifelong learner.

TIP # 37

You don't get what you want; you get what you ask for.

It's important to think about your future and determine what you want. The more you focus on a goal, the more likely you are to accomplish it. Some goals are so personal you may chose to keep them to yourself. It is difficult, however, to accomplish everything alone. The more you talk about your goals, the more real they become. Don't keep your dreams to yourself. If no one knows what you want, no one will be able to help you.

Jan was so upset when she discovered that someone else received the promotion she wanted that she quit her job. When she gave her notice, she hoped her manager would beg her to stay, but he did not. Jan did not get the promotion she wanted and left a job she loved because she had her heart set on something she never told anyone about, including the manager doing the hiring. She assumed others knew what she needed and wanted. How could anyone know when she kept it all to herself? Did she expect others to read her mind?

Most people are too busy dealing with their own issues and problems to worry about everyone else. If you want something, don't hide the truth, drop hints, or expect others to read your mind.

Speak up. No one will ever know what you want unless you say what it is. If there's something you want, whether it's a promotion, more money, or a favor from a friend, talk about it. Don't keep it a secret, and don't expect others to know what you want unless you tell them. Talk to the people who make the decisions—talk to those who can help you. No one will hear you unless you speak up. Tell people what you need and ask for what you want.

Be specific. Be specific about your requirements and expectations. Don't rely on others to speak for you. People can't fill in the blanks. It won't do you any good to hope for what you want if no one knows what you're hoping for.

Be realistic. People will take you seriously only if your requests are reasonable and realistic. Outlandish requests can't be fulfilled. Don't ask someone for something impossible. Make it easy for others to honor your request.

Be honest. If you're asked for your opinion, give your opinion. You don't have to agree with everyone else. Be frank about your point of view without being argumentative or alienating others. You need a better response than "I don't know" or "I don't care." It's okay if you have a different perspective as long as you're honest about the way you feel.

Be accountable. If you want something, it's up to you to get it. Be responsible for what you do and say.

Be direct. Don't make demands; make reasonable requests. Determine what you want. Then go directly to the person with the authority to honor your request. You will earn respect for knowing and stating what you want and will improve your standing with others.

Be inquisitive. No question is dumb or too insignificant to ask. You are expected to ask questions as you learn. If you want to know how you are doing, ask for feedback. If you want to know what it will take for you to advance, ask and find out. You are always better off asking than assuming, and you have a better chance of getting what you want when you are clear about what's expected.

Your future is up to you. Let others know what you need. There's no guarantee you'll get everything you ask for, but you will increase your chances.

TIP # 38
Don't compare yourself to others.

Life changes after graduation. Up until this time you have followed the path laid out for you. Although you found your own friends and interests to pursue, you and your classmates moved from grade to grade and shared many common goals. For most of your life, those the same age as you were progressing at the same pace as you.

Once you graduate there is no longer a clear path or peer benchmarks to follow. You decide your future direction. You'll find that some of your peers will continue their education; others will take a full-time job. Before you know it you will hear about former classmates getting married and settling down. You'll learn about those who achieved great things and others whose lives have taken a downward turn.

In previous generations it was common for someone to start off at a company and stay with that organization until retirement. Today, it is predicted that the average person will change career direction multiple times. The U.S. Department of Labor projects that recent and current graduates will have an average of 10-14 jobs by the age of 38.

I've often marveled at those who think they know what they want to do with the rest of their lives when they are in their teens or twenties. The path to take is so clear to some while others continue searching most of their lives. It can be difficult to predict what you will be doing 20, 30, or 40 years from now. And even if you have an idea, don't be surprised if you end up doing something else.

This is *your* life. You're on your own now. It's time to break away from others and make decisions based on what's best for you. Be an independent thinker. If you end up making the wrong choice, learn from it and move on. If a job doesn't work out, find one that does.

Don't compare yourself to previous generations. Don't compare yourself to your siblings, friends, or coworkers. Don't compare yourself to where you thought you'd be by now. Trust that wherever you are is the right place to be. Don't waste your time away, but know that time is on your side; you've got time to figure things out.

Set goals according to *your* desires. This is *your* life and you only get one shot at it. You can *learn* from others, but don't *compare yourself* to others.

TIP # 39
Everything takes time.

If you're in a hurry to get where you're going in life, slow down; you don't need to move so fast. As a recent graduate, you've been in school for some time and maybe you need to take a little time off. If you know what you want to do with your life, that's great— go for it! But if you're feeling overwhelmed by your many options and aren't sure of your direction, don't give in to the pressure to make a decision too quickly.

When surveyed about what they would have done differently after graduation if they knew then what they know now, a number of respondents interviewed for this book replied that they would have slowed down. Graduates face a lot of pressure to get a job and settle down but receive little encouragement to take time off or take their time making important life decisions.

Too many people rush through life. They complete one goal and quickly start working toward another. Are you in a hurry to get a job, get married, and start a family? Is that what you really want to do, or is that what you think you *should* be doing? If you're not sure, you're not ready to make a decision. Take time to reflect and relax. Let all you've learned sink in.

It may take years to become the person you want to be, so don't ignore the person you are today. Give yourself time to figure out what kind of work you want to do. Think about the city, state, or country in which you'd most like to live. Do you need to travel and visit other places before you decide?

Have you thought about the type of person you want to marry or the kind of marriage you want to have? Do you *want* to have children? Are you ready to be a good parent? Don't rush to take on more responsibility than you are ready to handle. Time is on your side. There's a difference between slacking and taking a little time off. Don't make excuses to avoid responsibility, but keep in mind that sometimes the most responsible choice is to wait to make a commitment to a job or a person. Never take on responsibility or obligations unless you're genuinely committed to meeting them.

Remember that patience is a virtue. It will take time for you to find an ideal job, and it will take time for you to earn and save the amount of money you want. You have to merit each promotion and pay increase you get.

Everything takes time, persistence, a game plan, belief in oneself, and the right attitude. Everyone starts somewhere. Even rich and famous people like actor Jim Carrey, software billionaire Bill Gates, and television icon Oprah Winfrey can tell a story of a time when things were different for them. Everyone must overcome struggles, challenges, and obstacles. Very few people start out at the top, but the tough times in life will help prepare you for the better times yet to come. Although it may be difficult to understand now, you will enjoy and appreciate what you have much more if you plan for it and work for it.

TIP # 40
Be yourself; you are enough.

On a plane ride home from Atlanta, I was thinking about all the work I had left to do before I could get my business up and running. After spending several days with Susan Bixler, a successful and respected image consultant in Atlanta, I had earned my certification as a corporate image consultant. Susan had written several books and established herself as an expert, and I wondered if I would forever be in her shadow. I wanted to establish my own credentials, not be the clone of someone else, yet I wasn't sure I was qualified to do it by myself.

I met with Gail, a friend of mine who is a psychologist, a few weeks later. I told her about some of my concerns and asked her to work with me on a few projects. I valued her insight and knew her credentials would be an asset.

Gail was flattered by my offer but declined the invitation to work with me. She leaned in closer and told me something I already knew but refused to believe. "You've got everything you need to succeed. You don't need me or my credentials." She knew I wasn't convinced and continued, "People might have awards and degrees decorating their walls, but many of them *hide* behind their credentials. They need to hear what you have to say. You don't need me or anyone else to help you—*you are enough.*"

Gail was right; she gave me some of the most valuable advice I've ever received. I began taking more risks and doing things *my* way. I reminded myself to be myself. I kept hearing Gail's words in my mind: *You are enough.*

It took time for me to find my own voice and establish myself as an expert. But only when I was true to myself, not trying to imitate someone else, did I really begin to excel.

Whether you believe it now or not, you really do have all you need to succeed. Be yourself. *You* are unique. You might have the same skills or interests as others, but only you do things the way *you* do. Be who you are; you can stand out and still fit in. People will respect you for being you. No matter how many people have come before you, there is no other you. Be yourself; *you are enough.*

TIP # 41
Pay attention to the proven practices of successful people.

Every tip in this book is written to help you succeed. You can read this or any other book written on achieving success, and although each successful individual has his or her own personal story to tell, there are some things almost all successful people have in common.

It's important to set goals and determine what you want, but knowing what you want is not enough to achieve it. Success doesn't just *happen.* You must be committed and motivated to succeed, work hard, develop good work habits, and maintain a winning attitude.

Most successful people have been where you are today. You don't have to learn everything on your own. Pay attention to the proven practices of successful people and increase your chances of success.

There are always exceptions, but generally you will find most successful people are:

1. **Committed.** Successful people believe in their vision, themselves, and others. If they say they will do something, they do it, and they do whatever it takes to get a job done well and on time.

2. **Driven.** Successful people are driven to succeed. They are purpose driven and driven in setting goals and then achieving them. They focus on their priorities, and they

are fearless, relentless, and willing to take risks. Driven to do well, they often exceed expectations.

3. **Team players.** Successful people understand the value of collaborative efforts. Emphasizing "we" more than "me," they bring people together and are able to appreciate and acknowledge each person's contribution.

4. **Innovative.** Successful people are creative thinkers and doers. They are not threatened by new ways of doing things; they think out of the box, generate new ideas, and are solution oriented.

5. **Optimistic.** Successful people are positive. They think positively, see potential, and focus on possibilities. They look for and see the good in other people, are "up" more than "down," and rebound quickly from a setback or problem.

6. **Diligent workers.** Successful people work hard, but because they enjoy what they do, it hardly seems like work. They don't watch the clock and anticipate the time to stop. They have specific tasks they want to complete, and only when they finish what they set out to do will they stop.

7. **Passionate.** Successful people are passionate about their work. Their personal resolve and enthusiasm are contagious and intriguing.

8. **Courageous.** Successful people are willing to confront problems and mend misunderstandings. They are willing to take a stand and when necessary are willing to stand alone. They give and accept honest feedback and always strive to improve. They are not afraid of failing or making a mistake and seek to learn something new when they do either.

Acquiring good work habits can increase your chances of success and help you maximize your natural talents and abilities. Identify and focus on the areas you should work on improving.

You don't have to learn the hard way or all on your own. Take your cue from those who are already where you want to be. *Pay attention to the proven practices of successful people.*

TIP # 42
Create and maintain a career portfolio.

Think of it as a scrapbook of your personal and professional achievements to be used throughout your career. A portfolio is another tool you can use to showcase your skills and help others learn more about you. Portfolios typically include an introductory or cover letter, a table of contents, your resume and a collection of documents representing your best attributes, skills, and accomplishments. However, it is up to you to choose what you put in your portfolio. It is for you and about you and meant to be a creative endeavor, so there are no strict rules you must follow other than to represent yourself in the best possible manner.

Your portfolio can boost your morale when your career is in a lull and give you an advantage when applying for a job or seeking a promotion. With a little effort you can put together a portfolio that will benefit you in many ways. You can utilize your portfolio to:

Help you prepare for interviews and make the most of each one you have. Before an interview you need to spend time doing research on a company. You'll want to prepare questions to ask and be prepared to talk about why you are the right person for the job. When you take the time to gather your best work and organize it into a portfolio, you will have an advantage. Putting together a portfolio forces you to ask, and answer, your own questions about what you bring to the organization—and those that are likely to be asked about you—in *advance.*

You will be better prepared and able to use your portfolio to back up the things you say. Most importantly, when you have prepared a portfolio relevant to the job you are seeking, you will be more likely to impress the interviewer and leave a positive and lasting impression.

Showcase your skills and capabilities. You can talk about how creative and hardworking you are, but chances are the interviewer has heard it all before. The candidates interviewing before you and after you are likely to say similar things. Providing proof of your past work and capabilities is more convincing than talking about what you have done and can do. Your portfolio provides evidence of projects you've done and accolades you've received, which enables the interviewer to get a better sense of you.

Set yourself apart by demonstrating your willingness to do more than expected. Although you may be asked to bring samples of your work to an interview, rarely is bringing a portfolio mandatory or expected. That is why if you do have a portfolio, it is perceived so positively. It demonstrates your initiative and commitment to doing more than expected. If you are up against another candidate who has a portfolio and you don't, you will be at a disadvantage. Having a portfolio will help you stand out among others and be more competitive.

Evaluate and focus on your strengths and accomplishments. Putting together a portfolio takes time. It requires thinking about, then gathering documents and testimonials that demonstrate your skills and most positive assets. Putting together a portfolio is a valuable exercise for anyone at any stage of a career. Achievements in the past you consider insignificant may be of great value. It is important to reflect on the experiences and accomplishments throughout your life that have made you who you are and to capitalize on them.

Maintain a record of your professional growth. Once you have a job, it is important keep track of the things you are doing and accomplishing. You may think you will remember over the years, but other than the big milestones in a career, it is easy to forget about things you've done. Keep track of classes and trainings attended, certificates and awards you've received. Save letters of appreciation and recognition along with copies of your best work and special projects you are proud of.

Refer to and use your portfolio during job reviews, when seeking a promotion, or pay raise. Your portfolio is the perfect tool to help you measure your progress and overall success. Keep track of your performance and your achievements. It will be useful throughout the years, whether you are making a career move, seeking a promotion, or requesting an increase in pay. Reminding your supervisor of your value by showing the things in your portfolio will increase your chances of getting what you want.

Bring your resume to life. Your resume should be included in your portfolio and updated as necessary. In addition, include samples of your work that support the information on that resume. Imagine being in an interview talking about a newsletter you wrote versus having the ability to *show* it to the interviewer. You will be able to bring your resume—and your skills—to life and have more effective interviews as a result.

Increase your presence on the Internet. Having a personal Web site that showcases your work and experiences also offers a comparative advantage when applying for work or seeking new opportunities. Consider creating an online version of your portfolio in addition to preparing one you are able to hand out in person.

TIP # 43

Put together your own personal advisory board.

It's tough to win a debate with my mother. I'm not one to back down from engaging in a healthy discussion, but I've learned that my mother is difficult to influence. When I was younger it wasn't easy when I'd try to convince her to let me do some of the things I wanted. One of the reasons is it wasn't only my mother I had to persuade. Before giving me an answer, she would consult with my dad, my grandma, my aunts, my friends' parents, or any others whose opinions she respected. I found it impossible to compete with what I now refer to as her "Board of Advisors."

My mother is methodical and doesn't make decisions in haste. It makes sense that she would want to seek the input of others before making a final decision. Her strategy makes sense. Businesses and organizations understand the value of having a board of advisors; if it works for them, why not for individuals too?

Although the people on my mother's "board" have changed over the years, she continues to bring the opinions of others into our discussions, especially when they agree with *her!* The more I've thought about her technique, the more I realize how beneficial it would be if we all had a board to turn to when we need a little perspective.

It's not uncommon to turn to others when making an important decision. Most of us have a few people we turn to, but it may be difficult for those close to us to be objective. Whether going through a transition, seeking input on a career decision, or dealing with a challenging situation, having people to turn to will help see you through.

Putting together a board may seem a bit formal, but it doesn't have to be that way. You don't have to make it structured or meet on a regular basis. You don't have to have meetings at all; you might be able to accomplish what you want through e-mail or the phone.

You don't even have to tell someone they are on your board, although you might get more from the person if you do. It's for your benefit to preselect and have people in mind that you can turn to when the need arises. The board you put together is for you to consult with for objective feedback and helpful advice; to see you through difficult times and make well-thought–out decisions.

The most effective boards have a cross representation of a diverse group of people. It is important to seek people with differing perspectives. Avoid filling your board with people likely to agree with you; look for those who will challenge your point of view.

Think about the people you admire and respect. Consider someone you'd like as a mentor. Think of a friend who cares about your well-being; someone who is a good listener. Look for those who share similar values, as well as those with differing points of view. You will benefit if the people you select are well connected; perhaps they will be willing to make introductions for you. Think of your board as a group of supporters for you to turn to in need.

You can grow your personal board slowly. You're not asking people to commit for life. Allow each relationship to evolve; decide together how to make the relationship work. Always inquire if there is anything that person would like from you. It is important to both give and receive. The more valuable the relationship is for both of you, the better.

Your board can work however you want. Some people check in with their board every month; others just a few times a year. Be careful not to lean too heavily on anyone; your board doesn't have the time nor desire to hear about every problem you have. Save your questions for the big issues that occur. Most importantly, listen very carefully to the advice you receive, especially when it isn't what you want to hear.

To get started, all you have to do is ask. Most people will consider the invitation a compliment. Wouldn't *you* be flattered if someone thought enough of you to ask you to be on their board?

TIP # 44
Dress for the position you want.

The moment you begin your job search, you must present yourself as the person you plan to be. You may be used to wearing what you want each day, like your favorite jeans and T-shirts, but if you want to be taken seriously, you'd better give serious consideration to what you wear.

When you dress for work, what *you* want to wear isn't nearly as important as what your *employer* wants you to wear. If two people applying for a job have similar credentials but one of them *appears* more qualified, that person has an advantage in getting the job. When all else is equal, the person who *looks* most professional and successful almost always wins.

When you decide what to wear to an interview, don't choose clothing based on who you are *today*; choose clothing that reflects the person you are about to become. Dress as if you already have the job, and you will appear ready to tackle the position and responsibility of the job you are applying for

There are many talented, intelligent, and capable people who create barriers for themselves; don't let your clothing be a barrier. Poor hygiene and inappropriate dress hurt your image. If it appears that you can't handle the basics of personal grooming, why should a potential employer think you can carry out the duties of the job?

If you want to be noticed for your contributions, don't draw negative attention to yourself. If you are ready to take on more responsibility and want to be considered for a promotion, make it easy for others to *see* how ready you are and look like the responsible person you claim you are.

I've heard from numerous individuals who attribute a promotion to their dressing better than they needed to. I've also heard from managers who didn't promote someone because that person didn't look ready to take on more responsibility. When you look as though you are ready for advancement, others assume you are ready.

Emulate the people who are where you want to be. If the managers in your company wear suits, start wearing a suit. That action alone will change the perception others have of you. The more closely you resemble management, the easier it is for others to see that you are ready to move into a managerial position. Even if you were unsuccessful when you tried to draw attention to yourself before, the change in your appearance could make the difference.

Don't dress for the position you have. Dress for the position you want.

TIP # 45

Get involved in life; work hard, and play hard too.

Some people live life on automatic pilot. They get up each day at the crack of dawn, go to work all day, come home with just a few hours to spare, and then go to bed. They wake up again the next day and start their routine over again.

I hope you'll do more than show up for work each day. Take on a new challenge, look for new and better ways of doing things; volunteer to work on a project. The more you contribute, the more value you bring to your organization. The more involved you are, the more you will get out of the work you do.

Life is what you make it. You can choose to get involved in life or sit back and wait and see how your life unfolds. You can choose to be a doer or a talker, a giver or receiver, a leader or follower. You can sit back and do nothing or get involved and ensure you accomplish something.

Work consumes many people, but it doesn't have to consume you. It's important to learn to separate your work life from your personal life. You shouldn't bring your personal life to work or make a habit of bringing work issues home with you.

When you work *harder*, you're not necessarily working *smarter*. Success isn't a result of the amount of time you put in each day; it's what you do with your time when you're working that counts. Don't waste your time away. Work on doing the most important things each day.

Some people work on weekends to catch up, but be careful if you are devoting the majority of your time working when you should be rejuvenating. Drawing the line between work and play has become more difficult. The concept of leisure is being lost, so much so that New York University sociologist Dalton Conley has coined a new phrase for the blurring taking place between leisure and work; he's coined it "weisure time." Technology has give us the ability to stay connected and be productive 24 hours a day. People are finding it more and more difficult to disconnect.

Everyone needs time away from work. It's good when you enjoy your job but important to have balance in your life too. Experience life and continue to learn and grow. The best way to learn is by *doing*. Get involved in your life.

Get involved with people. Develop strong relationships and connections with others. Keep in touch with former teachers, managers, customers, coworkers, and friends. These are some of your best connections, and staying in touch helps you build a strong network. It's easy to lose touch with people over the years, but it's enriching and beneficial for you to work at staying connected.

Get involved with mentoring. Spend time with people you admire, people who have done what you want to do, or people willing to help you and teach you something new. If your company has a mentoring program, enter it. If not, ask for a referral to one or find a mentoring program on your own. You'll find many people willing to help you if only you ask them to. You can learn a lot from a mentor—and from becoming a mentor, too. Stay involved in mentoring; once you're established in your career, offer to mentor someone who can benefit from you.

Get involved in industry associations and volunteer organizations. Do more than just join an association or send money to an organization; work on a committee, plan an event, or take on a leadership position. Don't join just because you think it will be good for *you*; join because you can contribute something to others too.

Get involved with your family. Spend time with family so that you know what's going on in their lives. Celebrate birthdays, anniversaries, and other occasions. Go out to eat, for a walk, a talk, or whatever you want. It doesn't matter what you do as long as you spend quality time with the people who are most important to you.

Get involved in your community. Read the local paper so you know what's going on, get to know your neighbors, and attend community meetings. Cast your vote when there's an election, learn about your elected officials, and become a part of your community.

Get involved in a cause. If you care about it, feel strongly about it, like to talk about it, and are passionate about it, do something about it. Your involvement (or lack of it) makes a difference. Don't sit back waiting for someone else to take the lead; step up and step out and take the lead yourself.

Get involved in a hobby. It will be easier to break away from work and give your attention to something else when it's something you really like to do. Get curious about something and take some time to learn more about it. Strive to have a variety of interests. It will make you a more interesting and well-rounded person.

Get involved in a league or club. Do you like to bowl, play basketball or cards, ride a bike, read, or ski? If you do, find other people who enjoy the same thing and join them. It's more fun to do these things with someone else and a good way for you to be held accountable when you know others are counting on you.

Get involved with your friends. Remember how much fun you've had just hanging out with your friends? Friends are good for you; stay in touch with your friends and hang out the way you used to. If you don't make your friends a priority and work at maintaining relationships with them, your friendships will slip away.

Don't take life too seriously. All work and no play is no good for anyone. Enjoy the fruits of your labor. Live life and enjoy life. Be sure you work hard, and play hard, too!

TIP # 46
Put people first.

You've been encouraged to work hard and to set and achieve your goals. You know it's important to be a good person too. But what does that mean to you exactly? When important decisions must be made, will you put people first? Will you favor *people* over politics, money, and success? Or will you step over people if doing so will help you advance socially or economically?

You can put people first and still succeed. You can have a family and have a career too. But you *won't* if you put work before family or if you value making money more than making friends. Relationships are important in every aspect of your life. What fun is it to win an award if you have no one to share your excitement? Is a celebration any fun if you're celebrating by yourself?

Everyone has something to offer, but you must be open to receiving what others have to give.

No matter how high you rise, you're never above anyone else. No amount of money you make or power you have will make you a better person. You have to work at being a better person. Don't let your success go to your head.

The best and most successful people rarely succeed alone. Watch any awards program and notice how often several people come forward to accept each award. Time and time again, those giving their acceptance speech exceed the time limit thanking and acknowledging others. Rarely is an award won through the efforts of one person alone.

It's been said a dying man never wishes for more time to work but wishes instead for more time to spend with the *people* he cares most about. *People* are what matters. Cherish your relationships.

Nothing is more rewarding than creating and sharing your success with other people. Surround yourself with supportive people, and you will soar. Pay attention to the people in your life. You'll never regret putting people first.

Someday it will be your turn and *you* will be called upon to accept an award. What do you see—lots of people with you or you standing alone? I hope you have people around you and you exceed the time limit while thanking them, too.

Social Skills

Maintain Good Relationships and Work Cooperatively with Others

TIP # 47
Use social networking tools to stay connected.

I was talking with a few recent grads about utilizing social media as a part of their job search. Krista said she joined LinkedIn after exploring it in one of her classes. At first she thought it was an "older" social networking site, because so many of the members own their own business or work in large companies. It wasn't until she started interviewing for jobs and then connecting with the people she met that she started to understand its real value for job seekers.

LinkedIn is the largest social networking platform designed exclusively for business networking. Krista is finding it easier to reach out to new contacts, and by building a network of career-related connections, she's hoping that her name will be remembered.

In addition to his friends and a few celebrities, Jason is following several advertising agencies and a few select media and marketing professionals on Twitter. He told me that Twitter didn't make sense right away. At first he saw he could "follow" publications like the *New York Times*, so he did. By following others on Twitter, he receives instant updates whenever they post something new. Jason started searching for publications focusing on advertising, which led him to a few companies. His list continues to evolve, and he finds new people and companies to follow based on who others are following. He says Twitter is both interesting and informative, because tweets (posts) cover a range of topics, from the atmosphere in the office on a given day to updates on big projects. Twitter's fast pace also allows Jason to stay connected to the latest news and social buzz.

Social networking sites—or platforms—have become a valuable tool for job seekers as well as those who are employed. Once they dabbled in Twitter and other "older" networking sites, the grads I spoke with all agreed it is important, and a good career strategy to participate and be visible. Some sites are strictly professional networking sites and will be used differently than other, more social sites. You, too, can benefit from being visible on these platforms. The following are a few basic guidelines for using the net to connect with others.

Constantly ask yourself, "What's the goal?" Joining social networking sites is the first step, but to be successful, you should always keep your goal in mind: Are you trying to make new friends or are you trying to land a job? Your objective should guide your use of each social networking platform. Dan Garon, an Internet communication consultant, stresses the importance of identifying your role on each platform you use and understanding your goal before you start participating. This will shape how you use each site and help you avoid the need for damage control. The number of platforms you are on isn't nearly as important as your participation; it usually pays to select a few sites and get the most out of each one. When determining your objective, consider not only what you want for yourself, but the value you offer others as well.

Think before you type, then pause before posting. You've probably heard about the things that can happen: A job offer is rescinded after reading a tweet on Twitter. Someone gets fired after posting an inappropriate comment about the company he works for, and on it goes. Anything you post has the potential to be read by anyone—today or years from today. If you are not careful, what is meant to be a harmless or humorous comment could come back to haunt you and your reputation.

Choose your friends and contacts carefully. Prospective employers routinely check out a candidate's Internet presence and social networking pages. Some will look a bit further and check out your friends and other contacts, too. They may even contact your friends to learn more about you. Think twice about the people you choose to associate with. Your friends and the people you associate with are a reflection of *you*.

Include a photo. Including a photo with your profile will help personalize your connections and make it easier for people to recognize and remember you. Most people include photos, therefore, not including one stands out. Others may wonder why or what you are hiding. Be sure the photo you use is a positive representation of you; a professional and friendly looking headshot is all you need.

Think quality, not quantity. Social networking is not about accumulating as many contacts as you can. You don't have to accept every request you receive, nor should you be more interested in the number of contacts over substance. It doesn't do you any good to have a huge list of contacts you don't know and are not able to utilize. The stronger your connections, the more likely they will be able to help you and open doors for you. The more you know about the people you are connected with, the more you will be able to leverage those relationships and benefit from them.

Separate your personal and professional life. For some, creating a separate profile for professional contacts is the way to go. Others have made the decision to dedicate certain platforms for professional use only. If a business contact initiates a connection on the platform you've designated for friends and family, you can direct them to the other platform. It's one way to keep contacts separate; another is to have two profiles on the same site—one personal, the other professional.

Keep your profile up to date. Think of your profile as a living, evolving document, and, an expansion of your resume. Complete your entire profile, making sure it represents you well. You never know who might find you or what someone might offer you. As you evolve, your profile should too. Updating your profile is another way for you keep track of your professional growth and accomplishments.

Reach out to others. Having a profile and a presence on social media is a first step, but it is not the last. Don't sit back and watch what others are doing or wait for others to reach out to you. Take the initiative; connect with people you know and new people you meet. Join groups; respond to discussions, write your own blog, or post comments on others. Keep people informed about you by posting status updates. Be willing to write recommendations when appropriate and ask others to do the same. The more value you add, the more valuable you will be to others.

Be authentic. There are no shortcuts with relationships. If you want to develop genuine and trusting connections, you must never abuse the relationships you've established. Don't become a burden by asking too many favors. Never pitch yourself or a product, preach, or send spam. If you have an ulterior motive and only care about your personal gain, it will be loud and clear to others and they will be less likely to help you. Give people a reason to want to follow you and stay connected to you. Aim to give more than you get.

TIP # 48
First impressions create lasting impressions.

Can you remember the anticipation you felt each year on the first day of school? The moment you walked into the classroom you probably had a good idea about whether or not you liked what you saw or whether it was going to be a good year.

As you search for a job or start a new one, the anticipation you feel might remind you of the way you felt at the start of each school year. You're embarking on a new experience, meeting people, and evaluating your new situation. With just a glance, you will make assumptions about the people you meet and they will make assumptions about you. Your (and their) instantaneous conclusions and decisions based on first impressions will affect your future. First impressions last much longer than the time it takes to form them.

The moment you enter a room and the instant you meet someone, the evaluation process begins. If you are dressed inappropriately or sloppily, are disorganized, or look worried, negative assumptions will be made before you have a chance to say hello. Business people are busy people, with little time to spare. No one is going to waste time getting to know someone who appears incapable or uncaring. Most interviews, meetings, and interactions are under time constraints. If you fail to make a positive impression within the brief amount of time you are given, you may never get another chance.

When you know what kind of impression you want to make and are able to convey it effectively to others, you increase your chances of getting the job you want and establishing yourself as a competent professional. You can't afford to have a bad day or an off moment; every interaction you experience is critical.

Within a matter of seconds the people you meet will be drawing long-lasting conclusions about you. Smile, make eye contact, and extend your hand when meeting or greeting someone. A *good* handshake bonds people together; a *bad* shake leads to mistrust. A strong and enthusiastic shake lets others know you are confident and in control. A half-hearted or wimpy handshake suggests weakness or apathy.

In business, shaking hands at the beginning and ending of an interaction is expected; in other circumstances, it is appreciated. A handshake adds friendliness to your greeting and reveals how you feel about yourself and others. Lack of eye contact, no expression, poor posture, or a questioning tone of voice weakens even the best shake.

When your hands are dry and warm, and you have a solid and complete grip of the other person's hand, you are saying, "I'm confident and ready to meet you." When your touch is steady and your squeeze is firm, the message is, "I'm focused and I genuinely care about you." And when the duration is brief and the "feel" assuring, you're saying, "I know what I'm doing. Don't worry about a thing."

You're competing with others who match your knowledge and ability, but you can differentiate yourself by the way you look, act, and connect with others by doing the following:

- Dress to impress the people you meet.

- Carry yourself confidently; act confident even if you don't feel confident.

- Hold your head high and look directly at the people you are greeting.

- Walk slowly and purposefully.

- Extend your arm and shake hands firmly.

The more prepared you are, the better your chances of making a positive impression. When you are prepared, you will feel more confident and be more present. You will find people are willing to take the time to get to know you, and you will get to know people on a deeper level.

It takes only seconds to form an impression, but the impact is long lasting. When your image and actions reflect your confidence, ability, and desire to succeed, it will be obvious to others. Know what kind of impression you want to make and do everything you can to create it *every* time you interact with another person.

TIP # 49

Take responsibility for yourself and your relationships.

I write a workplace advice column. As a result, I've learned a lot about people. Over the years, I've noticed a common theme among the many questions I receive.

People usually write to me because of a problem, and the problem usually is *somebody else.*

The troubles I hear about tend to center on the horrid boss, the irritating coworker, or the annoying customer. Every question I receive is different, yet the core issues and concerns are remarkably similar. I've been writing my column for more than 10 years, and I can recall only *one* letter I received in which the writer said, "I am the problem."

Don't get me wrong; there are bad bosses, bothersome coworkers, and unfair practices. I realize that the wrong people get promoted and the right people are let go. I know all isn't fair, bad things happen, and at times there's no bright side to look on. My job, however, is to give advice, and I try to provide some consolation.

I've noticed, too, that there is a common theme in the advice I give. Although each situation is unique, and I try to personalize my response, my overall message can be summed up in just a few words: *Take responsibility for your relationships.*

This isn't what most people expect or want to hear. Occasionally, I hear from a dissatisfied reader whose only reason for contacting me a second time is to tell me *I* am the problem!

If you struggle in your relationships or encounter problems with the majority of the people in your life, consider this: *Other people* might not be the problem; the problem might be the person looking back at you in the mirror.

It's much easier to focus on other people than it is to focus on ourselves, because we see them differently (and sometimes more clearly) than we see ourselves. We complain, we withdraw, we pout, we nag, and we lose sleep over other people, instead of taking a good look at ourselves. You may be powerless to change someone else, but you're the only one who has the power to change yourself.

Yes, there are difficult people; it's a fact of life. We don't get to choose our family members. The decisions we make about where we live and where we work give us some say in who our neighbors, bosses, or team members will be, but few people are able to hand pick the people they want to work with or live by.

Strong, healthy relationships require time, effort, and a *desire* to keep the relationship strong. Some relationships can't be resolved. Sometimes the best decision is also the most difficult.

I once heard a saying that has stuck with me over the years, and I try to live by the simplicity of the message. It summarizes the theme of my advice: "If it's to be, it's up to me."

Now it's up to *you: Take responsibility for yourself and your relationships.*

TIP # 50
Network, network, network.

When Lisa called to ask me to go with her to a party on Friday night, I said no. I'd had an exhausting week. I'd been working, studying, and trying to decide what to do about a shaky relationship I was trying to break off. I wanted to stay in my dorm room the entire weekend—*alone.*

"Come on," she pleaded. "Let's go check it out—we'll leave after 10 minutes if it's not any good. You *need* to get out and meet other people." Lisa was insistent, and I didn't have the energy to resist. I was sure I wouldn't meet anyone worthwhile or have a good time, but I let her talk me into going anyway.

Over 30 years have passed since that night, yet every time I see or talk to Lisa, she reminds me to *thank her* for *forcing* me to go to the party that night—and I *always* do. You see, the party she *made* me go to was where I first met my husband, Steve.

College dorm parties probably aren't the first thing you think of when thinking about networking. As I look back and reflect, however, I can see the events of that night were networking *working* at its best.

Networking doesn't have to be difficult and complex; it shouldn't be work at all. It doesn't always take work to expand your network. It can come from the things you *do*.

Do you: Talk to and keep in touch with your family, coworkers, customers, and friends?

Do you: Converse with your neighbors or teachers, store clerks, security guards, or drivers?

Do you: Maintain relationships with friends, former teachers, advisors, or bosses?

Do you: Attend weddings, celebrations, parties, or informal gatherings?

Do you: Start conversations with the people you meet while waiting in line or sitting on a plane?

Do you: Affiliate with a church or synagogue, belong to any clubs or organizations?

Do you: Volunteer, devote time to a cause, or help others out in any way?

Do you: Spend time on the Internet communicating and sharing information with others?

If you *do* any of the preceding, you *do* have a network of people. You're networking (or *doing* it) without even knowing. When you network to give and to grow, you gain.

Network to give. Develop meaningful relationships; it's not the *number* of people whose contact information you have that matters—it's the *number of people who matter* to you in your life.

The more genuine your relationships are, the better your network will be. Don't be consumed with what you *get* from your relationships; focus on what you can *give*. You'll find that the more you give, the more you eventually get. Staying in touch with people has never been easier thanks to technology, but it's nice every once in awhile to connect in person or by phone. Make the effort to meet some of your valuable connections for lunch or coffee. Let others know you are thinking of them every now and then by sending information or contacts their way. When you read an article you think would interest someone else, send that person the link, or better yet, print it out and send it the old-fashioned way—by mail.

Network to grow. Join groups both online and off; take a class, become part of a book, cooking, or other club. Join your alumni association, find a mentor, or take up a hobby or sport. Consider becoming a member of the local Rotary Club or Chamber of Commerce or volunteering at your favorite charity. Get away from your desk and take a break with coworkers. Invite a client (or your boss) to lunch. Grow each time you meet someone new. Grow by learning something new about the people you already know; learn from the experiences and opinions of others. Grow by learning, grow by doing.

Network to gain. Expand your knowledge, widen your interests, and reach out to others. Learn by asking, learn by listening, and by *doing* whatever you can to build strong relationships. Gain from giving and growing your network, and see your network *working* for you.

Network to *give*, Network to *grow*, Network to *gain*.

Network, Network, Network.

TIP # 51

Show up for events; your presence matters.

Melissa always felt uncomfortable when someone she knew experienced the loss of an important person. "I didn't know what to say or do," she told me. So, like many of us, she hesitated to call and stayed away, not because she didn't care but because she cared so much she didn't want to do or say the wrong thing. Instead, she rationalized, "They won't notice if I'm there or not."

Melissa's feelings are common. It's ironic that at times when people need us most, we hold back. Instead of attending to someone else's problem, we end up nurturing our *own*. Sometimes we *think* we know how someone feels, but we *don't*. That's why so many people turn to support groups for comfort. Whether it's an addiction, a trauma, or a loss, no one understands better than those who have been there.

Showing your support isn't limited to people who are suffering; it's important to be there for people in both good and bad times. You'll be invited to many events over the years and you may not be excited about accepting every invitation you receive. When you are busy with your own life, it can be difficult to take time away to focus on someone else's. Make an effort to attend. If you fail to be there for others, you will find others less interested in being there for you. Whether it's a wedding, baby shower, retirement party, reunion, or birthday, celebrate the special occasions in life.

By the time I heard about Kay's loss, it was *after* her father's funeral. Since I couldn't attend the funeral, I called to express my condolences and planned on sending a card. I didn't get around to sending the card for several months and hesitated before I did, wondering if too much time had passed.

Kay was so touched by my card she called to *thank me* for sending it, saying it came at the *perfect* time. The card I sent arrived on the three-month anniversary of her father's death—a day she was feeling especially sad and alone. She said the onslaught of cards and calls immediately following his death was a bit over-whelming, but receiving them helped her get through each day. By the time my card arrived, the others had stopped coming. Receiving my card reminded her people still cared.

It's never too late (and *always* appreciated) to let someone know you are thinking of them. When you can't be there in per-son, do the next best thing. Take the time to *personally* acknowl-edge the events of important people in your life. Send birthday cards, anniversary cards, and congratulation cards, too. Send sympathy cards to people who are grieving and notes of encour-agment to those who are ill. If you want people to be there for you, be there for others. Keep in touch, remember life's impor-tatnt events, and whenever someone does something nice for you, be sure to let that person know how much you appreciate it.

Sadly, Melissa learned about dealing with loss the hard way. "It does matter if you attend," she said. "I can tell you who among my friends was at the wake and funeral. Friends of mine who never met my dad came to the wake. It didn't matter if they stayed five or 50 minutes. It's a show of support and respect. *It matters.*"

She also learned how easy it is for people to say, "Let me know if I can do anything," but how hard it is to follow through. She said it helps to hear people say, "I'm here for you no matter what happens."

Show up for events and be there for people; your presence matters.

TIP # 52
Just say *"no."*

You might be used to hearing it but feel uncomfortable saying it.

You know it isn't hard to say but struggle with it every day.

You can hear "no" in your head, so why does "yes" come out instead?

You want to help others and make them feel good, but sometimes when you do, *you* end up feeling *bad*. Perhaps it's because whenever you say "yes" to something, you say "no" to another. It is impossible to do everything you want; time is too limited and life too busy. When you accept more to do than your time allows, you create needless stress for yourself. It's much better, although not always easier, to say "no" up front when you need to.

Saying no isn't easy. Adults of *all* ages struggle with saying it every day. "No" can sound harsh and negative. Even so, there are times *no* other response will do.

So what will you do if your manager asks you to dinner and you feel uncomfortable going? What will you say if the client you're with inappropriately touches your leg? Will you say *something* or *nothing* at all? Saying "no" in such situations is crucial, because it lets people know that they have crossed your boundaries.

What will you do when you're asked to head a committee, take on extra work, or help out a friend? What if you want to say "no" but aren't really sure?

When you're not sure how to answer:

1. **Consider your options.** Some requests are critical; they need to be done right away. Some people have authority; when your boss tells you to do something, you might have no choice at all. Know the difference between a command and an option. If you're ever unsure, *ask*.

2. **Get the facts.** Find out more about the request to make the right decision. "When do you need this by?" "Tell me what this is about." "How much time does it involve?"

3. **Take time to think.** Don't let people pressure you to say something you'll regret. Request some time to make your decision. "I need some time before I make a decision." "I need to look at my schedule." "I'll get back to you tomorrow."

4. **Make a decision.** Say "yes" when it is something you decide to do and "no" to everything else.

5. **Stand by your decision.** When you've taken the steps to make a well-thought-out decision, stick with it. You may disappoint someone, but it's better than disappointing yourself.

6. **Announce your decision.** If your answer is no, say "no." Don't *try* saying it, and don't make excuses for saying it. Say it any way you want:

No. No, thank you. No, I can't. No, I won't. Not now. No, I'm not interested. No, I'm not. No, you're not. No, we shouldn't. I won't be able to do it. Not a chance. I'd like to help you out, but I have to say no. I've decided not to do it. I decided against it. It's not going to happen. It won't work out for me. I'm saying no. No, I'm declining. No, I'm already committed. Thank you for asking, but no. No, it's not going to work out. I'm sorry to say this, but the answer is *no*.

Don't make it fancy or complicated. Speak up and simply say "*NO!*"

TIP # 53
Know the difference between an online and off-line friend.

Making friends is easier than ever before. It's common to have hundreds, even thousands of connections thanks to the Internet and social networking sites. But don't let the numbers deceive you; there's a difference between an established relationship and a contact you made online. True friends are hard to come by.

Even the most connected people can feel lonely. Online relationships have value, but do little to enhance your social life. If you spend most of your time online, even if you have lots of friends, you could end up feeling lonely.

Think about your favorite band or singer. You can listen to their music on radio, CD, iPod, computer, or television. You can read about them and follow their twitters, blogs, and Web sites, but nothing compares to seeing and hearing a live performance. Performing artists understand the power of connecting with their fans—it's why they tour. Attending a concert strengthens the bond. Getting together with a friend or business acquaintance in person strengthens relationships too.

Denise was talking with someone at a conference who commented on how calm and approachable she was; something he wouldn't have picked up on had they met on a networking site instead of in person. During the course of their conversation they started talking about motorcycles, something they both are passionate about. They made a memorable, likeable, long-lasting impression on each other. And, as a result of their conversation, Denise was able to introduce the person she met to someone that may lead to work in his field. Their ability to take cues from each other's facial expressions, tone of voice and body language enabled them to develop a deeper rapport much faster than an introduction online.

Your traits separate you from others. Your look, your character, your personality, wit and warmth are evident when people are with you, but more difficult to communicate online. The kind of connection and ability to relate that comes from a personal interaction is much more difficult to achieve on a computer.

Whether you like to mingle at "live" events or not, there is merit in doing so. It is advantageous to learn the ropes of socializing and networking both online and off.

The more people know about you, the better they understand you. The more people care about you, the more willing they will be to help you. Make your connections count; make them as *personal* as possible.

Whether you are looking for a job or to grow your network of business contacts and friends, utilize a variety of tools. Balance the amount of time spent socializing online and off. Attend business events and other gatherings that are of interest to you outside of work. Sharing common interests can make an initial conversation much easier. Once you know someone, making additional connections through that person is natural.

While it may not be possible for you to meet every person you are connected with in person, look for ways to get more out of your online connections. If you have information or a lead for someone, pick up the phone and make a call or send a personal e-mail.

Nothing replaces the connection that comes from a real friendship. It's nice to have the option of meeting someone for a walk, a talk, or just to hang out. Enjoy the benefits of connecting with people online, but be sure you still make the effort to get together every now and then.

TIP # 54
The company party is not a party.

If your idea of a good party includes heavy drinking, cozy (and cuddly) conversation, dirty dancing, or winning the title of *worst* karaoke singer, you're probably not going to think the company party is a party at all. I'm not suggesting you won't, or can't, have a good time; I'm merely suggesting you tone it down a bit.

Whether it's the company picnic, the holiday party, a convention, or someone's retirement or promotion during happy hour, social events can provide you opportunities to strengthen your relationships with coworkers.

When you work in a professional position, you are expected to behave in a professional manner at *all* times. If you behave unprofessionally, you are not fulfilling your obligations. Make the most of every opportunity you have, or you may not get the chance to prove yourself again. Act as if your behavior is being observed every minute, because *it is*.

If you wonder if your attendance matters, it does. You might not be *required* to attend, but your absence will be noted. When you are a "no show," you *show* you are not interested. This does not help you look like a committed team player or caring coworker.

If you're focused on the food, you're not focused on the people; don't attend on an empty stomach. Drinking alcohol on an empty stomach is likely to have a stronger effect on you. It's a good idea to eat something before the party; if you're watching the time and looking for food, you're wasting the time you should be talking with others.

If you can't decide what to wear, think *business event*, **not** *social event*. You are a professional; *look like one*. If it isn't a company picnic, don't even consider wearing jeans, tank tops, or shorts. If it isn't a costume party, don't wear anything so shocking or unusual that your clothing is the topic of conversation. If it isn't a black-tie formal affair, don't wear full-length, slinky, or sequined dresses or a tuxedo. And if it isn't a swimming party (which most business events are not), *never* bare your midriff, your buttocks, or breasts.

If you're planning on arriving fashionably late, make another plan. Late is late. There is nothing fashionable about it.

If alcohol is served, *think* **before you drink.** If you get wasted, you've *wasted* a valuable opportunity to demonstrate your self-control. You don't have to apologize or make excuses for not drinking, but when you drink and get drunk, you do. A small amount of alcohol is all it takes to affect your behavior.

If you want to stand out and be noticed, get up and move around. You are at a social event; *socialize*. Don't huddle in a bunch with your work buddies; get up and move around. People can't see you, let alone notice you, when you're sitting in the corner.

If you see people you do not know, introduce yourself. This is an ideal time for you to introduce yourself to those you don't ordinarily see or get to talk to, including company executives. But don't brown-nose, brag about your accomplishments, or ask for a raise or promotion; it is the *least-ideal* time to accomplish that.

If you are interested in someone, be friendly, but don't be a flirt. It is likely you will encounter people you are interested in getting to know on a more personal level. Most coworkers engage in casual conversation from time to time. It's natural to talk about vacations, family, and hobbies, but it can become awkward if you pry too deeply or offer too much information. If you are interested in someone, be discreet. Make arrangements to meet away from work to get to know each other better.

If you're hoping to work out problems or discuss the latest gossip, keep hoping. You're at a party, and conversation should be festive, so keep it light and upbeat. People look forward to celebrations. You don't want to be a downer and spoil the celebratory mood. Make sure *you're* not the topic of conversation back at work when the party's over!

If you don't know if you should bring a casual date, *don't*. Just because you're invited to bring a guest doesn't mean you have to. You're responsible for your date, and you might feel more relaxed without someone by your side. If your date gets drunk or acts inappropriately, it will be a negative reflection of *you*.

If you feel uninhibited, control yourself. I don't care how long you've wanted to tell your cube mate you think she (or he) is "hot"; this is *not* the appropriate time. Nor should you take over the dance floor or kiss your boss (or someone else's spouse) under the mistletoe. No kissing, no hugging, and no "hanging on" to people. Remember where you are. The party is an extension of your workplace.

If you want to leave and you don't see the people you'd like to thank, don't leave. Your host and hostess will remember who said hello and good-bye. Always do both, and never leave without saying thank you. It's the appropriate and most gracious thing to do.

TIP # 55
Always have a business card with you.

If you are looking for a job you know you need a resume. However, there may be times when you are out with friends, at a meeting, or other social event when you meet someone you'd like to connect with in the future. It may be premature, or even awkward to offer your resume at that time. If you want that person to remember your name and have your contact information, a business card will do the trick.

Consider creating your own business cards. They can be inexpensive to produce and small enough to carry with you wherever you go. A business card is a great networking tool that makes it easy for people to remember you, help you, and pass your name on to others.

My niece Allie called me for some advice the day before she was attending her first career fair. Although I didn't think she'd have time to put together a business card that night, I suggested she print her own business cards to hand out at future job and career fairs.

When she called me the next day to give me a report, she told me that the business cards were a big hit. I was surprised she was able to get the cards made so quickly. She told me she was determined to get them done the night before and that she was glad she did. She said that everyone she gave a card to was impressed and that she received many positive comments—all from potential employers!

The key to having a business card, whether you are employed or looking for a job, is to carry the card with you at *all* times, even when you think it unlikely you will need it. I learned this the hard way.

It was a beautiful sunny day in Ixtapa, Mexico, and my husband and I were relaxing on the beach. The couple next to us asked where we were from, and within a few minutes we were bantering back and forth.

David was intrigued when I told him about my business. "I am on the board of a company that could use your services," David told me. "I've got a meeting with them when I get back. I need to get your business card before we leave tomorrow."

My husband looked at me and said, "This sounds exciting. You've got your business cards with you, right?" I was *hoping* I did but wasn't really sure. After all, I was *supposed* to be on vacation. I was trying not to think too much about business.

Back in the room, I searched for my business cards. "Don't *you* have one of my cards?" I asked my husband. He didn't say a word, but I knew what he was thinking: *How can you have your own business, coach people toward success, and not carry business cards with you?*

I looked through my purse, my suitcase, and everywhere else, but I couldn't find even one business card.

David understood when I told him I must have given my last card away, which was easier for me to say than admitting I didn't bring any. So he exchanged cards with *my husband* instead, my name and number handwritten on the back.

Business cards are a tangible way to connect with others in the future. Having my business cards at home didn't do me any good and it won't accomplish anything for you either. Put some thought into *your* business card when you put it together and be sure to carry it with you and distribute it to others.

Include your name, e-mail address and phone number; if you have a permanent address, include it. If you're not sure where you'll be living, consider including the city and state or region you are in. Knowing what part of the country you are in can be beneficial for someone setting up interviews or looking to fill a position in a particular area.

If you are able to create a tagline or one sentence that describes you, your skills, and what you offer, include it on the card. It will help others remember you, and help you.

Although David and I exchanged a few e-mails after our return from Ixtapa, he never asked me to do any work for him. He didn't have *my* business card for the meeting and I'll never know if it made a difference to him, but I do know it made a difference to *me*.

I decided that no matter *where* I am, I will always be prepared and *always have my business cards with me!* I encourage you to do the same.

TIP # 56
Guard your shadow; it follows you wherever you go.

The time to start building and protecting your reputation is *now*.

You already know it's important to take care of yourself, because your physical and emotional health is essential to your well-being and ability to perform well. If you care about your health, you'll live a healthful lifestyle. If you want to stay close to your family and friends, you'll stay in contact with them. If success is important to you, you'll develop habits that lead to success. Thus, it follows that if you want to ensure your reputation is positive, you'll think about the things you do.

Your reputation is a result of everything you do—or don't do. Like a shadow, your reputation follows you wherever you go. You might not think the things you do today will matter years from now, but they will. Your character and integrity are at the core of your being.

You've seen it happen in politics: Candidates running for public office are scrutinized. Any wrongdoing or questionable behavior in someone's past can be brought to the forefront. Candidates' dreams have been shattered when scrutiny has uncovered their indiscretions. When the media and opposing political parties are determined to tarnish someone's reputation, they will stop at nothing, unless there's nothing in the person's past to use against them.

Even outside the political scene, your reputation follows you wherever you go. You won't have to look over your shoulder or have anything to worry about if you cultivate a reputation to be proud of. Decide what kind of reputation you want and what kind of person you want to be. Then live your life accordingly. *Think* about your reputation today and in the future.

Think about the kind of person you want to be. Think about the qualities that are most important to you. What characteristics do you want or need to work on? If you want to be a good person, what does "good" mean to you? How will you know if you are the person you want to be? Think about the way you want others to see you, and think about the way you see yourself. You can be the person you want to be.

Think about the things you *say*. Do you say hurtful things you later regret? Do you put people down, minimize someone's feelings, or lash out in anger? Saying "I'm sorry" is important but only when it is sincere. Even if you apologize, words can sting, and people may become leery of you. The more frequently you apologize, the less impact your apology will have. If you want to be viewed as a rational, thoughtful person, think about the things you say. When you choose your words carefully you'll have fewer regrets and won't spend time worrying (or wondering) about what you've said.

Think about the things you *do*. Your actions, not your *intentions*, matter most. What you *do* is what people remember. You can *tell* someone how important he or she is to you, but if you don't spend time with that person, your words are meaningless. You can *say* you're ambitious, but if you're not working hard, no one will believe you. Your actions reveal your *true* feelings. Do more and say less. Actions really do speak louder than words.

Think about the commitments you make. If you say you'll be there, be there. If you say you'll get something done, get it done. If you say you'll call, you'd better call. You are better off not committing than offering to do something but failing to follow through. Your words belong to you; you choose what you say you'll do. Until you give others a reason to doubt you, they will be counting on you and believing in you. Every commitment you make but break, no matter how small, damages your reputation. Don't overcommit, and be sure to honor the commitments you make.

Think about your limitations. You are human and can do only so much. If you try to be perfect or try to please everyone else, you'll end up disappointing others as well as yourself. Be realistic about the things you can do and have time to do. Think about what happens when you let yourself and others down. If you frequently fall behind or fail to accomplish what you set out to do, either someone is expecting too much of you or you are expecting too much of yourself. Know, accept, and handle your limitations.

Think about the way you treat other people. Do you treat everyone respectfully and courteously? Or do you give special treatment and pay extra attention only to those you think can help you? Do you choose your friends based on the qualities they possess or based on what you think they can do for you? Do you spend more time "buttering up" the boss than getting to know your coworkers? All people have value; when you fail to treat all people well, even those you do favor will notice. Besides, the person you bypass today could end up being someone you need something from tomorrow. Treat all people well.

Some things may seem so small that you brush them off as insignificant, but it can be a big mistake. Your reputation is built over time, and the seemingly insignificant things determine your reputation.

Be on the lookout; think about your reputation every time you choose your words, your deeds, and your actions. Everything you do and say will follow you wherever you go, just like a shadow. Guard yourself. Guard your shadow. Be the person you want to be by living your life purposefully.

TIP # 57
Stop talking.

"I dread my lunches with Jane," Leslie told me. "She delves into such detail; a five-minute story takes her 30 minutes to tell. She doesn't like e-mail, but when we talk on the phone, even if I tell her I only have a minute, she goes on and on and I can't get off of the phone."

Some people don't know when to stop talking. They think others want to hear every little detail, but they don't. Evan worked hard to increase sales in his territory. He found a solution to every problem, except one: his own. He never stopped talking. His coworkers said he suffered from "diarrhea of the mouth." I can't think of a less-desirable image.

I was greeting people as they walked into the training room. Typically, I get a two- to three-sentence response when I ask people about themselves, but when I asked Ron what type of work he did, his response never ended: "I just started a new job, but I'm waiting to hear about another one. If I do, I'll end up moving. I moved here three years ago for a job, but one year later, the company was sold. My girlfriend gave up a good job to come here. She has a good job now, but it took her awhile to find it. She wants to go part time to spend more time with our son. We got married last year, went to Vegas for our honeymoon. We wanted to go back for our anniversary, but didn't have anyone to look after our son. It's tough with no family here, so we don't get out much, but the neighbor took him one night. We saw a movie. It was the night of that awful storm. The electricity went out, and I had frozen meat in the freezer I had to throw out. I bought it to save money, but ended up wasting it instead, which is how I feel every time I fill my car up with gas...."

Ron went on and on. He was having a conversation with himself. Whether you are looking for a job, meeting customers, networking, or socializing with friends, when people ask you about yourself, they are asking for the 30-second commercial, not for the unedited version of your entire life.

People want to participate in a conversation; stop talking long enough to listen to what others have to say. If you want to increase your chances of receiving a job offer, making a sale, or impressing someone on a first date, you need to know when it's time for you to stop talking.

I know you want (and need) to sell yourself to an employer, a prospect, or someone you want to impress, but be careful not to oversell yourself. When you stop talking, you pick up cues you'd otherwise miss. If you like to hear yourself speak, listen to yourself ask the right questions.

Here are some good questions to help make a conversation successful:

"What's the biggest challenge you face in your business?"

"What type of work do you do?"

"How did you get into that line of work?"

"What do you like best about what you do?"

"Tell me about yourself."

You don't have to talk a lot to become more interesting. Some of the most interesting, successful, and popular people don't say much at all. They know when to stop saying "I" and make a habit out of saying "you." They listen more than they talk, and when you stop talking, *you* will too.

TIP # 58
Mind your manners.

Display good manners *with people.*

DO:	DON'T:
Listen attentively.	Interrupt someone.
Take an interest in others.	Ask personal questions.
Hold the door open for others.	Slam the door on someone.
Arrive on time.	Make someone wait for you.
Bite your lip.	Say it if it isn't nice.
Smile.	Wink, sneer, or snicker.
Look at the person you are with.	Eye someone up and down.
Remember names.	Assume a nickname is preferred.
Say "please" when making a request.	Make demands.
Show your appreciation.	Take advantage of people.

DO:

Turn off your cell phone.

Say "thank you" when complimented.

Drive defensively.

Accept responsibility.

Offer help.

RSVP promptly.

Send thank you notes.

Use good grammar.

DON'T:

Take a call when with others.

Refuse or negate a compliment.

Gesture at or intimidate drivers.

Cast blame on others.

Shun people in need.

Forget to respond.

Send e-mail instead.

Use slang or profanity.

Display good manners *at work.*

DO:

Keep your hands to yourself.

Greet coworkers each day.

Introduce yourself.

Attend meetings.

Treat men and women equally.

Work efficiently; focus on your job.

Dress for work.

Get to know your coworkers.

Wear name tags on right shoulder.

Initiate conversation with others.

Follow through on your promises.

Visit with coworkers over lunch.

Pick up after yourself.

Learn about cultural differences.

DON'T:

Touch (except to shake hands).

Talk too much at work.

Use first names unless requested.

Talk during a meeting.

Make sexual or sexist remarks.

Use work time for personal tasks.

Dress haphazardly.

Gossip about other people.

Refuse to wear a name tag.

Monopolize a conversation.

Break commitments.

Ignore others or leave them out.

Expect others to do it for you.

Ignore or judge differences.

(continues)

(continued)

Display good manners *when dining.*

DO:	DON'T:
Think before you drink.	Drink to get drunk.
Keep your hand available for greetings.	Become preoccupied with eating.
Put your napkin on your lap immediately.	Wipe your mouth—dab it instead.
Pass the salt and pepper together.	Pass one without the other.
Taste your food before seasoning.	Salt your food automatically.
Pass food counterclockwise.	Allow food to pile up by you.
Cut a few pieces at a time.	Pre-cut food and then dig in.
Spoon your soup *away* from you.	Blow on or slurp your soup.
Order something easy to eat.	Order messy finger foods.
Take your time as you dine.	Rush through the meal.
Chew your food thoroughly.	Talk with food in your mouth.
Position your silverware when done.	Push your plate away from you.
Excuse yourself when necessary.	Pick your teeth at the table.
Tip generously.	Eat out if you can't afford a tip.

You may have learned these rules before or think manners are old-fashioned. The truth is that manners *never* go out of style. They are every bit as important today as they were years ago. When you display good manners, you show respect for others. Treat everyone you meet courteously, regardless of age, gender, race, or ethnicity. When you do, you look good. You will be valued as an employee, friend, and colleague. Whatever you do, always remember to mind your manners.

TIP # 59
Balance screen time with face time.

Have you ever wondered what life was like generations ago? How did people manage without all of the modern conveniences we've become accustomed to? Can you imagine your day-to-day life without a television to watch, a computer to log on to, an iPod to listen to or a phone to use for texting and talking?

Sometimes I get tired of talking on the phone. I often wish I wasn't compelled to check my e-mail or turn on the TV and wonder if I do it out of habit. Sometimes I'm not sure if these things *simplify* my life or *complicate* it. Previous generations missed out on the technological advantages we have, and in some ways life was more difficult. In other ways, it might have been easier. They had fewer distractions and, as a result, more *face time*, which is something we are in short supply of.

Did you know that the average American child will spend more time in front of the television than in school? Do you have any idea how many adults spend more time interacting with a computer screen than interacting with people?

We've become a nation of "screen addicts." This is not a good thing; sitting in front of a computer, using your phone, or watching TV for prolonged periods at a time is *not* good for you. Research has found that TV watching leads to unhealthy eating habits and obesity. We eat too much of the wrong food and sit idle too much of the time.

Spending time in front of a screen doesn't help relationships or families either. Good communication is paramount to any relationship and can't compete with a television, computer, phone, or other electronic device.

Although e-mail, instant messaging, social networking sites, and texting often are used as a means of staying in touch with people, it is not equivalent to time spent face-to-face with someone. It is easy to hide behind electronic messages and escape the responsibilities of a real relationship and direct communication.

If you are in a relationship with someone and spend most of your time in front of a screen, you are putting your relationship at risk. If your job involves time in front of a screen, remind yourself to look up every now and then. If you have something important to communicate, do it face-to-face. Communication is more effective that way.

Technology has enriched our lives; we have the ability to get news in an instant and connect with people anywhere and anytime. Use it to your advantage, but remember: *Technology is no substitute for human contact.*

The next time you pick up the phone to make or take a call, *stop* **before you do.** Is the person you're about to talk to *more important* than whoever you are with? If so, complete the call. If not, put down the phone, face the person you are with, and have a conversation.

The next time you're about to log on to your computer, stop before you do. Look at your watch; it's easy to lose track of time when you use the computer. If you decide to continue, give yourself a time limit. Ask yourself: Is my time better spent interacting with *some<u>one</u>* or interacting with *some<u>thing</u>*? A computer screen is a thing; you're probably better off spending time with a person.

The next time you reach for the remote, *stop* **before you do.**

Do you want to *watch* **life or** *live* **life?** People tend to watch TV to alleviate boredom or loneliness. Are you bored? Are you lonely? Are you avoiding something or someone? *Do you think you should be turning on the TV or turning to someone instead?*

The key is balance; balance screen time with face time.

TIP # 60
Look for similarities, not differences.

I greeted the driver as I got into the backseat of the cab. It was a snowy night, and my flight had been delayed, and all I could think about was getting to my hotel and going to bed.

The driver was friendly, welcomed me to his hometown, and asked me why I was there. Although I typically like to strike up conversations, I wasn't really in the mood that night, but the driver was relentless. He wanted to hear about the conference I was speaking at the next day and was genuinely interested in learning more about me.

I began to respond to his enthusiastic manner and asked him a few questions too. He told me about his escape from Cuba when he came to the United States, about the boat he made out of old truck tires, and how he lived in hiding prior to his daring escape. He described his dangerous departure during a heavy rainstorm, how he almost died en route, and how he was miraculously rescued.

I was captivated by his amazing story of survival. He had such a positive outlook, was filled with gratitude, and so proud to be an American citizen. I learned about his three daughters, who ironically were close in age to my own three girls, and discovered his challenges and concerns as a parent were no different from mine.

When I got into the cab that night, our differences were obvious. I assumed we came from different backgrounds, worked different types of jobs, and lived very different lives. Yet, in less than an hour, I realized we had more in common than I thought. We both loved our families and had similar hopes and dreams for our daughters. We both enjoyed talking to and learning about other people. And it was through our differences that I was able to understand, in a way I never had before, why and how people risk their lives to come to America. As a result of our conversation, I was reminded how grateful I am to be a citizen of the United States, which I admit I often take for granted.

When I arrived at the hotel and got out of the cab, I smiled at Felix, and he smiled at me. "Good luck with the girls," we said simultaneously. We laughed and then did it again: "It was great talking with you," we said in unison.

I thanked him for the ride and handed him my money. I picked up my suitcase, and then, as if on cue, we smiled and shook our heads, turned around, and said good-bye.

As a result of meeting Felix that night, *I am different* when I meet people who are different from me. I find myself looking for our *similarities* instead of focusing on our *differences*. And you know what? More often than not, I end up finding what I'm looking for.

TIP # 61
Show your appreciation.

You are a unique individual. You have talents and abilities that differentiate you from everyone else. You are different, yet you are also more like other people than you may realize. Aside from common survival needs, people need to be acknowledged for the things they do and for who they are. Everyone craves appreciation.

People seek to satisfy this craving in different ways. Some people enjoy being in the spotlight; others are embarrassed by public praise. For some, it doesn't matter *how* they are acknowledged, as long as they are appreciated.

Whenever someone does something nice for *you*, do something nice in return; *show your appreciation*. Don't count on a call, an e-mail, or saying "thanks" the next time you see the person. Put your pen to paper and use the most effective (and impressive) way to say "thanks." Send a handwritten thank you note.

Have you ever thought about the way you go about opening your mail? Which pieces do you automatically throw in the trash, which ones do you put aside to open later, and which ones do you select to open first? Is it the bills, the solicitations, or the personal mail you receive that gets your attention?

Did you know that most people, whether they are aware of it or not, open personalized, hand-addressed envelopes first? We don't receive personalized mail every day, so we tend to *appreciate* it when we do.

You probably prefer to say "thanks" with e-mail; after all, it's less time consuming. It's also a less personal message. There's no envelope to open and no card or note to display, and there's a chance it might never get opened at all.

Everyone craves a little appreciation. Whenever someone does something nice for you (including interviewing you), *show your appreciation; send a thank-you note.*

Jacqlyn was looking for an intern. Of the 10 people she interviewed, only one sent a handwritten thank you note: That person was offered the job. When all else is equal, it is the little things that set people apart. Jacqlyn posts all of the thank you notes she receives on her bulletin board. It means that much to her. See for yourself the difference writing, and mailing a thank you can make.

When you show your appreciation to others, you will get back some of what you give. Appreciation is *always* appreciated. You can earn the cooperation and dedication of your coworkers by showing your appreciation. There are limitless ways to convey your appreciation. Here are just a few.

Seven ways to show your appreciation:

1. **Write a letter.** Go beyond a thank you note; write a letter expressing your sincere appreciation and how you've benefited from what the person did.

2. **Offer to run an errand.** If you're going out and will be near the post office, dry cleaner, deli, or coffee shop, ask if you can drop off or pick up something for someone.

3. **Help someone.** Show your appreciation by helping someone. Offer to make copies of something if you're heading to the copier, or deliver a fax you found in the fax machine. You can offer your help, but you will make a bigger impression if you do something without being asked.

4. **Bring a treat.** Does a coworker or friend like chocolate chip cookies, popcorn, or lattes? Get something the person will enjoy and bring it to him or her as a way of showing your appreciation.

5. **Be a sounding board.** Ask how things are going and listen to the response.

6. **Buy a gift.** Is your friend or coworker a cat lover? Get him or her a cat picture frame. Is he or she a golfer? Buy him or her a few new golf balls or other golf-related items. You don't have to spend a lot of money to show your appreciation. Never give something in the hopes someone will be indebted to you; give with no strings attached. And be careful whom you give to; some companies don't allow employees to accept or exchange gifts.

7. **Share information.** If you know that someone has a particular interest, bring in an article on the subject, give a subscription to a magazine or new journal, or talk about some information you heard.

When you acknowledge what people do, they will notice *you*. Showing your appreciation is a powerful motivator. When you value and appreciate people, you are fulfilling a basic human need. Get in the habit of noticing and appreciating what others do. They will benefit and so will you.

Self-Discipline

Be Healthy, Wealthy, and Wise

TIP # 62

Control your spending.

When I ask twentysomething's what they've found most challenging about life after graduation, money—and the lack of it—is frequently mentioned. "Everything is so expensive," Libby told me. "When I was in college and working part time I didn't think twice about buying something. Now when I find a great pair of jeans I'd like to have, I have to make the decision between buying groceries or the jeans. Lately, putting food in the fridge wins and the jeans stay in the store."

Working full time and living on your own may be a welcome relief, but the financial burden can be challenging. Many new grads are surprised to discover that the good salary they are earning is barely enough to cover expenses month to month.

Rachel is living paycheck to paycheck. Initially her salary seemed like enough, but she didn't realize how much of her earnings would be taken out for taxes, and hadn't considered the many other expenses she's responsible for. Over half of her paycheck each month goes to her rent payment. What's left goes toward utilities, insurance, cable, telephone, food, and entertainment, which includes shopping and going out with friends. She'd like to be able to save money but says she can't because she's barely getting by on the money she has. She says she is increasingly worried about her lack of funds and wonders how she will ever get ahead.

Money problems are a leading cause of stress, causing millions of people sleepless nights and other ailments. The inability to keep up with bills, mounting credit card debt, and concerns about the future can have a profound affect on your physical and emotional well-being.

Does money worry you or cause you stress? Do you wonder if you will have enough money to do the things you want? Do you control your spending, or does your spending control you?

Know where your money goes. The best way to avoid overspending and getting into debt is by knowing where your money goes. Start by keeping track of what you earn and what you spend. Write down *every* purchase you make and every bill you pay. Account for every penny for the next month or two. This is the only way to get an accurate account of what you are spending and will help you determine where you need to cut back.

Create a budget and stick to it. You can do it on your own, with the help of someone else or buy software to help you create a budget. Start by identifying your fixed expenses (rent or mortgage, insurance, car payment, utilities, phone, Internet, cable, other bills, etc.); determine how much you have left after paying these expenses, and then decide what to do with the remaining money. Having a budget enables you to make decisions about how your money is spent in *advance*. You always know exactly what you can and cannot afford. However, your budget is only as good as you are at sticking to it.

Plan your purchases. When my sister sees something she wants to buy, she keeps her eye on it and waits until it goes on sale. She shops around when purchasing larger items to ensure the best value. She rarely pays full price for anything. When you take the time to plan your purchases, you will save.

Impulse buying is tempting and may lift your spirits in the moment, but rarely is the pleasure long lasting. Most impulsive purchases are not essential. The best way to avoid impulse buying is to plan all of your purchases in advance and to budget for them. If you see something you want, put it on hold. Give yourself time to think before making a purchase. When you grocery shop, make a list and buy only what's on that list. If shopping and impulse buying is a problem for you, stay out of stores, malls, and shopping on the Internet unless you are shopping for something specific you have planned to buy.

Know the difference between a want and a need. You may *want* the latest version of the phone you have, but do you *need* it? Unless your phone isn't working or lacks features you *need,* it isn't essential. It's easier than you think to get rid of the some of the things eating away at your earnings. Start by reviewing your list of expenses, looking for items to cut. You might think cable television and premium stations are a must, but it isn't a staple in every home nor need it be in yours. It is nice to have, but the cost is high and likely something you could live without. The decision is yours. When you eliminate some of the nonessentials and have more money in your pocket, you'll probably find your desire for those things diminish, too.

Eat in. If eating meals out is part of your regular routine, think about making it something special instead. The latte you get each day, the fast food you pickup, the snacks you get from the vending machine, and the meals out with friends all add up in cost. Over the course of a year you can end up spending thousands of dollars on the food and drinks you purchase. Consider cutting back. Order plain coffee or tea instead of a specialty coffee drink; a small instead of a large latte. Bring your lunch to work; make meals in advance in larger batches and eat or freeze leftovers. Drink water instead of a soda—in your own reusable bottle. Limit the number of alcoholic drinks when out with friends. A few dollars saved here and there put many more dollars back into your wallet.

Think and live frugally. The more you cut back, the more you have in reserve. Getting into a frugal mindset can be easy. Want to see a movie? Wait a few months and rent the DVD. Can't wait? Attend the matinee and save.

Want to travel? Plan your trip in advance by taking time to shop around for the best travel deals. Want to read the newspaper, a magazine, or book? Cancel your subscriptons and get your information online. Spend time at the library and check out books for free.

Reexamine your phone, television, and Internet plans. Are you using all of the features you are paying for? Could you look up phone numbers and reduce the fees you pay for 411?

Living frugally does not mean you have to do without. It simply ensures you get the most out of every dollar you spend.

TIP # 63

Reduce your anxiety with technology.

"Be Prepared." It's the motto of the Boy Scouts of America. It sounds simple enough and the benefits of being prepared are clear, but often the anxiety in our lives stems from being *unprepared*. Being prepared is one thing; knowing what to prepare for is another.

We don't often view the proper use of technology as an essential component of being prepared, but it is. Technology can make our lives easier. It's when things go wrong that we realize how much we depend on the equipment we use. Not only is it frustrating to be stalled by technology, it can be immobilizing.

We don't plan on being hit with the latest computer virus or scam. We can't predict when a computer, phone, or other piece of equipment will malfunction, and we can't always prevent it from happening. But we are not helpless nor do we have to be victims. We can ease the stress associated with such problems by being prepared should something happen.

Backup your computer. My daughter was writing a term paper when her computer crashed. She was able to replace her hard drive, but thousands of photos and hundreds of school projects were permanently erased. She lost everything and had no backup. It was devastating for her at the time, but she learned a valuable lesson about the importance of backing up her computer on a regular basis. If you are working on a special or important project, backup the information more frequently. What's more, make sure the backup actually works.

We rely on our computers because they are reliable. Sometimes we forget that things can go wrong. I never planned on dropping my laptop, but I did. We don't anticipate our computer being hit with a virus, power surge, or even a cup of coffee—but it happens. A broken or missing computer is stressful enough without having the added worry about lost data. You can quickly backup your information on an external hard drive, CD, DVD, online storage service, or even another computer. If you use an e-mail account that stores messages online indefinitely (like Gmail), you can even e-mail yourself important documents and archive the messages; as long as you have access to e-mail you'll have access to the files. Whatever method you choose, set up automatic backups when possible or put a reminder in your calendar. The time it takes to backup your information is minimal compared to the time it will take to recreate all of your information should you lose it.

Backup and sync your cell phone. Mandy used her iPhone for everything. Although she was able to sync the information from her phone with her computer, she rarely did. It wasn't until her phone fell into the toilet that she realized the importance of syncing. She was able to replace her phone, but none of the information. Her calendar and contacts were wiped out. The music and photos she had accumulated were gone. She didn't remember the dates and times of her appointments and had to spend time searching for phone numbers and e-mail addresses. What she could have backed up in a matter of minutes took her weeks to recreate. Get into the habit of backing up the information in your phone—and keep your phone away from water, especially the toilet!

Protect your computer. I know people who've had their computers stolen, others who've been hit with a virus or identity theft. Do what you can to prevent such things and minimize your risk. Install firewall and security software and set it to update automatically. The investment up front is well worth the cost and will save you money should your computer be hit with a virus, a phishing scam, or other problem.

If you are toting around a laptop, treat it like the valuable item it is and with the utmost care. Never leave your computer in the car or anywhere unattended. Someone once told me they treat their computer like cash; you wouldn't display your cash or leave it lying around nor should you ever let your computer out of your sight in a public place. Think about not only the monetary value of your computer but the importance and value of the information inside.

Guard your personal information. Experts suggest using a different password for every Web site you visit, and changing that password every few months. It's a lot to keep track of, but well worth the effort. Be creative with your passwords and make it difficult for someone to access your accounts or steal your identity. The more complex you make your password the more difficult for someone else to figure it out.

Use privacy settings on social networking sites to restrict access to your personal information and limit the amount of private information you share. Even seemingly innocent information you disclose about yourself and your family could be used against you. I recently read about a home robbery. It turns out the burglars selected that particular home because they discovered the owner was out of town by reading a Facebook message. According to Carol Fredrickson, a personal safety expert, it isn't an isolated experience. The status updates you post on social media sites can lead to criminal activity. You may not think twice about posting the concert you are going to or your weekend away, but it could be an invitation for trouble. Fredrickson advises caution in the information you share and the need to protect your identity. Information on the Internet has made it easier for thieves to steal your identity. Never reveal your full birth date. The month and day is fine to post, but leave off the year you were born.

Never respond to e-mails requesting personal information, your Social Security number, or financial information. Don't click on e-mail links from financial institutions. Contact the company directly instead, but still be very cautious. Do not freely offer or verify personal information to anyone until you are certain who you are dealing with and know it is a legitimate request.

Your safety and security are important. Taking the necessary precautions is the best way to ensure you, your equipment, and your personal information stay protected.

TIP # 64
Be your own best friend; set aside time for yourself.

Have you ever had a *best* friend? It's fun to have a best friend, especially when the friendship lasts. I had a best friend who lived across the street from me. We were very young when we decided we would be best friends *forever.* I felt more secure knowing I had a best friend; it was nice to have someone I could count on. Our friendship was strong, spanning high school and college, but our friendship was put to the test when we went our separate ways as adults. When my best friend married, everything changed. She couldn't be there for me the way she had before, which I understood, but it left a void in my life. I had other friends, but no one replaced my best friend—until I met my husband.

My husband and I spent as much time as we could together when we were dating and after we married. Over the years, our lives changed and our responsibilities grew, and we found less and less time to spend together. There were times I needed my husband when he simply wasn't available. I had other friends, but they were busy managing their own hectic lives. I no longer could depend on others; I knew I needed to depend on myself.

No one can do for you what you need to do for yourself. What is a friend, after all? A good friend should be a bonus, not an obligation. I don't want to be a burden to my friends with every little problem I have—I want to *enjoy* my friends and want them to enjoy being with me. If you expect someone to be there all the time, you might end up disappointed. The older you get, the more you will see how busy everyone can be. It's not that your friends don't *want* to be there for you; sometimes they just *can't* be there for you. Instead of relying on everyone else, you need to rely on yourself.

As your responsibilities increase, your time alone decreases. If you don't pay attention, you can lose your sense of self in your work and close relationships. When the majority of your time is spent working and your free time is spent socializing, you'll have little (if any) time left over for *you.*

Friends are nice to have and many will come in and out of your life. The most important and long lasting friendship is the one you have with yourself. Be your own best friend. Develop a relationship with *yourself.* Depend on yourself. When you need to work something through, take some time to be with *you.* When you have a strong friendship with yourself, you will have better friendships with everyone else. When you're not a burden but are an easy-going friend, you're the very best kind of friend for others to have.

Time won't stop or suddenly become available. You'll never *find* time to do the things you want to do; you must *schedule time* for the things that are most important to you. You need to make *yourself* a top priority. It isn't selfish to take time for yourself; it is essential to your overall well-being.

Whether you set aside a few minutes or more each day, the time you set aside for you is *yours.* It's your time to unwind, your time to think, and your time to do *whatever* you choose to do. If you don't set aside time for yourself and make it a priority, who will?

Set aside time to unplug and unwind. Turn off the phone, the television, the computer, and even the clock. When you unplug outside distractions, you will be able to plug into yourself. Take some time each day to get away from all the busyness and noise you've become accustomed to. Instead, use that time to listen to your thoughts or to clear your mind and think of nothing at all. You can use this time to read, listen to music, take a shower, soak in a bubble bath, or call it a night and go to bed a little earlier.

Set aside time to journal. Journaling is good for your health. The simple act of putting your thoughts on paper is highly therapeutic. Journaling can help reduce stress, resolve problems, and help you understand yourself better. You don't have to be a good writer to journal. You don't have to worry about what to say. You don't have to read what you write to get the benefit, nor allow anyone else to read it either. Just put your pen to the paper or your fingers to the keyboard and let yourself go. Clear your mind and get in touch with your feelings. Keep a log of your life, and leave a legacy for future generations.

Set aside time to develop good habits. Make a habit of treating yourself well. Setting aside time for yourself should be a top priority. No matter how busy you are, never become too busy to take some time each day to do something special just for *you*. After all, you're the best friend you've got!

TIP # 65

Get in shape and stay in shape.

Ten years ago I changed my lifstyle. I was healthy in every other way, and I couldn't understand why I had little energy and frequent headaches. When a friend suggested I make an appointment with an acupuncturist and natural healer, I was skeptical, but I had nothing to lose but my headaches. I wasn't getting the results I wanted from traditional medicine, and I was willing to try *anything* to feel better.

The healer suggested a number of homeopathic remedies and supplements, but for it all to work, I had to drastically change my diet. Food sensitivities can cause all sorts of ailments. He gave me a strict diet to follow. It was difficult to stick to it, but my desire to *feel good* was stronger than my craving for any food or drink.

Within days I felt better. After a few weeks I had more energy. Over time, other people noticed the difference in me. I lost some weight, my skin was clearer, and I looked healthier (and some people said younger) than before. I was more in tune with myself and in control. Even my attitude changed for the better.

I've always been health conscious, and I thought I was eating healthy foods. As I paid more attention to food labels, however, I discovered I was ingesting all sorts of ingredients I couldn't even pronounce.

You, too, might think you are making healthy choices. Choosing a can of juice over a soda may seem better for you, but many juices have just as much or more sugar than a soda. You might select a muffin instead of a cookie or doughnut, but most muffins are high in fat, calories, and sugar. If you decide to eat a salad drenched in a high-fat dressing and topped with cheese instead of having a sandwich, you could be better off with the sandwich.

It's not easy to choose healthy foods when so many deceptive but unhealthy choices surround you. Select more food that is *grown,* not processed. Eat food that is *fresh*, not from a can, cellophane package, or a box. You don't have to be a vegetarian to be healthy; you need protein and can eat meat, poultry, and fish if you want, but the bulk of your diet should include lots of fresh fruits and vegetables, raw nuts, and whole grains.

You may be young and robust today, but statistics don't lie. A poor diet and lack of exercise increases your risk of heart disease, diabetes, cancer, obesity, and many other illnesses. The food you eat is one of the biggest factors in how you *feel* every day. When you feel sluggish, you might assume you need sleep when what you may need is to get up and move or eat more energizing food.

We talk about health and exercise, and we talk about losing weight. When it comes to getting in shape and staying in shape, there is a substantial amount of information on the subject, including the health risks of being overweight. Yet obesity continues to rise, and people become more sedentary every year.

You may look great, but are you as active as you were a few years ago? Are you gaining weight or staying the same? Once you've reached your final height, you should determine and maintain a final weight. Some people can eat all they want and remain thin because that's the way their metabolism functions, but most people's bodies do not work like that. No matter how thin you are or have been, you are likely to gain weight as you age.

You can avoid the gym and avoid the numbers on the scale, but you can't hide it when you are overweight and out of shape. Don't worry about looking or being *perfect;* focus on being healthy and living a healthy lifestyle. Don't just *get* in shape; *stay* in shape. You will feel better when you maintain a healthy shape and size. While some people stay in shape with little effort, most people have to work at it. As you consider your career and life goals, don't overlook *yourself.* Set realistic goals for your *health.*

The discipline it takes to stick with an exercise program will carry over into other areas of your life and benefit you in other numerous ways. For every excuse you can come up with not to exercise, there is a reason why you should.

Don't have enough time? Make time. Watch one less television show, make one less phone call, or get up 20 minutes earlier. Include exercise in your daily routine. Stretch while you brush your teeth. Take the stairs instead of the elevator. Park farther away and walk to your destination. If you can't find the time, look for it—it's there.

Don't enjoy it? Make it fun. Exercise with a friend. Listen to music or a book on tape while you exercise.

Can't get motivated? Reward yourself. Whether it's going out to dinner, to a movie, or watching your favorite show, reward yourself for exercising. Don't sabotage your efforts by rewarding yourself with a hot fudge sundae. If food is the reward that works for you, choose a healthier, less-fattening alternative. Better yet, reward yourself by doing something you enjoy but only if you follow through with your exercise.

Don't feel well? Exercise is good medicine. Move and you will feel better.

Don't want to? Get up and do some type of aerobic movement for 10 minutes; then reevaluate. Chances are your mood will change and you'll want to keep moving, but if you don't, at least you'll feel better knowing you did something instead of nothing.

Overwhelmed? Start small. Any movement is better than no movement.

Lonely? Find an exercise partner, take a class, or walk a dog. If you don't have a dog, volunteer to walk someone else's.

Bored? Make it fun. Watch television while you exercise. Find new ways to challenge yourself. Look—really look—at scenery, houses, or what's in your exercise room.

Tired and stressed-out? Exercise is a great stress reliever and can increase your energy, clarity, and stamina.

Hungry? Exercise can help curb your appetite. Drinking water is good for you and will fill you up too. Drink water before, during, and after exercising; drink water all day long!

The correlation between diet and health is proven. Exercise doesn't have to be hard work; you don't have to sweat or work out for an hour at a time to benefit. Only good things will happen as a result.

Always check with your doctor before starting a new exercise program, and once you get the okay, find the exercise best suited for you. Don't put it off any longer. Start moving and start reaping the rewards *today*.

TIP # 66
Neatness counts; get organized and stay organized.

Your boss has an important lunch meeting she must attend, and after discovering her car won't start, she asks you if you will drive her to the meeting. As the two of you walk to your car, you begin apologizing for the condition it's in. You regret not stopping at the car wash and wish you had taken the time to drop off the dirty clothes strewn across the back seat of your car. The dangling mirror and missing hubcap never bothered you before, and now you're wondering if your boss will notice. She waits as you remove the clutter from the front seat to make room for her to sit down. You're embarrassed when she sees your briefcase overflowing with papers and the number of empty soda cans and food wrappers in your car. You realize your car looks like a traveling storage shed, and although you hope it doesn't matter, you have a feeling it really does.

Neatness goes beyond personal appearance. The tidier and more organized you are, the more professional and in control you appear. A mess suggests *you* are out of control. The more organized you are, the more efficient you become. Your car, your briefcase, your desk, and everything you surround yourself with affect your ability to find things quickly and influence the perception others have of you.

The ability to find files and papers when you need them will save you time and reduce the stress that can evolve from not being able to find something when you need it. Your work area is not your private domain. It will be seen by others and should be kept neat at all times. You may be able to shut the door to your room at home and overlook the clutter, but your work space is part of a larger environment, and it is important to keep it clean. Papers piled on the floor are not only distracting but could pose a safety issue if you work in a high-traffic area.

Many people will get organized once or twice a year, keep things neat a short while, and return to their original mess. It is important to get organized and equally important to *stay* organized. It doesn't take much time to put things away if you do it consistently.

You will be handling lots of information. Try to handle things only one time before deciding what you will do with them. Putting things in a pile you plan to deal with later does nothing but create piles for you to deal with. When a letter, brochure, or memo comes to you, try to handle it only once. Make a decision about what you want to do with it. Do you need to give it to someone else, save it, file it, or throw it away? If you are not sure, put it in a special file or basket that you will go through at the end of the week, after you've had a chance to make a decision. When you go through the pile again, make a decision about each item, and get rid of what you can. Get into the habit of labeling and filing, not piling. Label your folders *and* your papers. Doing so will make it easier for you to find them later. Use baskets to help you sort your papers; you may still have a few piles, but they will be smaller and probably more organized.

Do routine maintenance to save time and minimize frustration. Keep pencils sharpened, staples in your stapler, and all of your tools working. Get rid of old food, containers, cups, and soda cans. Wipe down phones, keyboards, and shelves.

You never know who will notice what. Someone I worked with told me about a time she needed information from a coworker. He told her she'd find it in his computer, but his keyboard was so filthy she didn't want to touch it. Although her coworker was a nice guy, she said that incident changed her entire view of him. She couldn't imagine how anyone could touch that thing!

Neatness counts and is more than simply being neat. Living among clutter can clutter your mind. Take the time you need to get organized, and then stay organized. You'll be glad you did when you get the next promotion or award.

TIP # 67

No more excuses; deal with problems.

Problems are inevitable, but few are insurmountable. It may be easier to avoid your problems, but they never really go away unless you face them. It takes courage and discipline to tackle the problems you encounter. Are you up to the challenge? How do *you* deal with problems?

Do you view problems negatively? Problems aren't always a bad thing. The process of working through a problem can improve relationships, reduce stress, stimulate new ways of thinking, and produce positive changes. Confronting someone about a problem does not have to be unpleasant or combative. Every problem you face can teach you something new about yourself. Every problem can become an opportunity to expand your thinking, to learn, and to become a better, more compassionate person. View problems as challenges and catalysts for change.

Do you dwell on your problems? Obsessing about a problem and becoming fixated on it will not resolve it. In fact, it can do the opposite; the more you focus on what's wrong, the more you make out of it. Many problems can be easily resolved but instead are blown out of proportion. If you can't get your mind off a problem, the real issue may be your reaction.

Focus on finding solutions. Look for the lessons to be learned and ways to move past your fixation on the problem.

Do you ignore your problems? Ignoring a problem will not make it go away. You may be able to push it aside temporarily, but chances are it will surface again. Identify the reasons you prefer to ignore your problems. Are you leery of conflict, hurting someone's feelings, or being wrong? Consider that whatever it is you're trying to avoid could be the reason you're having the problem in the first place.

Do you blame others for your problems? If you have a problem with someone or something, it is your problem, not theirs. Take responsibility for your contribution to the problems you have; own your problems. Blaming others for your troubles perpetuates the problem. Be the example of how you want others to be. Work at resolving your problems and forgiving others.

Do you make excuses to avoid dealing with problems? It's not easy to admit you made a mistake or that you don't know how to do something. It's easier to avoid the truth, prevent an argument, and explain our shortcomings away. It's easier to lie than admit our lack of commitment. Be honest with yourself and others, don't sugarcoat the truth. Apologize when you've done something wrong, but don't let saying "I'm sorry" become easier than changing the behavior that is causing the problem. Be up front and tell someone when you are upset or unable to follow through. The only acceptable excuse is no excuse at all.

Every problem you face is an opportunity for you to do one of two things: Become a better person or let the problem get the best of you. You can acknowledge your problems or wait for someone else to do so. You can be solution-oriented or problem-oriented—the choice is yours.

TIP # 68
Freshen up!

After spending several days in bed sick with the flu, I was run-down and exhausted. All I wanted was to stay in bed, but I knew I had to get up. People were counting on me. I had a speech to give. I dragged myself out of bed and moved in slow motion. It took me twice as long as usual to wash and dry my hair and put myself together.

When I was finally ready to walk out the door, I felt like a different person. Considering just an hour before I was barely able to move or speak, I was amazed at my own transformation. Not only did I look much healthier, but I felt healthier too. As the day progressed, I felt more and more alive and like my usual self.

If I hadn't had to give a speech that day, I would have stayed in bed. If I had stayed in bed, I am certain I would have felt as lethargic all day as I did that morning. I am convinced that getting up and *freshening up* was the medicine I needed. Getting out of bed and out of my sick clothes and into the shower and my professional clothes helped me begin to heal and feel like my usual self.

We all have good days and bad days. Some mornings, you might be so tired you'll decide to forgo your morning routine. You might decide to hit the snooze button instead of taking time to shave, wash and dry your hair, or iron your shirt. If you look a little grungy, you'll probably tell yourself how you look doesn't (and shouldn't) matter. *But it does.*

Good personal hygiene is important. Basic grooming habits are important. You should bathe, use deodorant, and brush and floss your teeth *every day*. Your hair, undergarments, and clothing should be washed *frequently*. When you take care of yourself, it will show. You will look good, feel good, and *smell* good.

Create a freshen-up kit and keep it in your car or desk at work for the times when you are on the go. Include some of the following items along with any others you can think of:

- Comb, brush, hairspray

- Toothbrush, toothpaste, toothpicks, and floss

- Mouthwash, mints, breath spray or drops

- Razor and shave cream

- Stain remover pads

- Sticky lint remover or lint brush

- Static remover spray

- Sewing kit and safety pins

- Scissors, nail clipper, and nail file

- Mirror

- Extra pair of socks or pantyhose

- Extra tie, shirt, or blouse

- Extra undergarments

- Cloth for wiping shoes or spills

- Hand sanitizer

- Tissue

- Make-up and make-up remover

- Nail polish (use to touch up nails or stop a run in your nylon)

- Umbrella

Be fresh and stay fresh. Take time each day to freshen up!

TIP # 69

Plan your day.

Some of the best advice I ever received came out of a time-management seminar I took many years ago. In addition to learning how to manage my time, I learned how to *plan*. I realized planning involves more than writing down appointments and coming up with a list of things to do. Making a plan and *sticking to that plan* is the key, although it's not as easy as it seems. Planning isn't difficult to do, but doing the things you plan can be quite a challenge.

Setting goals is important; you need to identify the things you want and create a plan for your future. But don't overlook small, short-term goals. Your long-term success is a result of the things you do every day. Progress is a *process*. Setting goals and knowing what you want isn't enough to achieve it. You must have a plan and follow that plan. What you *do* each day will either move you closer to your goals or prevent you from reaching them.

We all have lots of things we want to do. The problem is that most of us have more things to do than time to do them. People are busy, but they are not always doing what they *should* be doing. Keeping busy can keep you from seeing what's happening to your time. If you try to do *everything*, you may end up accomplishing *nothing*.

We are bombarded by distractions. Your inbox has new e-mails, your phone rings, someone asks you for information. Every time you decide to do a random, unplanned task you lose your focus and take time away from all the things you have planned. The most effective way to manage all of the incoming information is to plan time for it. Failing to plan properly can lead to missed opportunities.

Dee, a television producer, missed an opportunity of a lifetime the morning she was late for work. One of the hosts of the show she produced became ill and a replacement was needed. By the time Dee arrived, a co-host was found, but the minute the executive producer saw her he expressed his regret. "Dee," he said "where were you when I needed you? You would have been the *perfect* guest host!" Dee missed what she says was a once in a lifetime opportunity that never presented itself again. Be on time: You can't seize the chance of a lifetime if you're not there to grab it. Proper planning can make the difference.

When you take the time to *plan* your day, you will be more focused. You'll know what you need to do, and you'll spend your time *doing* the most vital things. As a result, you will be more productive and increase your chances of achieving your dreams.

Plan your day every day:

Stop *thinking* and start *planning*. *Thinking* is different from *planning*. A thought is an idea, and ideas come and go. We can think about something we'd like to do but may never get around to doing it. When an idea becomes more than a passing thought and you decide to do something with it, you've made a decision—a *plan* to do it. A thought is intangible, a plan concrete; ideas are temporary. Unless you capture them and put them into action, you won't benefit from them.

Put it in writing. If you keep track of your appointments and the things you need to do in your *head*, it's time to put them someplace else. Take your pick; whether you use an electronic or paper planner, or keep a list, either one is better than storing information in your memory. You may be quite capable of remembering, but there's no reason to add that pressure to your plans. Use your head, but use it to put things in writing.

Be realistic. Making promises and commitments you cannot fulfill will lead to disappointment in yourself and others. Know what you will be able to accomplish within the time you have. Be honest with yourself and others. Telling someone in advance you will need more time to do something is better than saying you will have something done that you fail to do. People are counting on you and have deadlines to meet. Be realistic about your time.

Expect the unexpected. We seem so surprised when caught off guard. Traffic gets congested, the printer jams, packages don't arrive, computers stall, emergencies occur, and people get sick. We know anything can happen at any time. Why, then, are we so surprised when it does? The next time you schedule an appointment or meeting, block out extra time before it starts and after it is over. Don't be caught by surprise when traffic comes to a halt or someone has messed up your schedule—*expect and plan* for delays. Leave extra time in your schedule. When you expect the unexpected, you'll be prepared and able to deal with it because it won't be unexpected after all.

Keep information where you need it. People waste a lot of time looking for things. There's nothing more frustrating than needing information but not finding it. You will save time and reduce stress if you remember to keep information where you need it. When you schedule an appointment, write down the phone number, directions, and any other pertinent information in the same place you are writing the appointment. If you don't have enough room to write it there, be sure to reference where it is so you will be able to find it when you need it.

Plan one day at a time. Think about what you want and need to accomplish each day. Don't worry about all of the things you need or want to do this week, next month, or in three years. Focus on what you need to do *today*.

Set aside time to check e-mail and voice mail. Reading, listening to, and responding to the messages arriving all day can eat up more of your time than you realize. Plan specific times for checking and responding to e-mail and voice mail.

Underplan. Plan realistically and set yourself up to succeed. Be generous with your time when you plan your day; plan *extra* time for every task and appointment you have. Most people underestimate the amount of time it takes to get something done and then run out of time. Arriving a few minutes late to work or to a business event is *not* okay. A meeting called for 10:00 A.M. should begin at that time. Arriving five minutes early sends a completely different message from showing up five minutes late. You may think it's no big deal to run a few minutes behind, but it can be to others. Plan for interruptions and delays—make a plan you can follow that will help you get the most important things done. If you end up with little gifts of time between tasks, use that time for yourself.

Know your best time of day. Become aware of your timing and work with your natural rhythm. We all have certain times we are most energetic, sluggish, and tired. Plan your activities around the times you function best. If you're most energetic in the morning, use that time to get things done that take energy. Save your easier tasks for those times you feel less energized.

Know your plan. A plan doesn't do you much good if you don't know what it is. Take time each morning to plan your day. See how much of your time is committed and how much is left over. Think about the things you'd *like* to do, and then decide what *must* be done. Put your thoughts into action and writing; use a paper or electronic planner to express what's in your head. Know where you need to be and what you need to do. You won't be able to follow a plan if you don't know what the plan is.

Time is a precious commodity and favors no one; we all have the same amount of time to use each day. Spend your time doing the things that matter. Managing your time effectively requires planning and discipline. Take the time to learn time-management skills *now*. Consider taking a time-management class or seminar to learn techniques that will benefit you the rest of your life.

Don't let time control you; take control of your time. When you take the time to plan your day, you increase your focus and become more productive. You know what needs to be done and can spend your time doing it. As a result, you have more control over what you do each day and no longer feel that your days are controlling you. *Plan your day every day!*

TIP # 70
Smoke and booze; you lose.

Cigarette and alcohol advertisements feature young, vibrant, attractive models drinking, smoking, and socializing. They are surrounded by friends and lovers, and their sparkling smiles radiate happiness and good times. If advertising doesn't convince you that you'll look good and have fun if you smoke and drink, walk into any hot spot, be it a nightclub, bar, or restaurant, and you'll see a similar scene: young and vibrant people smoking (when and where permitted), drinking, smiling, and laughing.

If you are on the outside looking in, you might think you are viewing the "winners" in life. The message: Smoke and go on a drinking binge and you *win*.

You might decide you're a loser and wish you were meeting more people and having more fun. You might decide you feel better when you drink and more confident when you smoke. In fact, you might end up getting so much smoke in your eyes that you won't even see you are *changing*. And when you finally do take notice of the changes, you might not even recognize the person you see.

There is a downside to this "beautiful" life, and there is nothing pretty about it. Smoking and drinking are two of the most destructive habits people have. There are many misconceptions about the effects of both and many reasons why so many people do them. Do you see your reasons for smoking or drinking in any of these eight common rationales?

1. **Smoking is cool.** If you think smoking is cool, smoke a cigarette outside the doorway of a building, and observe the reactions (and sneers) of the people who have to walk through your cloud of smoke to enter.

2. **Smoking makes me look older.** If you think smoking will make you look older, it will. It won't take long for wrinkles to appear, and you will age prematurely and much faster than your nonsmoking friends.

3. **Drinking and smoking help me relax.** If you think drinking will relax you or a cigarette will calm your nerves, the effect will only be short-term. You will be on a vicious cycle. Your need to smoke and drink will increase and could become an addiction or worse.

4. **Drinking helps me forget my problems.** If you think drinking will enable you to forget your small problems, it might, but only because your drinking will create bigger problems to worry about.

5. **Drinking helps me feel less self-conscious.** If you think drinking will help you feel less self-conscious and make you more socially acceptable, consider that chances are good you'll do something stupid under the influence of alcohol, embarrass yourself, and feel even more uncomfortable as a result.

6. **Smoking and drinking will make me feel better.** If you think smoking or drinking will make you feel better, consider that you'll be trading one ailment for another. The short-term high you get is likely to result in a lower low when your addiction kicks in.

7. **Smoking and drinking will make me one of the beautiful people.** If you think smoking or drinking will make you more attractive, it won't. There's nothing attractive about

stained teeth or yellow nails, tobacco or alcohol breath, or a person unable to walk a straight line or speak without slurring his or her words.

8. **Society expects social drinking.** If you think you will be ostracized if you don't drink, you won't. It wasn't necessary to go along with the crowd when you were young, and it isn't as you age. Be true to yourself and don't feel pressure to conform.

The truth about smoking and drinking:

Smoking and drinking are addicting. You may tell yourself you'll be able to quit when you want, but quitting is extremely difficult.

Smoking and drinking are expensive. The amount you pay and how much you consume will only increase over time. The longer you indulge, the more money you throw away.

Smoking and drinking are bad for your health. Drinking and smoking increase your risk of numerous diseases, shortening your life span.

Smoking and drinking are dangerous. Drinking and driving is lethal, smoking is hazardous, and both are harmful to you and others.

Smoking and drinking affect your relationships. When your addiction is your focus and becomes more important than your friends and family, your relationships will suffer.

There's nothing good about smoking or drinking. It's easy to think you have your smoking or drinking under control, but that only means you don't realize when your habit starts controlling you.

If you don't smoke, don't start. If you do smoke, quit now, before more damage is done. And if you drink, drink sparingly or go without alcohol awhile to make sure you can. You might even find you feel better when you do. And if you think you have a drinking problem, admit it. You have lots of company. Don't be ashamed to feel powerless or unable to kick a smoking or drinking habit. Admitting dependency is one of the first steps in overcoming an addiction. You can do it.

TIP # 71
Learn how to de-stress.

Everyone experiences stress. Some people say life is more stressful today than ever before. Health care providers say stress-related disorders are on the rise. Approximately 75 percent of all doctor visits are thought to be stress related. Stress can be a motivator, but when mild stress turns into chronic or severe stress, it's time to do something about it.

- If you have frequent headaches or stomachaches, tight muscles, a bad back, or catch more than your share of colds or the flu, it could be due to stress.

- If you feel tired but cannot get to sleep or if you feel edgy, more irritable than usual, or sensitive and moody, it could be stress related.

- If your relationships become strained and people make more demands or seem needier, it could be their reaction to your stress.

- If traffic seems heavier, the days longer or shorter, the boss more demanding, or coworkers more bothersome, it's likely from stress.

- If you feel overcommitted, have trouble keeping track of appointments, fall behind schedule, or forget important information, the culprit probably is stress.

- If your motivation is down, your anxiety is up, and you're smoking or drinking more but eating less and less, the problem is most likely your stress.

- If you're eating on the run, your gas tank is empty, your bills are overdue, and your house is a mess, it's stress.

- If you have no time to yourself but bend over backward for everyone else, you pass the stress test.

Pay attention to triggers of stress and learn how to *de-stress* when stress hits. More important, do everything you can to prevent stress in your life. There are many ways to help counter and prevent stress. Incorporate as many as you can into your daily routine.

Here are 20 things you can do to make sure stress doesn't get the best of you:

1. Exercise. Stretch, do yoga, walk, run, or just move.

2. Eat a healthy, well-balanced diet. Drink less caffeine and more water.

3. Get enough sleep. Try going to bed and waking up at the same time every day.

4. Take breaks.

5. Listen to relaxing music.

6. Breathe deeply.

7. Express your emotions.

8. Meditate and visualize.

9. Resolve your problems.

10. Delegate or ask for help.

11. Say no. Don't take on more than you can handle.

12. Laugh.

13. Stick to a budget and reduce your debt.

14. Get organized.

15. Forgive yourself and others.

16. Create a relaxing environment.

17. Focus on one day at a time.

18. Pray.

19. Let go of your need to control.

20. Have fun.

Take charge of your time and your life. If you fail to control your stress, your stress will end up controlling you.

TIP # 72
Turn off the lights.

I've been living on my own for over 25 years and am self-sufficient. Yet anytime I am sick, I think about calling my *mom*. I know she can provide whatever I need, be it food, medicine, or advice. I could and should rely on myself for these things, but it's tempting to relinquish my responsibility to someone else.

Think about the times you acted irresponsibly. When you lived at home, if you didn't remember to take out the garbage, walk the dog, or mow the lawn, someone was there to remind you. If you failed to turn out the lights, turn off the iron, or turn on the alarm, someone else was there to do it for you.

Did you hear reminders often? Do you think your parents were trying to irritate you by nagging you? Think again. They knew the day would come when they would no longer be there to look after you, and they were only trying to *teach* you responsibility.

As an adult, you must look after yourself. You are free to do whatever you want. You can leave clothes on the floor and dirty dishes in the sink, and you can let garbage pile up if you want. No one will care (except maybe your spouse or roommate). But if you forget to lock the door or blow out the candles, you're putting yourself *and others* in jeopardy.

Your adult responsibilities go beyond taking care of yourself; you share the responsibility with billions of others to make the world a better place. Consider the effect your actions have on the environment and other people. As a responsible citizen, do what you can to help conserve energy, reduce waste, and stop pollution.

No one will notice if you fail to turn off the lights. It's up to you to notice. Do it because you want to live responsibly, not because someone tells you to.

Don't feel as though you need to do something big; it's the little things you do each day that help restore and save the planet and will prevent bigger problems in the future.

Turn out the lights. You really don't need to have every light in the house on when you are watching TV in one room. Conserve energy and save yourself some money. Get into the habit of turning on the light when you enter a room and turning it off every time you leave a room.

Don't shave in the shower. Even the finest hotels are encouraging guests to conserve. Fix the leaky faucet, repair the running toilet, and wait to wash your jeans until you have additional clothes to put in the washing machine. When you shave in the shower you are wasting running water. So turn the shower off when you shave, or make the decision to shave someplace else.

Lock up. Lock the doors and windows, both when you're at home and when you leave. An open window on the first floor or in the basement is an invitation for anyone to enter. There are ways to be safe and secure without being cooped up. Most police and fire departments will be happy to send someone out to your home or apartment to give you suggestions for making your home safe.

Make your bed. Even though you plan on unmaking it again in a few more hours, make your bed; you'll sleep better if you do. A freshly made bed is inviting, and taking the time to make it is habit-forming. When you get out of bed in the morning, make it right away. It doesn't take long and will set the tone for a well-structured and organized day.

Hang up your towel. It takes only a few seconds, but take the time to hang up your towel and you'll see how much faster it will dry. Don't wash it—use it again and again. When you use a towel to dry off after a shower, you and the towel are *clean*. Why wash a towel every time you use it? How dirty can it get when you use it only to wipe yourself dry?

Reset your thermostat. In the winter, you will be cold. In the summer, you will be hot. Dress accordingly. There is no sense wearing a heavy winter sweater in the middle of the summer because the thermostat is set so low. Set it to be comfortable. Consider its harmful effects on the environment and on your finances.

Reuse and recycle. Recycle your newspapers, bottles, containers, and cans. Do your part to prevent excess waste. Drink from a reusable cup instead of from a new paper cup that you throw away. Buy larger, value items rather than the more expensive and smaller items. There are tons of waste polluting our environment—don't add more than absolutely necessary.

Choose conservation over convenience. Walk to the store; don't drive. Take public transportation. Join a car pool. Ride a bike. Run your errands methodically—don't drive all over the place. Think about our dependence on oil, the price of gas, and the problems from pollution. Then think about alternative ways to get where you're going.

Turn everything *off*. If it's been turned on, turn it off. Turn off your curling iron, turn off your computer, and turn off the coffee pot. Blow out candles, and remember clothes dryers can cause fire too. Always look things over before you leave a room, go to sleep, or leave for the day, and get into the habit of turning everything off.

Over time you will remember the things your parents told you to do. If you become a parent, you'll tell your children many of the same things your parents told you. You won't do it to bother them; you'll do it because you *care*. You'll want to *protect and educate* your children in the same way your parents tried to protect and educate you.

TIP # 73
Trust your instincts.

You can call it what you want: a gut feeling, a premonition, or just a hunch. You might refer to it as your intuition, your inner wisdom, your conscience, or that little voice you hear in your head. At times you may think you're being silly and try to ignore the feelings you have. Relying on your instincts is not something most of us have been encouraged to do.

- Have you ever had a strong feeling about something yet no basis for the feeling you felt?

- Have you ever felt ill when there was nothing physically wrong?

- Have you ever felt anxious for no apparent reason or had a feeling too vague to explain?

- Have you ever suddenly thought about someone right before the phone rang, only to find that person calling you?

- Have you ever had a song on your mind moments before it played on the radio?

- Have you ever had a premonition about something before it happened?

- Have you ever had a dream that came true?

- Have you ever lost your energy around certain people?

- Have you ever wavered about a decision you had to make?

- Have you ever felt uneasy about someone or something but didn't know why?

If any of these things have happened to you, your intuition has been in touch with you. Some of the things you consider coincidences may not be as much of a fluke as you assume. Pay attention to the subtle and not-so-subtle signs you receive; you may be more intuitive than you think. Learn to discover the ways in which your intuition communicates with you. It might be a feeling, thought, or physical or emotional sensation. Whatever it is, it's too important to ignore.

Children are naturally intuitive, and chances are at one time you were too. Children trust their feelings until they are conditioned to *think* instead of *feel*. When you were young and afraid, you didn't have to deny your fears. If you didn't trust someone, you could run and hide; you weren't compelled to conceal the way you felt about someone. As you matured, you didn't want to appear foolish, so you (and everyone else) learned to deny such feelings.

If you've ever had a bad feeling you've dismissed as irrational, you were working *against* your intuition. Start working with your intuition instead. Your instincts can *protect* you. Your initial reaction is always your best safety measure. If something seems odd, it probably is.

Trust your feelings; how you feel *does* matter. Allow your instincts to alert you to dangerous situations, prevent you from making mistakes, and guide you in making important decisions. Don't argue with your intuition. If something or someone doesn't feel right, there's a good chance something could go wrong.

Your feelings are not right or wrong. Don't try to justify the way you feel. Let your feelings guide you. Trust your instincts.

TIP # 74
Get a tetanus shot.

I had an appointment with my doctor for my annual check up. As we caught up with each other, I told my doctor about the books I was writing. She has always enthusiastically supported my work and was exceptionally enthused about *this* book. She wanted to know all about the tips and made me promise to reserve a copy of the book for her. When we concluded the exam, she wished me well, and just as she was about to open the door and leave, she turned to me and said, "Tell them to be sure to get their tetanus shot." I half-heartedly agreed, thanked her for the idea, and said good-bye.

I was still in the development stages of my book, and although I wasn't sure if writing about health fit in with the concept, her advice stuck with me. It wasn't until my daughter developed a sinus infection that I saw my doctor again. After she checked my daughter, I asked her if she was serious about her idea for the tip "Get a tetanus shot." She was and I asked her to tell me more.

She explained how everyone should have a tetanus shot every 10 years. By the time most people graduate, many will be due for a shot, but the last thing most people think about after graduation is going to the doctor. The more she explained, the more I understood the importance of this tip. "I want all the young, healthy people to stay healthy," she said.

Whether you're graduating from high school or college, you'll be busy preparing for and entering the next chapter of your life. Finding a place to live and work and starting a new job can be all consuming. You'll have even less free time once you are working full time. You'll no longer have yearly health forms to complete for school, and no one is going to make you an appointment for your annual checkup at the doctor or dentist. Your health is now in your hands, where it belongs.

Take good care of yourself. Don't wait until you are sick to see a doctor. Do it while you are healthy and increase your chances of staying that way. Prevention is the key.

Take charge of your health and take preventive health measures:

- Find a doctor and a dentist. If you don't have one, ask around for recommendations.

- Get annual checkups.

- Brush and floss your teeth every morning, evening, and in between.

- Eat a healthful, well-balanced diet.

- Drink lots of purified water.

- Limit your alcohol, caffeine, and sugar intake.

- Maintain a weight consistent with your height and build.

- Exercise.

Your long-term health is a result of the habits you develop today. Invest in yourself and your health. Do all of these things, and remember my doctor's advice. If you haven't done it yet, go and get a tetanus shot. Keep health records and get your tetanus shot every 10 years or so.

TIP # 75
If you wouldn't say it to someone's face, don't say it.

Your ability to get along with people is important. So is your ability to adapt to the different types of people you meet.

The relationship component of a job can be crucial. If your friendships are strong and you feel you belong, they enhance your overall work experience. If you feel left out or alone and have conflicts with others, however, it can make going to work every day feel like a chore. If you never figured out how to deal with the troublemakers in your life before or how to get along in a group, you may find yourself facing some of the same issues you've struggled with in the past. But if someone annoys you, discredits you, or spreads rumors about you, you don't have to respond as you did before; you can choose a new way to respond.

If someone you work with becomes a nuisance, what will you do?

If someone is spreading rumors about you, what will you do?

If you see the supervisor you loathe at a bar with someone other than his wife, will you remain silent or tell your friends at work?

If you can't stand the smell of your coworker's aftershave or the way he smacks his lips when he chews, will you tell him? Will you tell others about him?

The office grapevine is alive and well; gossip is just as prevalent at work as it was in school and it is not easy to ignore. You can pay attention to it and learn from it, but be careful about adding to it. Spreading rumors and gossip about other people can damage reputations and hurt relationships. Having something said *about* you often hurts more than something that is said *to* you.

The next time you're ready to say something you shouldn't or if what you are about to say could hurt someone, think twice. If you wouldn't say it to someone's face, don't say it; you'll sleep better at night.

Build trust. If someone tells you something in confidence, keep it to yourself.

Be direct. If you have a problem with someone, speak directly with that person.

Get to the source. If someone has been talking about you, don't talk about them or what they say to everyone else; go directly to the source of your problem.

Avoid spreading gossip. Don't spread rumors; be the roadblock where rumors stop.

Don't talk about other people. Steer your conversations away from talk about other people and toward something of greater value.

Speak well of colleagues. If you want to say something about someone, think of something positive to say.

Remain silent. If you don't have anything nice to say, don't say anything at all. You've heard this before. Now's the time to apply it.

Demonstrate a Positive Attitude

Make Your Life a Little Easier

TIP # 76
Your attitude is your choice.

One spring my family and I attended one graduation open house after another. It was a gloomy day, and although most of the events took place outside, some hosts had set up their garages and family rooms just in case the weather wouldn't cooperate. It didn't. By the time we arrived at the third open house, it began raining. The parents of the graduate hurriedly took down the outdoor setup and squeezed everything into the garage, which was filled with bikes, toys, and tools. We barely had a chance to say hello before we helped the other guests carrying trays of food, tables, and chairs from the backyard into the garage. There was little room for all the people and the food, and the parents complained, blaming the weather for ruining the day.

I felt sorry for the parents, not only because the weather was bad but because they seemed so surprised. They had no alternate plan. They relied on the unpredictable weather, rather than on themselves, to make the party a success.

According to Petra Marquart, an authority on customer service and author of *The Power of Service*, other people can affect your mood in the same way the weather does. "Attitude," she says, "is the *emotional climate* in which we live." If you feel down at the end of each day or drained after spending time with friends, there's probably a reason. According to Marquart, it could be because you're working next to "drizzle" or hanging around "dark skies."

Anyone whose mood depends on other people, environmental factors, or other influences beyond their control is going to be unpredictable and unreliable. Imagine trying to have a meaningful relationship with such a person. It's not easy being around people whose moods change as quickly and frequently as the weather does.

No one can predict the weather with total accuracy, yet we follow forecasts and make our plans accordingly. When you plan an outdoor event or activity, you *hope* the weather will cooperate, but you know you shouldn't count on it. If you don't have an alternate plan or the flexibility to adapt, you shouldn't plan the event outside. The weather may be unpredictable, but your attitude doesn't have to be.

If the weather ruins your plans, you have a right to be disappointed. You can rant and rave, but no matter what you do, it won't change the weather. It didn't deliberately ruin your plans, and guess what? *The weather doesn't care.*

When it "rains on your parade," your parade isn't ruined unless *you* ruin it. Your *reaction* to the rain affects the outcome more than anything else. Of course you're let down, but you don't need to wallow in your sorrow. The rain may have dampened the *event*, but it doesn't have to dampen your *spirits*.

The weather is unpredictable; people are too. Don't rely on either to make you happy. You can *prefer* sunshine over rain or an easy-going coworker over a difficult one, but you will have to accept and deal with whatever you get.

You are not powerless. You can weather any storm. Be your own barometer. You choose your attitude—you control your response. Do you want to be a cloud of dread or a ray of sunshine? **You** decide; *your attitude is your choice.*

TIP # 77

Make someone's day.

Make someone's day. It's one of the simplest, most gratifying things you can do. There are countless ways to make someone's day. Start by looking for things you can do. There's no need to spend money or take up a lot of your time; it really is the little things that count. Make someone's day a little better, and you will find that your day is a little better too.

Seven ways to make someone's day:

1. *Acknowledge hard work and effort.* Sometimes you have to stay up late, get up early, and go out of your way to get something done. You feel good about the things you do, but it's nice when others notice too. You can do that for your coworkers. Do more than say "nice job"; acknowledge someone's dedication, efforts, and hard work. When you do, you can be sure you will make someone feel appreciated, and it will make his or her day.

2. *Offer encouragement.* A little push or an extra vote of confidence will help anyone in need. When someone else believes in you, it's easier for you to believe in yourself. When was the last time you offered your support or asked someone (and wanted to hear) how he or she was doing? How often have you said, "Keep it up; you're doing great. I know you'll make it?" Look around. Do you see someone losing hope? Does anyone seem afraid? Why not encourage that person? Your encouraging words can make a difference—they can *be* the difference between someone's failure and success. Offer your encouragement and you will surely make someone's day.

3. *Be there.* Be there for people. Be there for *their* needs, not yours. Be there to listen, and be there to share. Be there in good times, and be there in bad times. Be there to laugh, be there to cry, and be there to lend a helping hand. Be there to show you care; be there because you care. Be there because you *want* to, not because you *ought* to. When you are there for someone, you will make that person's day.

4. *Do something unexpectedly.* Pick up the check, hold open the door; send flowers, or deliver balloons. Bake chocolate chip cookies, make a lunch or reservations for dinner, make a big congratulation sign, or decorate the room with streamers. Do someone a favor, clean up someone's mess, pay someone a compliment, or leave a wrapped present on the desk. Send a card, or call to say hello. Wait patiently, listen calmly, or ask how someone feels. Do something simple yet thoughtful, but whatever you do, do it unexpectedly. When you do, you will make someone's day.

5. *Say it.* You know how you feel, you know what you think, and you know how much you care. But no one else will know unless you tell them so. If you think it, say it: "I enjoy being with you." "I'm proud of you." "I love you." "Thank you for being you." No one knows how you feel; no one can read your mind. If you have something to say, why not say it? When you do, you'll make someone smile, and you will know you've made someone's day.

6. *Pay attention.* Notice what you see. Notice what you hear. Notice *everyone* you see. Don't walk by; stop and say hello. Notice someone's haircut; notice the photo on

the desk. Notice someone's positive outlook; notice when someone's upset. Notice when someone's excluded; notice when someone is ill. Pay attention to detail, for the more you notice, the more you'll see how very important paying attention can be. Pay attention. Make someone's day.

7. *Get excited.* Get excited, as excited as you'd be for yourself. Get excited for someone's promotion; celebrate when someone reaches a goal. Get excited over someone's new purchase; be happy for the money that person saved. Get excited about someone's vacation. Congratulate someone who gets a raise. Get excited about someone's good fortune. Get excited about someone's success. Get excited about making a habit of making someone's day *every* day.

TIP # 78
Consider yourself fortunate.

Most people fail to realize how fortunate they are until they no longer have what they should have been grateful for all along.

How often do you call the important people in your life to say hello or "I love you?" When was the last time you watched the sun rise—or set? Do you take time each day to stop and smell the roses? Do you appreciate the comforts of home, the food you eat, or any of the modern conveniences you've become accustomed to? Do you plop into bed too exhausted to give thanks for all you have? If you're too busy to think about how fortunate you are, *slow down.*

Gratitude is *good* for you. When you are grateful for what you have, you don't think about what you lack. When you are grateful for the little things as well as the big things, you add pleasure to your life. Sometimes it isn't until we lose the things or people we take for granted that we realize what we had. Absence really does make the heart grow fonder.

A friend of mine hadn't realized how fortunate he was until he was thousands of miles away from home. Being away from his daily routine provided him with ample time to *think*. He thought a lot about the things he missed the most and the lessons he was learning while he was away. When he returned home after serving his country at war, he sent a letter to his family and friends.

I was touched by what he wrote. It caused me to think about my own good fortune, about the things I take for granted, including my freedom, which people in some countries lack. I realized that my problems pale in comparison to the problems of others.

My friend gave me permission to share part of his letter. When you read it, I hope you, too, will stop and think about your own good fortune. No matter how big your problems may seem, there's a good chance you are more fortunate than you think. The following are a few of the lessons my friend, Command Sergeant Major Duane Fredrickson, learned while he was away:

- It's the little things in life that make a difference, like sunny side eggs (we only got the powdered version) or a Starbucks coffee.

- I learned the value of making the best of all situations. Rather than complain, I endeavored to find the positive and create fun.

- I gained an understanding of what it means to have nothing.

- I learned sand can reside in places you and I have never imagined; I took four showers in a row to rid myself of the dirt.

- I learned that roach motels will catch centipedes, crickets, and spiders as well as cockroaches that are four-inches long. (I put four of these motels around my bed and they filled up so quickly that I needed to replace them once a week.)

- I have a new appreciation of the true value of friendship and realize I've taken my friends for granted.

- I discovered at times I've taken those I love the most for granted too and realized how very important they are to me.

My friend traveled thousands of miles away from home to learn some of life's most valuable lessons. He is fortunate because he returned home safely and was able to share what he learned with others.

You don't have to travel far to realize how much you have to be grateful for. Some of the most important things in your life are right before your eyes. Take the time to notice and appreciate what you have. *Consider yourself fortunate.*

TIP # 79
Look on the bright side.

Think positive. Be optimistic. Don't be so hard on yourself. Smile! Things will get better. Sleep on it. Stop complaining. Tomorrow's another day. It won't hurt your eyes to look on the bright side. Sometimes it's easier said than done. Perhaps you try but can't always find a bright side to see.

Would you like to feel better about yourself? Are you looking for success? It's on the bright side. Do you want health and happiness, peace of mind, and a new perspective? Just look on the bright side of things. Are you seeking more joy and less stress?

You'll have it when you look on the bright side. Here's how to get started:

Change your view of the news. Whether you watch the news on TV, listen to the radio, read the paper, or view it online, it doesn't matter how you get the news as long as the news doesn't *get to you.*

News can be depressing; much of it generates stress and fear. You should know what's going on in the world, but you don't have to dwell on it. There's no need to listen to the same news reports several times a day.

If the news makes you anxious, don't watch the news at night; you might find you sleep better when you don't. Make a decision about how much news you want to hear and when you want to hear it. Seek positive news. There are good-news sites on the Internet, and you'll find some good-news programs on TV. Talk less about the bad news you hear and more about the good. You can change your view of the world by changing your view of the news.

Make sense out of senselessness. Some things make no sense: a six year old brings a loaded gun to school, a drunk driver gets his fifth DWI, a newborn baby is found in a dumpster, and on it goes. You can shake your head in disbelief or look for the reasons why such things happen. Do people need to be more responsible? Do our laws protect us? What can be done to stop such senselessness? What would you like to see changed? It will help if you read *into* the news you hear rather than just read *about it.*

Do something. You may not be able to change the world, but you can change *something.* Don't sit back and complain about the problems you see; *do something.* Get involved; join an organization; write to your legislators, send a letter to your newspaper, or post your thoughts on an Internet bulletin board. Volunteer your time, donate needed goods, or send a financial contribution. Talk about what can be done. Educate those who do not know. It doesn't matter what you do as long as you *do* *something*, no matter how small—and it's better than doing nothing at all.

Look for the good in the bad. It's a fact of life; bad stuff happens. Life is *not* a bowl of cherries, and it's seldom fair. Both good and bad fortune is distributed randomly and inequitably. You can throw up your arms in despair or try to find some good in the bad. It's painful when a relationship or job comes to an end. However, endings often spur new beginnings; the things you learn from each experience often lead you to something else. The end of one relationship might result in a healthier, more loving relationship. The loss of a job often leads to a more challenging, better-paying job. Loss can lead to gain, pain can fuel compassion, and bad can turn into good.

Focusing on the good doesn't take away from the bad but can make it easier to bear. The good is not always apparent right away, but if you look, you'll find something positive.

Put on a happy face. You don't have to feel happy to look happy. Sometimes looking happy can help you to feel that way. Don't try to solve all of your problems; just start by doing one thing differently. Changing the expression on your face may seem too simple to do any good, but try it and see for yourself what a difference it can make. Your expression can literally change your life. Even if you have nothing to smile about, smile anyway. The more you smile, the better you will feel; your life will begin to change for the better.

Appreciate what you have. Have you ever wanted something so much it occupied your mind? Do you remember the excitement you felt when you finally got what you had been waiting for? How long did the good feeling last? Days, weeks, months, or years? We anticipate but too often fail to *appreciate* the things we have.

Do you appreciate what *you* have? Start with the basics; if you're able to move, see, speak, and hear, be thankful. Some people struggle every day to do the things you take for granted. Take time each day to think, write, or talk about the things you appreciate. The more grateful you are, the more you will find to be grateful for. Don't wait until it's too late; appreciate what you have while you have it.

Replace negative thoughts with positve thoughts. When you have a good outlook, and it shows, you will find it easier to meet people and make new friends, increase your chances of career success, improve your relationships, and make everything you do more enjoyable.

Look on the bright side. Life is what you make it; you can look for, and see, the dark side of life or choose to look on the bright side of things. It's your life, and you can decide how dark or bright you want it to be. What you look for is what you'll see.

TIP # 80
Enjoy the ride.

Have you ever been on a roller coaster? Did you like it? Would you be willing to ride it again? Some people like the roller coaster. Others prefer the merry-go-round. Which do you prefer?

Some people fear the roller coaster. They focus on the problems and risks. Some people hold back; others let go. Some people scream, others weep, and some make no sound at all. Some people try to conquer their fears and decide to go for a ride. Others refuse. They sneer as they stand on the side and criticize those who try.

Some people prefer the merry-go-round because it moves slowly and provides a better view. It's a relaxing ride but not nearly as exciting as a roller coaster. You know what to expect on a merry-go-round; you know you keep going round and round.

Life is a lot like a roller coaster.

Life is unpredictable, with lots of twists and turns. At times it moves very slowly. At others it moves too fast.

Life is a thrilling adventure; you never know what will happen next. One minute you're up, and the next you're down. Life is filled with highs and lows.

Some people look forward in life; others look back. Some people look at everything, yet others see nothing at all. Some people focus on pleasure, but others concentrate on pain. Some people resist; others relax.

Life can seem brief or appear to last a very long time. No matter how thrilling, a good roller-coaster ride always comes to an end. The same is true in life. Strive to make sure you don't reach the end of your life until you've had *the ride of your life.*

TIP # 81

Life is *not* a game.

Some people think of life as a game. There are similarities between life and games; both can be played, both have rules, and both turn out winners and losers. Those who view life as a game might approach their lives methodically, living their lives the way they'd play a game of chess. Others might take more risks, gambling with life the way they gamble with money.

There are differences between the two, however. Games distract you from life; the more you play, the less you pay attention to the more important things in life. You can play a game as often as you want; you can play until you *win.*

In life, you get only one chance to *play. When your life is over, the game is over.*

Life is *not* a game. Life is the real thing. Life is unpredictable; you can play it right and still lose. Life is not always fair; one wrong move, one bad choice, is often one too many in life. Take a chance with your life and it could be the last chance you get.

Life isn't always fun, but it can be if you decide to make it that way. *Enjoy your life.* Take risks, but don't engage in *risky behavior.*

Think about the things you do. Don't *play* with your life. You are young. You have a bright future. Protect your life.

Don't play with your safety. Don't ignore proven safety measures. Safety measures and safety gear have one purpose: to keep you *safe*. Wear your seat belt, wear a helmet, and wear knee and elbow pads. Wear a life jacket, wear sunscreen, and protect your eyes by wearing sunglasses. Wear a jacket, a scarf, hat, gloves, or mittens when it's cold. Your safety is in *your* hands; be safe.

Don't play with money. You can make your money grow or throw it all away. Don't pay with a credit card if you don't have the money to pay for the bill when it comes. No bargain is a bargain if you'll be paying interest on it for years to come. Save some of your money. Don't spend everything you have. Put some money aside for a rainy day. Think twice before making a purchase, no matter how small. Skip the candy bar, cup of coffee, or can of soda each day, and save the money you would have spent. In just a few years, you will have saved thousands of dollars. Save more, and you'll have more. The habits you develop today will affect you financially for the rest of your life. Learn how to manage your money.

Don't play with the law. Keep the law on *your* side. If you choose to break the law, you will pay the consequences, and you will have a record that will haunt you the rest of your life. Every time you apply for a job, you will be asked if you've ever been arrested or convicted of a crime. Do you see yourself as a criminal? Whether you do or don't, other people will. Take or sell illegal drugs and you are taking a big risk. Take something from someone and you are stealing, whether it's a small amount of money from someone's drawer or an item from a retail store. If you exceed the speed limit, cheat on your taxes, drink and drive, or break any other law, you are taking a huge risk. Laws are meant to protect you, and you can protect yourself by obeying the law.

Don't play with people's feelings. Be honest with yourself and others. If you are in a relationship you know is going nowhere, but the person you are with is looking for commitment, don't string him or her along. If you have a problem with someone, don't tell everyone else—tell that person. Treat others the way you'd like to be treated. Don't use people for what you hope to get. You'll get more when you give of yourself and treat people well. The more in touch you are with your own feelings, the easier it will be for you to feel for someone else.

Don't play with sex. Your body is not a toy, and sex is not a game. Don't say *yes* if you want to say *no*, and know that *no* means *no*. Don't confuse sex and love; if you want love, you won't get it by having sex. If you aren't comfortable talking with someone about your feelings or the decision to have sex with him or her, *don't*. If you think sex belongs in a committed relationship, be sure your partner thinks the same way. Anytime you decide to become sexually involved with someone, you put your life at risk. You can and should practice safe sex, but nothing (other than abstinence) provides you the assurance you need against pregnancy or disease. Sex is not a game. Don't play with sex; play it safe.

Don't play with your future. Think. Your future is at stake in everything you do. Do you envision owning a home, getting married, or having children? Do you want to start a business, run a marathon, or travel the world? Do you want to be healthy and maintain a youthful appearance? If there is something you want to do, start planning *now*. Every decision you make and everything you do will either help you accomplish your goals or make them more difficult to achieve. The future may seem far away, but your future is a result of what you do, starting today.

TIP # 82

Don't take rejection personally.

Rejection can be summed up in one word: OUCH! It *hurts* to be rejected, but it doesn't have to. Rejection can be good for you! As the saying goes, no pain, no gain. The struggles and setbacks in life will provide you with some of life's most valuable lessons.

Rejected? Put it in perspective.

- Rejection is a part of life. You can't always get what you want. Accept it and expect it to happen. When you are rejected, it isn't always about you.

- Rejection is inevitable. Consider it an aspect of your education. You can try out for the school play, the soccer team, choir, or any position you want. You will either make it or you won't. There usually are more people trying out than there are positions available. You or someone you know will experience rejection. It doesn't mean you are no good; it means other people fit the guidelines better.

- You can apply to as many colleges as you want, knowing you will reject those you choose not to attend and assuming some colleges will reject you. Most schools can accept only a certain number of new students each year. Why take it personally—thousands of others will be rejected too, so join the club!

- It takes courage to approach someone new. Salespeople do it all the time. Even the best salespeople hear "no" far more than they hear "yes," but they don't give up; every "no" they hear brings them closer to a "yes." It's a numbers game; why don't you play along?

- When you apply for a job, you set yourself up for rejection. If you aren't asked for an interview, it doesn't mean you are no good—it means there are more-qualified applicants than you. While your goal is to get your foot in the door, the goal of the person in charge of hiring is to find the best person for the job. Part of that job is rejecting a certain number of applicants. If you never get a call for an interview, don't blame yourself—blame your resume! If you interview for a position but don't get the job, it doesn't mean you did poorly; it means someone else did better!

- When someone wants to end a relationship with you, it doesn't mean you are unworthy, even if someone else tries to tell you so. Anyone who would say such a thing is the one who is unworthy. You may not want a relationship to end, but when it suddenly does, the relationship (or other person) probably wasn't as great as you thought. If someone hurt you in the end, think about the hurt you would have experienced if you had stayed.

- If something you said or did makes someone so mad they won't talk to you, don't take it too personally. Just as you must control your anger, other people must control theirs. Most anger is misdirected anyway. The person may be upset with him or herself or someone else but decided to take it out on you. Welcome this type of rejection—you don't need people like this in your life.

- When someone is harsh with you, judgmental, or critical, don't assume you are wrong. A person who finds fault with everyone else generally is unhappy with him or herself.

Rejection is seldom a personal affront. Learn what you can from each experience; then move on. The way you feel about what happened will change over time. You will see things differently in the future. Every successful person has been rejected—and more than once.

TIP # 83
Respond; don't overreact.

Life is full of surprises. No matter how prepared you think you are, you never know what each new day will bring. It has been said that whatever happens *to you* in life is less important than *how you respond* to what happens. You may not be able to control everything that happens, but you *can* choose your response to the things that happen to you.

If someone accused you of something you didn't do, how would you respond? Would you take time to *think* about your response or allow your emotions to take over and react without thinking? When you're upset, do you tend to talk quickly or slowly, loudly or quietly? Do you yell and pound your fist or become tongue-tied and shut down?

If you were a patient in an emergency room, would you prefer a doctor who responded calmly or reacted emotionally? How would you feel if the doctor who was to care for you began screaming hysterically, swearing, or yelling? Doctors are always expecting the unexpected. An emotional reaction won't help anyone under such circumstances. When you are a patient, your life depends on a doctor's ability to respond calmly and effectively.

Most emotional reactions and overreactions are due to an element of surprise. No one *expects* an accident. You don't *plan* to lose your job, miss a meeting, or lose a valuable item. An emotional reaction to such events is not unusual, but the question is whether or not it is *helpful*.

Losing your temper or your composure when your flight is delayed, when you're stuck in traffic, have misplaced your keys, or are dissatisfied with the service you receive is neither appropriate nor acceptable. In contrast to other things in life, such inconveniences are hardly worth becoming agitated over, yet these types of incidents provoke emotional reactions all the time.

You might try to respond calmly, but trying isn't the same as *doing*. Saying "I'll try" is like saying "I might" or "I'm not sure I can." Do you *try* to go to work or do you go to work? Do you *try* to exercise, or do you get up and move? Do you *try* to remember a friend's birthday, or do you remember it? You either do something or you don't.

You can *choose* your response the same way you *choose* the clothes you wear, the food you eat, the TV show you watch, and the words you use.

If you tend to overreact, think about more effective ways to respond. Don't wait until the next time you feel your emotions taking over; identify what *isn't* working and what kind of response will work better instead.

Sometimes the best response to a person or situation is *no response*. If you aren't comfortable responding at the time, saying "I need some time to think" or "I'm not sure how to respond to your comment" is preferable to saying something you'll later regret. When you take time to think things through, you are *responding*, not *reacting*, to what happens. You will have fewer regrets, make better decisions, and exercise self-control.

TIP # 84
Learn to laugh at yourself.

When was the last time you had a really good laugh? Not just a little chuckle, but a *hearty* laugh? When was the last time you laughed so hard you had to stop to catch your breath or had tears running down your face? If you can't remember, it's been too long.

Laughter is *good* for you. In addition to the aerobic benefits you gain from laughing, laughter can reduce stress, lower blood pressure, and ease pain.

If you want to laugh but have nothing to laugh about, don't despair; what's funny to one person isn't always funny to another. Identify your own brand of humor, and if you look, you will find things to laugh about.

You don't have to be funny or have a lot of funny things happen in your life; just look for the funny things that happen each day. Learn from comedians, who know how to turn a common occurrence into a hilarious event. Comedians aren't afraid to look silly; they thrive on their humiliation. An embarrassing moment often is the basis of a hilarious story to tell. Some of your best laughs will be the result of your most embarrassing moments *if* you are willing to see the humor in what happens instead of the humiliation.

Not long ago, I slipped and fell in the detergent aisle of the grocery store. It happened so fast I wasn't sure how I ended up on the floor. My daughter was at the other end of the aisle and I expected her to help me, but instead she was walking the other way. She wanted nothing to do with me. I felt rather sorry for myself and was about to get mad, but when I saw her laughing uncontrollably, I wanted to know what she thought was so funny. As she told me what she had witnessed, I started laughing too. The more we embellished and talked about the details, the funnier it became. For the rest of the shopping trip, we couldn't look at each other without laughing. My stomach muscles were sore, not from falling but from laughing so hard.

Learn to laugh at life; learn to laugh at yourself.

Lighten up! Don't get too worked up about the little things in life. Will the thing you're stressed about today be remembered a year from now? Will it matter five years from today? Don't hang on to perfection or stress; learn to *let go* of the things you can't control.

Accentuate the funny side of life. You'll find humor almost anywhere if you look for it. Do you ever watch late-night television? David Letterman is known for his top-ten lists; Jay Leno for his headline segments. These segments bring out the humorous, unusual side of the day's events. Don't overlook the more unusual side of life; accentuate the funny side of things.

Use humor. A little humor can go a long way. Observe comedians and other people you think are funny. Listen to the way they talk about themselves and about life. If you heard a joke that made you laugh, write it down and read it again—consider sharing it with someone. You don't have to be armed with jokes or try to entertain your friends, but be willing to laugh with others, and don't be afraid to laugh at yourself.

Get up and go out. Get up and go out to a comedy club, a funny movie, or a play. Go to a bookstore, a coffee shop, or to visit a friend. Go roller skating, bowling, or anywhere you haven't been. If you feel like a fool doing something you haven't done before, it can be fun *and* funny.

Have more fun! All work and no play will hurt anyone's funny bone. Make sure you make time for fun times. Play fun games, tell funny stories, and do something fun for yourself. The more fun you have, the more likely you will find something to laugh about.

The next time you're feeling ill or a little blue, laugh and see what it does for you. Laughter really is the best medicine. Laugh yourself to good health.

TIP # 85

Change is inevitable; misery is optional.

When Ann Ulrich's husband came home from work with "that look" on his face, she knew what it meant; he had been fired. She knew she had to do *something*. She decided to throw a party to celebrate her husband's job loss. Her husband was less enthusiastic about the idea, but once he redirected his anger and frustration over his job loss into planning his celebration, his perspective changed. As they planned the details of his job-loss celebration, they both grew increasingly optimistic about the turn of events and the possibilities the future held.

The original "I Got Fired! Party" was a success. Not only did her husband benefit, but she did too. As a result of her experience, she founded a company, Celebrate Transitions, Inc. to help others learn how to celebrate their job loss too.

Job loss is not something typically celebrated. There is no right or wrong response to being fired. Everyone reacts differently, but few react joyfully. Losing a job is rarely considered good news. But it forces you to take a good look at your life and yourself, whether you want to or not. Throwing a party is both a positive and proactive response to job loss. It is easier than calling everyone you know and telling the same story repeatedly and a great way to network and let others know you are looking for work.

Change isn't easy; anything you can do to minimize the stress you feel is beneficial. There are many uncertainties in life, but change is constant.

You are evolving and changing too. Just look through an old photo album to see how much you have *changed*. You've changed physically since the day you were born, and you will continue to do so. Your knowledge changes, and so does your perspective.

Your experiences, both good and bad, have shaped your view of the world and are part of you.

You can *resist* change or you can accept and embrace it. You can make it easier or more difficult. Either way, change will occur. It is inevitable. If you resist change, what are you resisting? Are you:

Denying the truth?

Trying to control things you have no control over?

Saying no to new opportunities?

Opposed to different or better ways of doing things?

Resisting new knowledge?

Limiting your potential?

Change is inevitable, and it can be *positive.*

- Change can help you face and conquer your fears.

- Change can lead to better relationships, a better job, and a better life.

- Change can teach you something new.

- Change can produce compassion.

- Change can broaden your perspective.

- Change can motivate you to take action.

- Change can be good; focus on the positive aspects of change.

You don't have to *like* change to *accept* it; you can learn to cope with change. Only you can choose whether you will resist or accept it. *Celebrate* the changes that occur in your life.

TIP # 86

Sometimes you have to let go.

Some things are worth fighting for, but others are better off left alone. You should fight for what you believe and work hard for the things you want. Hold on to your dreams, your values, and your self-respect. Hold on to those you love. Hold on, but don't hang on; know when it's time to let go.

Letting go isn't easy, but neither is hanging on. When you let go, you give up control. Giving up is *not* the same as giving in. When you give something up, you release it; you free yourself of your need for control. Trying to control what you cannot is a daunting task. The longer you hang on to something, the more you hurt yourself. You deplete your physical and emotional energy when you try to have power over anything that is out of your hands.

- **Let go of your fear.** If you're hanging on because you are *afraid* of letting go, let go of your fear; you've nothing to be afraid of.

- **Let go of your need to be right.** If you're hanging on because you don't want to be wrong, let go of your need to be right.

- **Let go of your need to control other people.** If you're hanging on to a relationship because you don't want to lose someone, it's likely you've already lost him or her. You can't make someone love you, want to be with you, or be the kind of person *you* want him or her to be.

- **Let go of your grudges.** When you hold a grudge, you hold on to your anger and you hold yourself back. Don't allow your anger to get the best of you. The person you forgive isn't the only one who gets a break—you will feel better too.

- **Let go of your need for perfection.** No one is perfect and neither are you. What's the point in setting standards too impossible to meet? Set your standards high, but make sure they are within reach.

- **Let go of guilt.** No one can *make* you feel guilty. Anyone can try, but guilt is something you bring on yourself.

- **Let go of your judgments.** You are not superior and have no right to criticize or pass judgment on others. Look inward instead of outward. The more you look for and find fault with others, the more likely you are to see that similar weakness within yourself. Focus on what you can control; focus on you.

- **Let go of worry.** Worry does nothing but cause more worry. No amount of worry will prevent something from happening or help you deal with it if it does. Worry is a waste of time. You can't predict the future. Life is unpredictable. Stop worrying, stop predicting, and start enjoying life and living.

You can let go and still hang on to your hopes and dreams. You can let go and still fight for what you believe. If you can't change it, resolve it, or control it, do the one thing you can do: Let it go.

TIP # 87
Put on a happy face.

You've heard many messages about the impact of your attitude and the importance of maintaining a positive attitude. It isn't difficult to understand that a cheerful disposition is preferable and that optimism is something to strive for. If you want to make yourself and others feel better, look pleasant, and be happier, just put on a happy face.

You've probably heard it or even suggested it yourself: "Snap out of it." "Don't worry." "Be happy." "*Look* happy." If someone suggested these things when you didn't feel like snapping out of it or smiling, the encouragement to do so may have made matters worse. When you are feeling down, being told to cheer up will not necessarily make you feel any better, but the truth is it could.

A positive attitude will help you in many ways. When you have a good outlook, and it shows, you will find it easier to meet people and make new friends, increase your chances of career success, improve your relationships, and make everything you do more enjoyable.

Thinking positively is *good* for you in other ways too. Studies have found a correlation between mental health and physical health. Positive people tend to be healthier than their negative counterparts. An optimistic outlook is good for the immune system; the more positive you are, the stronger your immune system is likely to be and the better able you are to fight off illness and disease.

Happy, emotionally healthy individuals *live longer* than those who are unhappy, negative, and pessimistic about their future. One of the simplest ways to change your attitude is by *smiling*. *Smile* and your eyes sparkle; *smile* and you appear friendly; *smile* and you soften the lines in your face; *smile* and you look happier; *smile* and you *feel* happier too.

Don't underestimate the value of the expression on your face. Think about the times you've looked at someone and could tell he or she was mad or sad. We speak with our faces although we may never say a word. It's easy to tell when someone shouldn't be disturbed; we understand the silent language when someone's face says "leave me alone."

If you aren't meeting the right kind of people or finding the job you want, the reason could be as simple as the expression on your face. Not sure? Look around you and notice the people you see.

How many *look* happy? Compare those who look happy with those who don't. Which are you attracted to?

Work on improving your attitude. Look on the bright side. You don't have to feel happy to look happy. Sometimes looking happy can help you to feel that way. Don't try to solve all of your problems; just start by doing one thing differently. Changing the expression on your face may seem too simple to do any good, but try it and see for yourself what a difference it can make. Your expression can literally change your life. Even if you have nothing to smile about, smile anyway. The more you smile, the better you will feel; your life will begin to change for the better. People will smile back. Some people may even speak to you. You've got nothing to lose. If you want to improve your attitude and live a long, healthy life, you have to start somewhere. Why not start with your face?

TIP # 88
Learn to give and receive compliments.

I hardly recognized Sherry when I ran into her unexpectedly at the mall. I hadn't seen her in some time but had talked with her on the phone about the operation she had to help her lose weight. "You look wonderful," I said. I was about to be more specific, but she interrupted me. She rolled her eyes and said "Wonderful? Are you kidding? Look at me. I'm a mess! My shirt is stained, my hair is greasy, and my clothes are practically falling off of me. You need to get your eyes checked."

I was dumbfounded. Sherry had lost a substantial amount of weight since the last time I saw her. She *did* look good. I wasn't scrutinizing her, and I wouldn't have noticed any of the imperfections she was determined to draw my attention to. Instead of focusing on the positive outcome of her weight loss, she focused only on the negative, pointing out all of her perceived flaws.

Sherry not only made herself look bad, but she made me look pretty bad too. Rather than listening to and accepting my compliment, she *criticized* me for giving it. As if that weren't enough, she contradicted everything I said.

Sherry isn't the only one who has trouble accepting a compliment. Most of us want reassurance and praise, yet when we actually get it, we don't know what to do with it. When we feel insecure or undeserving of the praise we receive, we tend to refute it.

Think about your reaction to the compliments you receive. Do you graciously accept other people's comments? Consider a compliment as a gift. When someone gives you a gift, he or she hopes you will appreciate and accept it. Imagine how you would feel if you gave someone a gift, but instead of graciously accepting it, the person gave it back to you. When you receive a compliment, it might make *you* feel more comfortable to reject it, but think about the impact on the person who gave it to you. That person might feel uncomfortable when you do.

Accept the compliments you receive, and be generous in giving compliments to others. Do you look for, and talk freely about, the positive things people do? Or do you feel threatened, afraid that doing so will make someone else look better than *you?*

When you make someone else look good, you make yourself look good too. Look for the good in others, and then tell people what you see. Be careful you don't use flattery; a genuine compliment comes from *within.*

Make it easy for others to receive your compliments; be sincere, specific, and succinct. And make it easy for others who compliment you; don't debate or negate a compliment. Accept and appreciate it. A simple "thank you" is all you need to say.

Be a generous giver and a gracious receiver; learn to give and receive compliments and see for yourself how rewarding both can be.

TIP # 89
Be a cheerleader for yourself and others.

You don't have to be a big fan of baseball to know about the World Series or a die-hard football fan to be familiar with the Super Bowl. These are two of the biggest sporting events held each year. These offer a time when people gather together to watch and cheer, and do you know why? Because it's more fun than watching, cheering, or celebrating alone.

Would a game be as exciting to watch, or as thrilling for the players to play, if there were no fans cheering them on? Professional athletes rely on their fans to cheer them on, but they aren't the only ones; *everyone* does better with a little encouragement. You don't have to play a professional sport to surround yourself with fans.

Who surrounds *you?* Are your friends and family on your "team"? Do they want you to win? Will they celebrate your success? Do you hear more cheering or more jeering? Are you a cheerleader for others? Can you feel happy (not envious) for another person's success?

You're fortunate if you have people cheering for you, but the most important cheerleader in your life is *you.* You need to be your biggest fan. You have to rely on yourself. Only *you* can motivate you. It's important to have support from others, but ultimately, your motivation comes from *you.*

Listen to yourself. Do you speak highly of yourself and others? Do you criticize more than you praise? Are you more inclined to say "good job" or "you could have done better," "I'm doing okay" or "I'm feeling great," "I told you so" or "at least you tried"? Listen to the things you say; if your words aren't supportive, *you* aren't supportive.

Be a good sport. Are you happy for the successes of others, or do you compare someone else's success to your own? Is your attitude consistent, or are you a fair-weather fan? When times are tough, do you give up on yourself and others or keep cheering on? We all need a boost when the going gets tough, and we need encouragement to go on. Be a cheerleader *all* of the time; be consistent.

Cheer for yourself. You won't feel like a winner if you call yourself a loser, and you'll find it difficult to accomplish much if you tell yourself you can't. Tell yourself the things you need to hear repeatedly. The more you cheer, the easier it will be to believe in what you hear yourself saying.

Cheer for others. Do you find fault with others or look for what's right? Do you point out problems or look for solutions? Do you hold people back or push people forward? Are you inclined to say "keep it up" or "give it up," "you're doing the best you can," or "you could have done better?" The more you cheer for others, the more they will cheer for you.

Celebrate your triumphs. Remind yourself of your successes by creating your own hall of fame. Proudly display the awards, ribbons, and certificates you receive. Save the nice notes and cards you get so you can read them when you need a cheer to get you going. Display pictures of happy and special moments in your life, and look at them often or anytime you need a boost. You don't need to win the World Series to feel you've accomplished something big. Celebrate the little things and the big things and cheer yourself on.

Learn a new cheer. If you don't know how to cheer, you can learn. A cheer must be sincere; make sure you *sound* excited. Start slowly; work on a new cheer each week. Practice saying the cheer until you feel you've got it right. Here are a few cheers to get you started:

Way to go!

You did it!

WOW!

You're really coming along!

Congratulations!

Good job!

You outdid yourself!

This is fantastic!

Right on!

You've learned fast!

That's great!

You're almost there!

I'm so proud of you!

TIP # 90

Avoid toxic people and environments.

I regretted answering the phone. I didn't have time for a long talk, but with this particular person our conversations always went on longer than I wanted. I was thrilled when I heard a knock at my door and my dog started barking. My caller heard it too, and we both knew I had to hang up the phone.

I greeted my neighbor and thanked her for coming to the door and helping me escape from what would have been a long and dreaded phone conversation. Her response surprised me. "You need to do a little housecleaning," she said. Before I could respond, she made it clear she thought my house looked fine. "I'm talking about the woman on the phone. If she has worn out her welcome, why do you keep inviting her in?"

My neighbor's advice sounded a bit harsh at first, but it did make sense. She got me to think about the "stuff" that was creating a "mess" in my life. I thought about the people I wanted in my "house" and those I could do without. Why did I give so much time to someone when it created so much stress? If someone came calling, I let that person into my life, but worse yet, I kept knocking myself out trying to be a perfect host!

When someone adds more stress to my life than I can handle and I feel uncomfortable around that person, I need to evaluate what the relationship means to me. I barely have even enough time for the people I *do* want in my life. I must decide whom I want to spend time with rather than allowing other people to make such important decisions for me.

Do you allow toxic people in *your* life? If you aren't sure, find out. Ask yourself the following questions.

Am I choosing to be with this person out of habit or convenience? People tend to spend time with the people they work with, live by, and or share common interests with. Would you go out of your way or travel a distance just to be with this person? If not, do you have a real friendship or one of convenience?

Do I feel good about myself when I am with this person? Does he or she treat you respectfully? Does this person try to change you, criticize you, or control you? Pay attention to how you *feel* around this person. A healthy relationship feels good—a toxic relationship can literally make you feel ill.

Do I want to spend time with this person? Who initiates your get-togethers? Does this person want to spend time with you, but you don't feel the same way? If you are responding to someone else's desire to spend time together, make sure you want to spend time together too.

Are my needs being met? Are you giving and giving without getting anything in return? Are your needs important to the relationship, or do they take a back seat to the needs of someone else? Do you have a voice in the relationship, feel listened to, and cared about? Not all relationships are split 50/50. It's fine to give more than you get as long as you choose to have it that way. But if you give and *hope* you'll get something back, or spend the majority of your time meeting the needs of others, you're likely neglecting your own needs. You deserve to get something back. Your needs are important too.

Does this person have qualities I look for in a friend? What qualities do you look for in a friend? Does this person possess these qualities? Are you proud to call this person your friend? Does he or she fit in and get along with your family and friends? Do you look forward to his or her calls and your time together? Or do you try to avoid this person and make up excuses to avoid being with him or her? If you don't see qualities you value in someone, why do you keep this person as a friend?

Am I being too nice? In the preceding account, I talked on the phone with my "friend" because *she* wanted to; I held back *my* opinion because she wouldn't listen, and I allowed her to monopolize my time. I didn't want to hurt her, so I tried to be nice but ended up hurting myself in the process.

Am I willing to work at the relationship? Good relationships take time and effort but shouldn't drain you emotionally or leave you feeling frustrated. Is this person important enough to you to work at improving the relationship? If you don't care enough about someone to make the relationship better, you probably don't need the relationship.

Is this a toxic relationship? If you are unhappy with the way someone treats you or talks to you, or if you feel stuck and hope things will change, think seriously about why you stay in the relationship. If someone hurts you physically or emotionally by yelling, blaming, shaming, teasing, scolding, smothering, or controlling you, you are in a toxic relationship. Toxic relationships can destroy you. Reevaluate the relationship. You have options. Talk with someone who can help you, and consider seeking professional help.

Beware of toxic people, relationships, and environments. A person can be good *to* you yet not good *for* you. Whether at work, home, or somewhere else, pay attention to the way you *feel* around other people. Do a little housekeeping; clean out the "stuff" that's either "messing" with you or *messing you up.*

Areas of Distinction

Rise Above the Ordinary and Live an Extraordinary Life

TIP # 91
Volunteer.

It's important to live intentionally. You need to know who you are and where you are going. The more focused you are, the better off you are. The busier you are, the more productive you are. Ironically, it's the people who are the busiest that we rely on the most to get things done. But time is precious, and you may find more things you'd like to do than you have time to do them.

You might be inclined to say no when you are asked to volunteer, but think twice before you respond negatively. Volunteering is always optional, but it can be very worthwhile and it's something you should consider carving out the time to do. When you share some of your talent and success or some of what you have with others, you will enjoy and appreciate it more. There will always be people with more and people with less than you. Pay attention to both, but pay special attention to those who can use your help.

You don't have to make a big commitment to volunteer. In fact, you need to be careful not to overcommit. If you try to do too much, you won't help anyone. Be selective and carefully choose the volunteer opportunities that appeal most to you. Then get involved and commit only to those things you can see through to completion.

You don't get paid money when you volunteer, but what you get is something money can't buy. You get the personal satisfaction that comes from doing something good, and you may get experience otherwise unavailable to you. When you volunteer and improve life for others, your life will change for the better because it will improve too.

Look for volunteer opportunities through work and outside of work. If you don't know what kind of opportunity you want, there are volunteer organizations that can use your help and help you figure out what you're most suited to do.

- Volunteer one day or evening a week, once a month, or a few times a year; it doesn't really matter as long as you find time to volunteer.

- Volunteer to donate money, food, clothing, or whatever an organization needs. Or, instead of buying and sending cards on a special occasion, send a card from the recipient's favorite charity informing them you've made a donation.

- Volunteer your home; house a foreign exchange student, or offer to hold a meeting or event at your home. Become a foster parent; there are many children needing temporary shelter and there are just as many abandoned pets.

- Volunteer your expertise. Charities and organizations need different types of expertise. Share your knowledge with others and help out an organization or person in need.

- Volunteer and do something you are passionate about. You're bound to learn something new and meet other passionate people who share your interests too.

- Volunteer to mentor others. Become a big brother or sister. Give encouragement; be someone's life coach. Get involved in a mentoring program.

- Volunteer to help out a friend or neighbor; volunteer to help the sick, the elderly, or anyone unable to care for him or herself.

- Volunteer selflessly; volunteer because you want to give, not because there's something you're hoping to get. Volunteer because you want to do something for someone else, but don't be surprised when you benefit from volunteering yourself.

TIP # 92
Make a difference.

Lois was only 52 when she died. People came from near and far to honor her memory and celebrate her life. Anyone in attendance wanting to pay tribute to her was encouraged to speak up, and people of all ages, from every walk of life, stepped forward to share their stories.

Rebecca, the first to speak, both laughed and cried as she talked about her best friend. "Lois thought I was so funny, she wanted to hire someone to follow me around to write down everything I said. I'm here to tell you that I'm not the one worth writing about—Lois is. She had a way of making me feel so special; she made *everyone* feel special."

Everyone who got up to speak told similar stories. Lois wasn't famous or featured in the headlines, but she had a profound impact on those who knew her. She made a positive difference in people's lives.

Lois accomplished what many do not; she lived a happy and meaningful life. In his book *When All You've Ever Wanted Isn't Enough*, Harold Kushner says people do not fear death as much as they fear leaving a life that had no meaning. What people fear most is the thought that their life hasn't mattered—no one wants to be forgotten. The happiest people, he says, aren't those who *pursue* happiness but those who, by being good people, live meaningful lives.

Some people are deeply connected to the importance and purpose of their lives, while others are not. Everyone finds meaning in different ways. Some people seek significance through their work and accomplishments; others rely on their relationships or the deeds they perform. How do you find meaning in your life? What do you hope to accomplish during your lifetime? What's the most important thing you want to do? What kind of person do you want to be?

Who are the most important people in your life? How do you want to be remembered by them when you are gone? In what ways would you like the world to be different because of *you*?

You might think what you do doesn't matter, but it does. You might think one person can't make a difference, but one person can and often does. Think about the individuals who have influenced *your* life. Then ask yourself if they know who they are. If you haven't done so yet, be sure to tell them the difference they've made. When you do, you'll be making a difference in their lives too.

You're on this earth for a reason, and it's not to take up space. No one can tell you what you are meant to do, but there is a reason. Search for your purpose.

As you begin to build your life, the end may seem far away. You want to think about living, not dying, but you should think about the legacy you want to leave behind some day. Start thinking about it *now* and start making a difference today.

TIP # 93
Cross the finish line.

No matter how many projects you start, your achievements are a result of what you *finish*. It doesn't matter what you think about doing or plan to do; you get credit only for what you *complete*.

People don't *plan* on stopping a project in the middle or as they near the end, but all too often they do. Some say it's because of a fear of failure; others say it's a fear of success. The best antidote for fear is to face and conquer it.

You won't end up where you want by quitting. The only way you win is when you *cross the finish line.*

How many books have been bought but never read? How many photo albums have stayed empty with no pictures because we're too busy to fill them? How many songs have been written but never sung? How many manuscripts are being written but won't ever be finished?

Why do we make promises we cannot keep? Why do we start things we never complete? What gets in the way? What gets in *your* way?

Do you quit when you think you cannot win? If so, stop thinking about winning and start thinking about *doing.* Did you know that *winners never quit?* Those who quit will never win.

Do you say yes when you want to say no? If so, how will you motivate yourself to see the project through? Remember, you can't please everyone. Say yes only to the things that are most important to you.

Do you have things you know you'll regret if you don't get them done? If so, put these tasks at the top of your list and make it a priority to finish them. You may never get another chance to tell someone how you feel—or to visit someone who is terminally ill. If you wait too long, you might be too late to do anything at all.

Do you have a list of things you don't want to do but feel you *ought* to? If so, determine how important it is. If it's important, you should do it. Exercise is important, and we all ought to exercise, but we don't because it's easy to procrastinate. If you wait to exercise until your life depends on it, it could be too late.

Do you have things you plan on finishing *someday*? If so, decide *when* that someday will be. The someday you're waiting for may never come unless you assign a deadline to it.

Do you have things you plan on doing when you find the time? If so, you need to realize you will never *find* time. You have to *make* time to do the things you want to do. If you haven't found more time by now, chances are you never will.

Do you have things you'd like to do that aren't important? If so, cross them off your list and put them out of your mind. Focus on doing only the most important things.

Do you have things you want to do but aren't sure you can? If so, you can do anything you set your mind to. Find the strength to see it through, and consider asking someone to help you.

Do you have trouble finishing things because you're never satisfied? If so, focus on *doing* your best, and stop worrying about *being* the best. You'll never get much done if you're striving for perfection.

You don't get credit for the things you *think* about doing or *plan* to do someday. You get credit only for what you *do* each day.

Make a list of all the things you want to do; then decide which tasks are most important to you. Focus on the most important ones and make a plan to get them done. It's easier to finish when you carefully consider what you start.

Be a *doer*, not a quitter. You let yourself down when you stop short of a goal, but you will feel like a winner every time you **cross the finish line.**

TIP # 94
Follow your heart.

When it was time for Colleen to declare a major, she wasn't sure what to do. The subjects she enjoyed most were those people told her she couldn't do anything with professionally. Under pressure to find a career, she declared accounting as her major after doing well in the accounting class she took.

At times she wondered if she had made a mistake, but she pushed her concerns away and stuck with her decision. After graduation, Colleen got a job with a large accounting firm. She was compensated well and her success made her the envy of her peers, but she remained dissatisfied. Although she did well at her job, she didn't really like working in accounting.

Whenever she mentioned her frustration to family or friends, they told her she would be crazy to give up such a great job and career. Assuming they knew what was best for her, she listened to their advice instead of listening to herself and following her heart.

After working at a job she loathed for seven years, Colleen's physical and emotional health began to deteriorate. She suffered severe anxiety attacks and could no longer ignore the circumstances that were affecting her health and well-being. Her idea of success didn't match what others told her success was.

It took some time, but when she finally paid attention to her heart instead of her pocket book, she quit her job, took a different one in a public relations firm, and went back to school. As a result, her health and her peace of mind improved.

Colleen knew all along what was best for her, but instead of following her heart, she followed the advice of others. Look inward, not outward, to find the answers to your most important questions. No one knows better than you what's best for you.

Consider carefully the advice that others give you; pay more attention to the advice you give to yourself. Use your head, but don't ignore how you feel. Sometimes you just *know*. Some feelings are too difficult to explain, especially to others who have difficulty listening to their hearts.

When your head and your heart tell you two different things, carefully consider your choices. Look at all sides, the risks, and consequences. If your feelings are stronger than what you *think* is right, get out of your head and follow your heart.

TIP # 95

Love the work you do.

Whether you work full or part time, you will spend more time at work than almost anywhere else. Are you willing to spend the majority of your time (and your life) working at a job you dislike, or do you want to spend your time doing something you enjoy?

When you enjoy the work you do, it won't feel like work at all. You will feel, and know, that you're doing the work you were meant to do. Don't worry if you're not sure what you're meant to do just yet. It can take time to figure it out.

Pay attention. Pay attention to your activities, both in and outside of work. Notice what you are doing when you feel most energized and alert. Which tasks do you enjoy doing most and which the least? Can you detect a lifelong pattern, or are you establishing new interests and habits?

Find your passion. If you could spend your time doing anything you wanted, what would you do? If money wasn't an issue, would your answer change? If you had so much money you could give some away, who would you give it to? Think about your interests. What are your favorite things to do? What subjects interest you most? What topics are you inclined to talk about, think about, or read about? Do you have a talent or skill you'd like to improve? The answers to these questions can help guide you. Start by identifying the things you are most interested in or most enthusiastic about. Your interests and enthusiasm indicate your passion.

Look for meaning in your work. If getting a paycheck is the only thing motivating you to get out of bed and go to your job each day, you need to find more meaning in your work. Look beyond your compensation; look for something you can give. Can a coworker use your help? Can you make a client smile? Can you find a way to challenge yourself? The more meaningful your work is to you and others, the more satisfied you will be doing it.

Do more than get by. Are you arriving at work each day eager to do a good job? If you show up physically but are absent emotionally, *you* aren't showing up for work at all; only your body is. If you are getting by and doing the bare minimum, it won't be too long before you say good-bye to your job. There are plenty of bodies for hire but too few outstanding employees.

Don't let your job define you. You are not your job, but when you love your job it will be a *part* of who you are. Some people lose themselves in their work. Work shouldn't be an escape from life but a part of life. It's important to get good feelings from your job, but make sure you get good feelings other places as well. Work hard at work, but work hard at your outside relationships and hobbies too.

Money isn't everything. Money can buy you many things, but one thing is certain: Money will *not* buy you happiness. A study that appeared in the *Journal of Personality and Social Psychology*, published by the American Psychological Association, put money at the bottom of the list of the psychological needs that bring happiness and fulfillment. Self-esteem, competence, and a feeling of closeness with others were at the top of the list.

Some people love every job they have, not because each job is ideal but because they find the good in what they do. Some jobs are better than others, but no job will make you happy if you are unhappy. If you are consistently dissatisfied, think about making changes within yourself before you look to change jobs again. You can find work you love but only when you're ready to.

TIP # 96
Believe in yourself.

This is *your* life. Decide how you want your life to be. You can either stay where you are or set yourself free to become the person you know you can be. You can accomplish anything you want as long as you *believe*.

If you believe you can't succeed, you probably won't. You are more likely to succeed when you believe you can. Your beliefs create your reality; you choose what you believe.

The dance team had been through a rough season. Participating in one of the most competitive divisions in the state, they hadn't done as well as they had hoped. Their dream of representing their division at the state conference was slipping away.

The upcoming competition would determine which teams advanced to the state level. The girls were excited about the dance they choreographed, but their confidence was waning. They wanted to do well, but they didn't think they had a chance.

Many of the dancers' parents (myself included) felt frustrated with what seemed to be biased judging inequities, but with little time to spare we realized even *our* attitudes needed adjusting. Up until now, our role was to raise money for the team. With just two weeks to go until the big competition, we knew no amount of money would help the situation.

The girls had the talent and ability to make it to state. The only thing missing was the *belief* they could. As members of the dance team booster club, we parents were determined to "boost" the girls' spirits and "raise" their thinking to a higher level.

We came up with a plan. Each day for the following two weeks, a group of parents showed up at practice to encourage and cheer the girls on. We knew the dance team could do well, and we told them so. We celebrated their effort with banners, posters, mementos, and pizza parties. We embarrassed them (and ourselves) as we entered the gym shaking pom-poms and noisemakers.

We had serious moments with the girls too. We read inspirational stories and poems and all got together to watch a few movies about an underdog who becomes the champion. One day we surprised each girl with a copy of the book *The Little Engine That*

Could, by Wally Piper. A classic children's tale, it reinforces the power of belief in oneself.

The story is about a little engine that manages to pull itself over the top of a steep mountain. The bigger engines that said, "I cannot watch," as the little engine slowly pushes up the mountain while saying "I think I can—I think I can—I think I can" over and over. It became the dance-team mantra.

The girls were having fun again, and it showed when they danced. The competition day arrived, and right before they were about to perform, they huddled together to chant their new mantra.

Two weeks prior, going to state seemed impossible, and the team assumed they *could not* win. Everything changed when they changed their thinking. Once the girls realized they *could* do well, they **decided** they *would* do well. Because they believed in themselves and believed they would make it to state, they did.

The girls credit the parents, but the credit goes to the girls. Nothing we did could have helped unless the girls were willing to help themselves. The parents always believed the girls could win, but the girls' belief needed to come from within.

When you cast doubt on yourself, you create doubt in everyone else. When you believe in yourself, you won't need reassurance from anyone else. Instead of assuming you *can't,* why not assume you *can?*

Some people believe they are destined to fail; others believe they will succeed. What you believe has *everything* to do with what you achieve. It doesn't matter what others believe you can or cannot do. What matters is what *you* believe you can do.

Martin Luther King, Jr. *believed.* He had a dream *and* the courage to share it with others.

Helen Keller could not hear or see, but she managed to have a *vision;* she accomplished more than most, despite the number of obstacles she faced.

Marilyn Monroe, Elvis Presley, and the Beatles were all told they wouldn't succeed, but they *did*. They didn't believe what others predicted their fate would be.

No one else knows what's best for you. Only you know what you believe. Look for the motive when someone tells you what you should or shouldn't do. Is this person thinking about what's best for you? Anyone who discourages you might be discouraged himself. Perhaps he (or she) once had a dream and let it slip away. It's not easy supporting someone else's dream if you've given up on your own.

It hurts to stop believing. When you give up on yourself, all you're left with are thoughts of what *might* have been.

Life is full of choices. Decide *now* how you want your life to be. You can't be wrong about a decision if it's right for *you*.

Have a vision—picture the way you want your life to be. Believe in your vision. Believe you will rise each time you fall. Believe you are meant to reach your dreams.

TIP # 97

It's not what you earn, it's what you do with your earnings that count.

What do you envision when you think about your goals and plans for the future? Do you hope to own a home someday? Will you ever want to purchase a new car, furniture, or better computer? Is travel important to you? Have you thought about what it will take for you to qualify for a mortgage or loan?

If you don't know all you need to know about money, you're not alone. The knowledge you need for a secure financial future is not included in the curriculum of most schools. Your ability to do the things you want and to live the lifestyle you choose is dependent not only on what you earn but also on what you do with your earnings. If you spend and invest wisely, you will watch your earnings grow.

After working at his full-time job, Chris earns extra money working as an umpire and as a hockey coach. His days are long, but he is determined to pay off his student loans as quickly as he can and save enough money to buy his first home. He watches over his money and calculates every purchase. He brings a bag lunch to work and prepares his evening meals in advance to avoid the temptation of eating out or picking up food. He dropped his membership at the gym and runs outside instead. Everything he does is well thought out with one goal in mind: To get and stay out of debt and to be in control of his finances.

To some, Chris's approach is too extreme. His friends tease him about being cheap and encourage him to spend more of the money he is making. But he laughs it off. He's made the choice to get and stay out of debt, be in control of his finances, and work toward a stable financial future.

Perhaps you've saved money and invested wisely over the years and will continue to do so. If you are like most young adults today, however, you've freely spent the money you've had.

This is an important time in your life. Think about the things you want to achieve, accomplish, and accumulate. Make plans and set goals, not just for the things you want to do, but also for how you will afford to do these things. Reap the benefits of getting a handle on your finances *now*.

Save. No matter how little you earn, you can and need to save some of your earnings. A little money saved each month goes a long way. Save for a rainy day, save for a big purchase, save to give you peace of mind. Make the commitment to put away some amount, no matter how small, out of *every* paycheck. Make arrangements to have it automatically withdrawn from your paycheck and deposited into your 401(k) plan at work and employer-matched retirement funds, a personal savings account, or your own IRA.

Ellie started putting away a minimum of $100 per month when she began working. She's been *paying herself first* for the last six years and has close to $10,000 saved. Had she kept the money she is sure she would have spent it, yet she managed to get by without it. She feels secure just knowing the money is there and has curbed her spending as a result of her desire to see it grow.

No one knows what future circumstances will be; one way to plan for the unforeseen is to be financially prepared for the unexpected expenses that arise. Having an emergency fund to see you through a job loss or transition, an illness, or any other unpredictable circumstance will make it a little easier to get through a difficult time.

Pay with cash. When you pay with cash you spend only the money you have. Purchasing something on credit is easy. Paying it off is not. When you pay with credit it is tempting to charge up more than you have to spend.

If you aren't able to pay with cash or check, a debit card is the next best thing. But even debit cards can cost you. Many cards will approve purchases your balance doesn't support, which can lead to additional charges.

Lauren was stunned to discover she had accumulated close to $500 in overdraft fees one weekend. She had plenty of money in her account from the check she had deposited, but, unbeknownst to her, the bank was holding the funds, pending approval. Monitor your accounts closely. Overdraft and other bank fees add up and will cost you. The best way to avoid added costs and overspending is to pay with cash.

Get and stay out of debt. Few people plan on getting into debt, yet millions of people are deep in debt. It can take years to get out of debt and restore your credit score. Your intentions may be to pay off the balance on your credit cards each month, but it is easier to charge something than it is to pay the amount of your accumulated charges.

Consider the true cost of the purchases you make. An item on sale may end up costing you *more* when put on a credit card. If you pay it off over time instead of when the balance is due, miss payments, and incur late fees, you might end up paying *more* than the item is worth!

- Avoid the temptation to use your credit to purchase items you cannot afford.

- Keep your balances low enough on your credit cards to pay them off each month.

- Pay your bills on time to avoid additonal interest and late fees.

- Keep your credit score in check. A good credit score is important now and in the future.

Invest in your future. The time to start and get in the habit of investing is now. If you aren't sure about the best ways to invest in your future, seek the advice of someone who does. Utilize the many resources available to help you. Find information on the Internet. Read books or consult financial experts. Take advantage of free services. The best source you have, however, is *you;* you are the one who will decide what you do with your money. You work hard to earn the money you make; make the most of your earnings.

Live within your means. You don't have to deprive yourself by living within your means, but you do need self-discipline. Saying "no" to something you want can be difficult. When you resist the temptation, think of it as saying "yes" to your financial welfare instead. Living within your means is not a punishment, it is a reality check. Managing your money can be overwhelming, but it doesn't have to be. Adapting to a lifestyle you can afford gets easier over time. The reward is your financial security.

TIP # 98
Be a successful student of your own failure.

Most people seeking success do everything they can to avoid failure. We expect to succeed; we revere the most successful people and pity those who fail. Failure is viewed negatively, and we *fear* it. We're embarrassed when we fail. We often hide our failures and keep them to ourselves.

Yet most people fail before they succeed. Think about some of the successful people you know. How did they get where they are today? Have they always been successful?

Abraham Lincoln failed many times in his career but went on to succeed. He was defeated in elections and rejected for political office numerous times, but it didn't stop him from running again and becoming one of America's most recognized and respected presidents.

Thomas Edison failed thousands of times before he successfully invented the light bulb. He succeeded because he kept trying and never gave up.

Louisa May Alcott was told by an editor that she'd never write anything people would want to read, but that didn't stop her from writing. She went on to write the legendary *Little Women* and a number of other works.

Sylvester Stallone experienced his share of rejection and failure. His script for the movie *Rocky* was rejected more than 30 times before it was accepted, produced, and became a smash hit.

Michael Jordan was cut from his high school basketball team, but that didn't stop him. He kept on playing and trying and succeeded at his game, becoming the National Basketball Association's most famous player.

Barbra Streisand faced rejection; she was frequently told she wasn't pretty enough to succeed, but she didn't give up. She's a successful singer, actress, songwriter, and movie director.

Steven Spielberg dropped out of college. Now he's a blockbuster movie producer and director using his platform to both entertain and educate his audiences.

J.K. Rowling, creator of *Harry Potter,* was broke and unemployed when she wrote her first manuscript. Once a struggling single mother, she's now one of Britain's wealthiest women.

Walt Disney suffered financial problems and a nervous breakdown before achieving fame and fortune and founding an animation and entertainment empire famous throughout the world.

People can fail many times and still succeed but only if they refuse to accept defeat. Successful people view failure as a temporary setback rather than a permanent resolution. They persevere, refuse to give up, and try over and over again. Don't be afraid of failing; anticipate failure—it's an important part of success. The more you look, the more you will see the benefits of failure.

Anticipate failure. Do what you can to avoid taking a big stumble or making mistakes, but don't be surprised when you do. Anticipate failure before success, knowing that most people fail many times before they succeed. When you acknowledge that you might fail, it will be less upsetting if you do.

Study and learn from failure. Be a student of your own failure; learn from your mistakes. Take the time you need to evaluate your failures. Determine what went wrong and why. Decide what needs to change and what you will do differently the next time around.

Let go of failure. Don't dwell on your failures. Instead, focus on your successes. Take the time you need to regroup, but don't wait too long to pick yourself up and start over again. Each time you fail, you're one step closer to success.

Give yourself credit for trying. Don't be ashamed of failing. Don't be too hard on yourself or think you're a fool; you didn't do anything so wrong. You've got nothing to be embarrassed about.

People fail all the time. Those who never fail are those who never *try*. You're already ahead of others because you are willing to try.

Try again. Don't let your errors stop you from trying. If you want to move forward, you have to try over and over again. The more you try, the closer you will get to reaching a victory.

TIP # 99
You can make it through challenging economic times.

As I was being introduced at a recent event, I was standing back-stage as the announcer read my bio. As he mentioned the name of my most recent book, *How to Get a Job and Keep It,* there was laugh-ter among the audience, something I had never experienced before. I wasn't sure what prompted such an unusual response until I thought about it later that evening. I don't think people were laugh-ing because the title of the book was *funny;* I'm convinced the laughter reflected the uncertainty and fear among the crowd due to the recession and challenging economic times we were living in.

When economic times are tough, you can ask anyone and you will get an earful about how bad things are. Plenty of articles are written about businesses going bust, increasing numbers of the unemployed, and other documentation to assure us that all is *not* okay.

During a recession most people simply want to keep the jobs they have. Those who are unemployed need all the help and reas-surance they can get. I can't think of many people who *want* to read a book about how to get a job and keep it, but the reality is that we *need* information about protecting our careers whether we want it or not.

No, it isn't funny, but we laugh anyway. The fear of losing a job and not being able to find one is real.

I'm frequently asked what advice I have for people looking for work when times are tough.   The truth is that much of my advice and the concepts I talk about are timeless. There will always be competition for jobs. Each of us needs to do what we can to give ourselves a competitive advantage, regardless of the economic circumstances.

When the economy is strong and jobs aplenty, people are more relaxed—and often more *lax* in the effort they exert both on the job and in preparing themselves for what's next.

If you are looking for work and not finding what you want, be flexible. Even when all you hear about is a lack of jobs, keep in mind that there still *are* positions to be filled. You might not find your ideal job during challenging economic times, but there are opportunities for those who seek and create them.

Whether you are currently employed or looking for work, the following tips will help you manage the uncertainty of your future in both the good and the not-so-humorous, difficult times.

- Take care of yourself; don't look to your company, your boss, or anyone else to take care of you.

- Keep your resume up to date (whether you are employed or not).

- Be prepared: Ask yourself, "What if I lose my job—what will I do?"

- Develop new skills, take a class; diversify.

- Make the most of the job you have; be someone who adds value—someone irreplaceable. It may not save you from being laid off, but it could make a difference.

- Be proactive. Don't wait for the dreaded news of a layoff to make change—start preparing for change today.

- Use your youth to your advantage; many companies prefer hiring new grads

- Network. Keep in touch with classmates, teachers, former colleagues, etc., and continue to build your network. Your connections and relationships, if nurtured and tended to, will remain constant

- Tune out the doom and gloom. Avoid spending time with negative people. Keep away from people who only talk about how bad things are. Tune out the doom and gloom media.

- Look for the lesson to be learned. The challenges we are forced to face help us to learn and grow if we are willing to look for the lesson.

Most importantly, remain optimistic. Nothing lasts forever; this difficult time will pass. Try to find a reason to laugh. They say laughter is the best medicine; it might be just what you need to see you through a challenging time.

TIP # 100
There's no business like your own business.

This book includes information about how to find a job and achieve career success. Finding a job and working for someone else is a great way to get started on your path, however, it is not the only route nor must it be a permanent destination.

Many people dream of being their own boss. I've been an entrepreneur most of my life. When I was 10 years old I held a day camp in my parent's backyard. When I was 11, I printed up flyers and knocked on doors in search of babysitting jobs. I started working at a *real* job as soon as I was able at the age of 15. I took out my first loan after graduating from high school to become a Mary Kay consultant. I was hired for my first sales opportunity when I was 20, at a time when few women were in sales. At 22, I became an independent contractor with a sales organization and ran my own sales business for over 15 years. The knowledge I gained and the success I had over the years prompted me to start my own training and consulting firm that has led me to where I am today.

Owning and running a business has many advantages, but it isn't always as wonderful as it seems, nor is it for everyone. The reality is that being a sole proprietor can be a tough, long, and lonely road to travel. There are no guarantees when you are in business for yourself, but that hasn't stopped me, and it doesn't have to stop you either.

A survey conducted in December 2007 by the Kauffman Foundation for Entrepreneurship recently found that four out of 10 young people ages eight to 21 would like to start their own business in the future. Sixty-three percent of respondents agree that, through hard work, they have the ability to start their own business. Another 37 percent did not close the door to entrepreneurship, saying they were just unsure about it.

According to the survey, the top reasons for becoming entrepreneurs included the desire to use their skills and abilities, build something for their future, be their own boss, see their ideas realized, and earn lots of money.

The upside to owning a business is well touted, but it's the downside that needs to be carefully considered before making the leap. There are many perks to being in business for yourself, but it is far from easy. There is little financial stability until a business gets off the ground—and it can take years until it does.

You may have a brilliant idea, but it takes more than creativity to keep a business afloat. You need to know how to run a business too, or have the resources to hire someone to run the business for you. Managing a business is not for everyone, but it can be most gratifying if you do it right and the business succeeds.

When it comes to starting a business, there are few barriers. It is easier and less expensive to start a business today than in years past, thanks to the Internet. And, with an abundance of information at your fingertips, you have the ability to get answers to many of your questions instantly.

Some people are innovative and it is an idea or invention that gets them started. Other ideas for products and services are the result of a personal experience or realized need. For some it is the frustration of not finding a job or the demands of working for someone else that lead to self-employment.

Over a million new businesses are started each year—proof that the entrepreneurial spirit is alive and well. However, according to the Small Business Administration, more than 50 percent of small businesses fail within the first five years. Business ideas aren't hard to come by; it's putting the idea into action that people find more challenging. Starting a business isn't easy, but keeping it afloat is even more difficult.

Reading and hearing about the success of other entrepreneurs is inspiring, but sometimes misleading. By the time we hear about someone's success you can bet there were many misses along the way. It takes time to grow a business and see a profit.

There are certain qualities many accomplished business owners and entrepreneurs have in common. Do you think you have what it takes to start your own business?

Do you have self-discipline? When you are the boss, no one is going tell you what time to start or end your day or keep track of what you need to be doing. You will need to have the self-discipline and motivation to put in your time. You will be the one to create and do the work that needs to be done. You will need to monitor and keep track of your progress; no one else will do that for you. Do you have the discipline you'll need to do the work and see things through?

Do you have self-confidence? Confidence is an essential characteristic of almost all successful entrepreneurs and business owners. You must believe in yourself and the product or service you represent. You will need to be the cheerleader for your idea even when your belief in what you are doing will be questioned and challenged. You will face many obstacles and naysayers when you are on your own. Does hearing someone say it can't be done get you down? Do you have the self-confidence you need to face the adversity?

Do you have stamina and determination? Starting and running a business requires hard work and long hours. Being your own boss can mean doing the work of many people. Successful entrepreneurs aren't deterred by negativity or setbacks; it fuels their fire and the resolve to succeed. Do you have the stamina and determination to hang in there when the going gets tough?

Are you self-reliant? When you are in business for yourself, you and only you are accountable and responsible for your results. Setting and achieving goals are in your hands: Are you able to admit when you've made a mistake and change course when necessary? Are you willing to take 100 percent responsibility for what happens?

If you are determined, tenacious and willing to take a risk, then you might just have what it takes to launch your own business. Put your ideas onto paper and into action. Opportunity awaits you!

TIP # 101
Never give up on your dreams.

I was working on writing my final few tips when my daughter, Stephanie, and I were talking about my dreams for this book. She asked me *why* I decided to write the book. There were and are so many reasons that I had trouble giving her a simple answer. Writing this book was something I wanted to do, but even more, it was something I was *compelled* to do.

When I came up with the idea for this book, I assumed it would be similar to other projects I've done. It wasn't. Because this is a book about *life,* with each tip I wrote, I looked closely at how I was living it in my own life. I couldn't write authentically about something I hadn't dealt with or didn't know about, so in the process of writing I discovered work I had to do. As I encouraged you to grow and change, I was growing and changing too.

If anyone had told me when I was younger about the things I'd be doing today, I wouldn't have believed a word. In fact, no one else would have believed it either. I wasn't a failure, but I wasn't much of a success either. I can't say I've struggled as much as some people, but I've had my share of challenges and obstacles and have learned many of life's lessons the *hard* way.

It's one of the many reasons I wrote this book. I don't want you to struggle more than you have to. I want you to understand what's expected of you, what works, and what doesn't. I want you to make the most of yourself and your life. Most of all, I want you to believe in your dreams—to know that anything is possible. It doesn't matter who you've been. Your future success is a result of who you become.

People frequently assume I'm a journalist or communications major, but I am not. I wasn't a star student in any classroom, and I didn't graduate from a prestigious university. However, I'm sure I would have received all A's if I'd been graded on what I learned as a student of *life*. I've always been a dreamer and determined to excel despite the adversity I faced.

I know you've heard it before, but have you ever really thought about what it means to *never give up on your dreams?*

It takes courage to dream. It's lonely when you have to defend something only you can see. It's not easy when people question your motives or discourage you. It takes strength to hold on to a dream you fear is slipping away. *Will you hold on to your dreams?* More than anything, I hope you do.

You have everything going for you. You've just completed the first few chapters of your life. Part of your story is written; the rest is yet to be told. *You* are the author and you've got empty pages to fill. Only you can determine the details of the story that will eventually be a reflection of the way you've lived your life.

Writing a book isn't easy. Some people have a tough time getting started; others struggle when they reach the end. It's not easy facing yourself. You won't always like what you see, but through the experience you will learn and grow. When you reach the final chapter you will see how close you came to fulfilling your dreams. You can either wait or decide now what you want your outcome to be.

The *only* reason I've accomplished anything, including writing the final words in this book, is because I *dared to dream* and *never quit.*

There are 101 tips in this book, and there is valuable information in each and every one.

The message I leave you with, however, is most crucial and is what I wish most for you:

Never **give up on your dreams.**

Appendix

Extra Credit Bonus Insights

I had no idea what I would find when I began my research for this book. I had plenty of my own advice to offer new graduates, and I had a feeling others had just as much to say. I wanted to provide the right mix of advice and didn't want to miss anything important. There's so much I wish I had known earlier in my life and I was sure there were others who felt the same. They did, and they responded to my request. I asked a selection of people working in a variety of industries the following questions:

What advice would you give to a recent graduate about to enter the "real" world?

What is the best advice you ever received and how did it affect you?

What's the most important lesson you've learned since your graduation?

If you had it to do all over again, what would you do differently?

Many people selflessly offered to share their personal stories, words of wisdom, and hard-learned insights. The majority of responses came through e-mail, although I did conduct a number of interviews over the phone. Some people offered their comments and asked for no attribution, preferring to remain anonymous. Others requested only their names be used. Still others included their names, titles, and company information, and each quote that follows has been attributed according to the wishes of the person who gave it. All, however, contributed because they want to help you, the new graduate, get a jumpstart on your personal and professional success.

Experience really is the best teacher, and you will learn the most from your own personal experiences. No matter how many times you hear something, it will always have more impact when you can relate firsthand to the information you receive. However, the more knowledge you have and the more aware you are, the better able you will be to make good decisions and deal with whatever you face. These insights can help prepare you for what's ahead and help guide you as you grow and make important decisions about your future.

This extra section is filled with bonus tips for you. You get "extra credit" for reading them, but the real credit goes to each and every person who took the time to respond. These insights represent the various responses I received, and I am sure you will find value in what is here. For easy referencing, these insights have been broken down into the same categories as the other tips in this book. I am sure you will enjoy reading what others have to say and will benefit from their experience and I trust you'll refer to these insights often.

WORK SKILLS

Find a job in a company that you are passionate about. Take any job necessary to get your foot in the door and be prepared to prove yourself over and over again until they can't help but notice your pure and total genius. Make yourself indispensable. Do not expect them to see said genius until you have consistently exhibited it over and over again. Work really hard. But don't forget to stay well rounded outside of the job as well. If you get lost in the job, you will lose yourself when you lose that job.

Carrie Heckman,
Vice President of Marketing,
Civilian Pictures

Growing up we all hear, "Just do your best." Well, one of the hardest lessons for me to learn was that sometimes your best is not good enough....Sometimes you will lose the game, the client, or the account. At times like these, I look at the process. Did I do everything I could to achieve the outcome I wanted? If you did everything you could...that is your best. You may not be a winner, but you win because you gave it your best.

Susan Edwards, M.S.,
3D Productivity Consulting

Making mistakes is one of the critical ways that people learn. It is okay to make mistakes; however, it is important to keep making new mistakes. When you make a mistake, it gets you curious about how to fix it. Don't spend time trying to find the source of whom or what to blame; figure out what you can do to prevent the mistake from happening next time and move on.

Robbin Walker

Think of each job you have in your career as a learning and growing experience. The first few may not be the "job of your dreams" but work hard, focus, and keep a positive attitude. Do this and you'll develop yourself into a valuable resource, and people will notice. Never quit without another job lined up. Eventually you'll be the executive admiring a recent graduate with the same dedicated work ethic!

Alexander M. Costakis,
Managing Director,
Hollywood Stock Exchange, LLC

As hard as it may seem, doing a good job for your employer because it is the right thing to do makes all the difference in job satisfaction. Can you imagine the uncommon reactions from bosses and coworkers when you respond to criticism and even unfair treatment when you are motivated by doing the right thing. I strongly advise...be on time, stay a little later than most, and if you promise a deliverable, then [meet the] deadline.

Steve Hall, C.P.C.,
Senior Consultant, FGP International

It is important to remember that it takes time to prove yourself to a company. Have some patience. Go above and beyond what is expected and learn from everything you can and your opportunities for getting ahead will come.

Let someone know what you want—a boss, another manager, someone you can trust. It's hard to get what you want if no one knows you want it.

Be flexible, be open to new opportunities, take some chances, and you'll have an interesting and rewarding life. Many people will never know the "right answer" to the question, "What do I want to be?" but they can have a fun ride trying to figure it out.

Anonymous

I have learned that it is really important to have some expertise, knowledge, or skill in one thing versus a little bit of knowledge in many things.

Robin Stein

Whatever you do, love it. No matter how small the task, put your all into it. When I care about what I'm doing, I not only enjoy my work more, but I take more from it—skills, insight, etc.—that I can apply to bigger jobs in the future.

Laurie Katz,
Director of Publicity, Facts On File, Inc.

One of the things I learned about being in the career services industry is that a recent grad's first job sets the pace for his or her entire career. This is why it is important for them to not take the first offer that comes along.

Linda Matias,
President, CareerStrides and the
National Resume Writers' Association

One way or another, as pressured as I felt at the moment, as overwhelming as it all seemed, it all gets done. Once I truly embraced that concept, I was healthier in my outlook, relaxed more, and was more balanced. I still work very hard. But now I know to trust that it all gets done.

Maggie Mortenson

Don't enter any job thinking your diploma will get you through because it will not. The diploma only opens the door, but you still must prove yourself. I would tell any young person entering the business world "you must earn the respect and confidence of your coworkers and superiors."

Anonymous

Over the years I've worked in both large corporate settings and small businesses, in all sectors—private, nonprofit, and profit. The most important things I wish I'd known when I graduated are: (1) to do even the smallest and most menial tasks cheerfully and well, and (2) to realize that my job was to make my boss look good. It all starts with doing the small stuff.

Anonymous

One of the first things for a graduate to realize is that your first job may help determine the direction of your career, but it is not the only determinant. This means that one has to consider a given job at hand from many different perspectives [other] than just the immediate role or job definition. [Such as] what skills does it [the job] use and what skills may it help develop?

Shefaly Yogendra,
Technology Policy and Strategy Consultant

Your degree is an accomplishment. It doesn't entitle you to anything. The effort you put forth and the attitude that you approach your work and others with can either help you or hurt you...as you enter the work world.

LaChel Hird,
LarsonAllen

While employee benefits are important considerations, ask a prospective employer about their corporate culture. If they value their employees as one of their best assets, you may be on the path toward a rewarding and fulfilling career.

Sandra D. Bullock,
Vice President Institutional Sales,
Wells Fargo Brokerage Services, LLC

Be cognizant of the environment that you choose to work in. Toxic work life can infect, negatively, all areas of your life. Realize that you do have choices and yet, that doesn't mean you won't have to work hard. Keep your options open.

Peggy L. McNamara,
Author of *My Tender Soul – A Story of Survival*

Find a mentor and maximize the relationship. Focus on what will make you successful in the company culture and key things you can do to stand out.

Danielle Devine,
Vice President, Public Relations,
Johnson & Johnson Personal Products Company

COMMUNICATION SKILLS

Be trustworthy. Don't get involved in the gossip mill. Keep confidences. Keep your word.

Anonymous

Admit mistakes as soon as possible. These can impact company monies and your professional reputation, so it is wise to address these quickly to prevent bigger issues. An employee who readily admits he made the mistake earns more respect than the employee who doesn't own up to the error.

Anonymous

Be a sponge—listening is critical. Don't feel compelled to comment on everything; it's okay to be in [a] learning mode.

Danielle Devine,
Vice President, Public Relations,
Johnson & Johnson Personal Products Company

Never lie. None of us has a good enough memory to remember everything we've ever said to everyone. Conversely, almost everyone possesses a gift for remembering everything anyone ever said to them. If you're caught in a lie, your credibility is damaged for a long time, if not forever. That's too high a price to pay. Tell the truth or remain silent, but never, never lie.

Sharron Stockhausen,
CEO, Expert Publishing, Inc.

My mother once told me that "Confidence is a double-edged sword. Possessing too much or too little can be disastrous. Use it wisely and you will get ahead."

An individual's confidence level says much about the person, and nowhere is it more scrutinized than in a job interview. Job interviews are usually a one-shot chance to get the door opened further. A candidate is judged from the minute they enter the room. Character assessments are subjective and are made from a person's carriage, posture, and diction. Too little confidence is offensive and can be construed as someone who thinks they know it all. Success is reached when the candidate has the ability to discern the degree of confidence the interviewer is looking for and give them what they want. In other words, a successful candidate doesn't…sweat and knows when to keep his/her mouth shut.

Anonymous

Practice communicating! Take informal courses on interviewing techniques; learn to clearly articulate ideas, with concise and brief answers; get to the point; do not go off on tangents; utilize examples in your discussions; discuss how you can help the other (company, or person, or business, etc.)

Be prepared! Separate yourself from the rest of the crowd by being ready, well prepared, punctual, and do one thing different, better, and more special than the others. Leave something behind, make an impression, ensure they remember you, ensure they talk about you, stay focused, and be patient.

Henry Stein

Listen to friends; sometimes they see you better than you see yourself. I only hope that young people starting out have a good support system and can communicate with people that they trust to help them find what it is that they really want to do with their lives.

Anonymous

Always seek to improve your communication skills, both verbal and written. You'll never regret, on a personal or professional level, your improved ability to influence the world you live in.

Danita Bye

Talk to knowledgeable people about your concerns. It's your life. Ask lots of questions.

Anonymous

LEADERSHIP SKILLS

Be yourself. There is nothing more attractive than genuineness and authenticity.

Maggie Mortenson

The best business advice I ever got was that, in the long run, people hit only what they aim at. It is a bit corny, but I think true. I think that Thoreau said it first. The worst business's quote I ever heard was "ready, shoot, aim".... This was considered a truism during the dot-com boom. That didn't work out very well.

Barry Poltermann,
CEO, Civilian Pictures

The best advice [I received] was provided by my father, who instilled in me qualities of high standards, high ethics, high morals, and offered me the advice that taking the high road would pay off most of the time, while trying to cut corners or cheat one's way through might pay off some of the time, but not often enough to make a difference.

Henry Stein

View all things as a learning opportunity. This will keep you fresh and open to innovative thinking. By striving to keep this as my mantra I am amazed at the opportunities that have been opened to me and the things I've learned along the way. It has also given me the confidence to share what I've learned with others.

Attitude is critical. A positive attitude allows you to be more likeable, approachable, and seems to be character strength in a leader during times of crisis.

One characteristic that I have observed in my own boss and many others that I have had the privilege to meet is "humbleness." There is no room for egos.

Marilyn Williams,
Executive Assistant to CEO, Best Buy Co., Inc.

Be an insatiable learner. You competition is getting better every day . . . you need to keep learning, stretching, and growing your own skills and beliefs. Commit to excellence in all that you do. Your work is your reputation.

Danita Bye

Many times life offers choices or opportunities that may look scary—because you might fail, because you might be laughed at, because it may turn out different than you think—but simply the opportunity itself will, no doubt, be a growing experience that will make you stronger and more self-confident. This is especially true as a young adult when so many opportunities present themselves in a variety of ways.

Maureen Fischer

Make a great plan. I believe that moving forward in life is what makes life interesting. Being afraid to try something new, not being challenged, waiting until you are forced to make a decision rather than making your own choices are things that make life boring...keep challenging yourself...find your own way.

Carol Rockler Chesen,
Edina Realty, Inc.

The biggest challenge for graduates is the difference in expectations from school to work (no excuses, no grades, etc.). The most important attribute is to show how you take responsibility and solve problems (rather than wait to be told, blame others, etc.)

Sherron Bienvenu, Ph.D.,
Professor Emerita, Emory University

The best advice I've received is from my former boss, Craig Palmer. He told me about the rule he uses called the "Three I's." You use this rule to help in decision making. The rule is, "What you Initiate, think through all of the Implications and the Impact it may have in all directions." The Three I's are Initiate, Implications, and Impact.

Here's how it works. [Ask] exactly what do I want to initiate? (In one sentence, what is the crux of the idea?) Next, [ask] what are the implications? Lastly, if the idea is used, what are the ways it could impact others?

Debi Cain-Rivord,
TwinCities West Chapter of the International Association of Administrative Professionals (IAAP)

SOCIAL SKILLS

People are the corporation or the school or the small business. The world of work is very diverse. Work is about more than just being smart and knowing the technical parts of your job—it is also about building relationships (one person at a time), connecting with others, and being respectful to [sic] any differences that may exist. Be "real"—everyone may not like you, but the people who do like you will like the real you.

Robbin Walker

Attend company functions, even if you have to attend alone. It is important to show you're supportive of any company event, if possible. You also will be enriched by meeting other people in your company.

Anonymous Office Manager

Get involved in company events, fund-raising, etc. If the company is dedicated to raising money for the United Way, join a committee. Always talk with your manager/supervisor first to let them know your plans and assure them that this committee will not interfere with your job performance. This participation will enable you to do some good and your name will be known within the company as a team player. Ensure you follow through with anything you commit to.

Anonymous

My advice would be to treat others as you would like others to treat you, and have a mind-set for service.

Mark Neumann,
Comptroller, Essex Property Trust

Early on in my high school and college years I was taught by some very special role models that if you help enough other people succeed, then you will indeed find potentially greater joy than if you focus on your own needs to the exclusion of others.

Steve Hall C.P.C.,
Senior Consultant, FGP International

My advice is to those who would love to live in a specific region of the country. Aim your job search very specifically at that area. It is much harder than you might think to move after you have held a job in another region for a period of time. You are invested in staying with that employer, you may marry someone from that region, your friends are there, and so on.

Suzanne Nelson

Treat everyone you meet with respect and honesty. You never know when or where your paths will cross again in this ever shrinking world. People are bridges to other people, opportunity, and success.

Karen Winner

I've learned not to prejudge people and situations. So many things are not what they seem . . . . Give things time…see more; meet more people; try more situations, both comfortable and uncomfortable. Be open to change because it's the only guaranteed situation you're going to find.

Anonymous

I've learned that as independent as I am, and like to be, I still need help from other people to achieve my goals…I need others to think highly of me, speak highly of me, and want to help me, which means I have to do my part first: To always give and speak well of others so that I can receive the same.

Peggy L. McNamara,
Author of *My Tender Soul – A Story of Survival*

It's not what you know or how well you did in school—it's getting your foot in the door! The best way to do this is to use your existing network of friends, relatives, and acquaintances. Be shameless.

Be sure to send each one a thank you note and tell them how helpful they were and ask them to keep you in mind if they hear of anything. Then be sure to send them a note when you do get a job, and thank them again for their help. You will then have a large mentoring group in your own industry to call upon for advice and other referrals. Be sure to update them on your progress and send them all holiday cards. Also, ask them what groups you could join that would be helpful for the industry and for networking in general. Then join the groups and keep active.

Anonymous

Always keep your eyes and ears open through friends, family, and acquaintances. You never know who is looking for employee prospects…never write off previous friends/relationships—you never know when they will come back.

Nancy Shiff

Know that life's daily annoyances really aren't important. The most important elements in anyone's life, at any age, are family, friends, health, and happiness. The rest is "small stuff."

David Abramsage,
Writer, HGTV's "Designers' Challenge"

Work hard, but always remember that good relationships with those you value are more important than any paycheck! Good relationships, like anything worthwhile, take lots of hard work.

Anonymous

Become familiar with current events—read a national newspaper and a local paper. This should be done no less frequently than once each week, daily, if possible. Reading a current events magazine once in awhile is a good idea as well.

Anonymous

SELF-DISCIPLINE

Climbing the corporate ladder, making money, working long hours is no guarantee of personal happiness or measure of success. Finding the right balance between work and play is a key component to success and happiness...the scale of balance will shift depending on where you are in life. I think everyone should check in with himself or herself periodically and ask: Am I having fun? Am I focused at work or am I distracted? Where's my mind—here today, or thinking about the future?

If you're overworked and not taking time for yourself, distracted at work, and worrying about the future, it's time for realignment. Listen to the message your body is giving you.

Sandra D. Bullock,
Vice President, Institutional Sales

Be patient. Very seldom do you begin your career at peak. Develop an appreciation for what you learn and accomplish along the way to your goals.

Anonymous

Education counts! Getting an education is so important and will make a difference for the rest of one's life.

Anonymous

Find what you enjoy doing and build a career around it. Don't assume you already know by virtue of your major.

Rock Anderson,
Director of Recruiting Services and Diversity, Siemens Corporation

Follow your heart and your head. Years ago when I was younger, my motivation was money, promotion, status, etc. I was successful, but it felt empty. My heart urged me to pursue writing. My head told me to pursue financial success. Now, many years later, I know that I could have listened to my head and my heart and found a way to satisfy both. That's what I'm doing now and I'm very happy.

Wanda Craig,
W. B. Craig & Associates, Inc.

Keep a rolling account of your achievements, both at the workplace and outside (community, charity work, etc.). Review your strengths and weaknesses objectively and identify what skills, beyond the obvious and [the] technical/functional, you used in a given situation. Examples of such skills might be persuasion, team motivation, leadership, conflict resolution.

Shefaly Yogendra,
Technology Policy and Strategy Consultant

Write down your goals. Some people do this in December; I like to do it around my birthday every year. I have goals in every area: personal, financial, spiritual, professional, etc. Think about what you want and focus on what's really important.

Danielle Voorhies,
Strategic Angle Marketing

If I could do anything differently, I would have followed my instinct and passion. It may have been difficult but I think I would have been happier with my career. I would have taken the risk instead of the safe way out.

Darlene Moss,
Career Development Coordinator, West Stanly High School

Follow your gut instinct. Sometimes when making a decision or hearing information, I turn it around in my head before acting on or absorbing it. However, sometimes I get an immediate "feeling"—a gut reaction—and I've learned that I should listen to it. If something seems "off," it probably is.

Keep learning. No matter what career you choose, most likely it is evolving all the time. To be successful, you need to actively pursue education and keep up to date with current trends.... Continuing education doesn't mean you need to continue going to college or take night classes. It can be as simple as attending a one-hour program once a month or a few-days program once or twice a year. Unless it's so expensive you can't afford it, sign up and consider it an investment in your future.

Debi Cain-Rivord

Focus on family and friends. They are the ones that will be there after you've been laid off, switched jobs, and struggled with bad bosses and companies. They will be your foundation and support during the inevitable changes in the business world.

Even when all you want to do is slam the alarm clock to stay in bed, knowing that your family and friends support you will help you peel away those warm protective sheets and deal with another day. Keep plugging away. Don't give up!

Michael Fisk,
Manager, New Media, MGM Studios

Trust the process. Being as impatient as I am, I tend to want things to happen right now, and the world doesn't always work that way. Trust the process simply means that if you go out every day and do the best you can with what you have, the results will show—eventually.

Anonymous

Your life is a sacred journey and path. Follow your vision with passion and take pride in the things of the heart which matter to you. Be unwilling to compromise your integrity. As you stand before it, at the end of each day, the mirror reflects your image's perspective. This reflection is the only one you must answer to.

Cary Brayboy,
Certified Personal Trainer,
Founder of Grey Wolf Fitness

As a new grad, remember, the most important step is to find that first job. Preferably in your field, but any job will get you into the world of work, and following a routine—getting up in the morning, learning the responsibility of being somewhere on time, putting in a full day of work, learning how to work with different people, etc. Also keep in mind that even if your first job is not your "dream" job or the job you want, to work hard, and learn as much as you can. Find a way to learn skills that can be used to get that next job up the ladder.

And if your salary is not what you want, remember, with experience comes better pay and better jobs. No matter what the profession, if you put the time, effort, and your all into it, the financial aspect of the career will eventually come.

Also, don't compare your job or your salary to your friends and other recent grads. People start out doing different things in different ways, and always remember it's not where you start, but where you finish.

Matt Krumrie,
Writer

I would encourage you to know who you are and what your values are and revisit those every time you need to make a major decision, whether it be personal or business.

Anonymous

Save money! When you get that first job you see an immediate rise in income. Start saving before you get used to spending the extra money. Maximize all 401(k) and employer matched retirement funds. If your employer matches, you save double.

Anonymous

Take 100 percent responsibility for yourself and your relationships. Too many people go through life with the attitude, "I am only 20 percent or 50 percent responsible for the success of this project or this relationship."

My dad used to say, "We create our own problems." Before I blame others, [I] first look in the mirror and ask myself, "What did I do or fail to do that may have caused this situation to occur?" There is a tremendous feeling of freedom when we are willing to accept responsibility for our actions or inactions.

Mike Norman,
President, Michael D. Norman & Associates

Believe in yourself—nobody knows you better than you....Listen to your heart. Do what you love, and you will do it well, and find a way to make money at it.

Anonymous

Look at the future and make choices based on your dreams. Finish your education while you are young and head for the big time.

Anonymous

The best advice I ever got was "Finish" from an author. He said there were many great writers in the world, but not many of them finish. Don't think that anything you choose is a life sentence. People change direction all the time and everything you do can help lead you to another exciting chapter in your life.

Wendy Baldinger,
Singer/Songwriter

The challenge for the graduate . . . is how to keep current and what to pay attention to. My "keep current" system is my rule of three. If I hear it, am exposed to it in any way three times, I check it out because something is going on. The "it" can be a book, a concept, [a] term, a company, a person. Whatever "it" is, I check it out.

My passionate commitment to being a lifelong learner and professional in my field is to read each day for one hour. . . . I heard that if you read for one hour a day in your field, in time you will be as knowledgeable as the perceived gurus in that field.

Beth Fischer

Go get some experience. Travel. Work at a non-profit or Starbuck's (where you will probably end up anyway for the next six months while you are searching). Get involved. Make a difference. Learn. Go to grad school (most definitely, go to grad school). Make mistakes. Have fun. Raise some Cain. You are still at an age where you can get away with it.

Don't be 40 years old with 15 or more years work experience and have nothing to show for it but a mortgage and a paunch. You will need those memories of good times as the work gets harder and the responsibilities such as marriage and kids come around.

There will always be time for work.

Rob Gelphman,
Principal, Gelphman Associates

If you have things in your life emotionally or physically that are stopping you from being the person you want to be, put considerable energy into working on those things. These may seem like personal issues, but they can dramatically impact your ability to make good business and career decisions, and they can impact your behavior on the job.

Beth Spencer

Don't let your age stop you from getting the education you want to change your life. Be willing to start at the bottom of your chosen profession.

Betty McMahon Buman

Don't think you're going to get your dream job immediately. It is going to take a lot of hard work, perseverance, and soul searching. Think with your head, but listen to your heart too.

Bonnie Blumenthal Stein

You're responsible for your own fiscal survival. This means that the majority of your activity from the minute you get out of bed until your work day ends is centered around making money. You have no control over your schedule whatsoever. You have to be in the office when your employer says you have to be, with little room for negotiation.

Anonymous

DEMONSTRATE A POSITIVE ATTITUDE

Stay open to different opportunities. It's okay not to plan every detail of the future. Sometimes you "fall" into opportunities that are better than anything you could have predicted or planned in advance.

Laurie Katz,
Director of Publicity, Facts On File, Inc.

I'd be less inhibited by fear. Fear will do you in every time. Don't be afraid to take risks, don't be afraid to stand alone, don't be afraid to ask questions, don't be afraid of rejection or failure. Everyone falls down; the people who are successful are the ones who get up and dust themselves off and keep going.

Try to excel no matter what you do—giving your all is very important, and people will recognize that you're a hard worker. But know that there is no shame in failing— the only shame is in not trying.

David Abramsage,
Writer, HGTV's "Designers' Challenge"

The only person you can really control in your life is yourself. Therefore, learn to really like yourself—put a lot into your life so you will be comfortable with who you are.

Leslie,
Interior Designer

A recent graduate may feel intimidated or insecure due to lack of experience. I would suggest they act confidently, even if they're not. I would also recommend talking to someone who has done what they want to do. We can all learn from someone else's experience. Whether they are going to further their education or look for a job, the world is a scary place and you have to be competitive. Look people in the eye, give them a firm handshake, and sell yourself. Look for opportunities and make it happen.

Anonymous

Money isn't everything. Family, friends, and loved ones will ultimately make you happy.

Walter Keen Wilkins,
Research Manager, Earthlink, Inc.

The best advice I ever got was from my dad. He told me that if I worked hard, treated people with respect, and always did my best, that I could have any career that I wanted. He suggested that I find out what made me unique as that uniqueness would make me stand out from the other grads. He said that I was the only one who could limit my dreams.

Carol Fredrickson,
Violence Free

Figure out what your unique abilities are. I think too many people choose careers for the wrong reason. . . . I think when people are doing what they love and are inherently good at, work doesn't become a burden.

Anonymous

Be true to yourself, be honest, have balance in your life, always maintain a sense of humor, listen, and treat others as you would expect to be treated.

Beth Sterling,
VP Sales, BizRate.com

Follow your heart, dream big, and be persistent. If you get knocked down, dust off the dirt and strap your shoes on better. Look at everything as an experience and a stepping stone to the next level. There truly is no bad experience—it's all good learning. And the learning should never stop. Risks are something you need to take to get to where you want to go. Just look before you leap.

Holly Jo Anderson,
Veritas Marketing, LLC

Realize that the company will hire you only if it is to their benefit and not to yours. Remember, the purpose of Human Resources is to screen you out. They do not hire you; they just keep you from being hired.

Ernie Simpson,
President, Wizardco International, Inc.

Some voices are more equal than others . . . expect to have a voice, expect to offer an opinion, and at the same time, don't expect to have everything go your way. Cream rises to the top . . . don't ever feel you are too good to do anything you are assigned. It isn't the task you're completing that establishes your worth; it's your attitude. Be positive, and you'll rise to the top.

Anonymous

AREAS OF DISTINCTION

Everyone is on his or her own timetable, his own journey, and that success is defined by oneself, not by peers or the media or society. The path that you take to success is right for you. It might not be the path traveled by everyone else, and that's okay. And sometimes the road less taken is indeed the most interesting path of all.

David Abramsage,
Writer, HGTV's "Designers' Challenge"

Learn how money works first. Learn how and how much to save, how to protect yourself, and how to take advantage of different tax structures legitimately.

Usah Christi

It would be wise . . . to talk with someone working in his/her chosen field of employment and residence to become at least slightly more conscious of current practices, trends in practice and ways of life, including local politics, where the person plans to live.

Anonymous

Fresh out of high school I loved music and cars. Without a real vehicle for music I went with the auto industry. Years later I was camping in a remote island with no power, no phones—nothing. But I had a cell phone and pager so BMW could reach me on vacation. When I returned home I handed in my resignation and went to audio school. Twelve months later I was hired by a firm in Dallas and sent out on a Rolling Stones tour. Since then I've been around the world with multiple national recording artists, and although the money is not quite as much as before and the work is grueling at times, it was the best move I've ever made. I have no regrets. Find your passion.

Mical Caterina

Get involved. Make a commitment to keep learning and growing as an individual. Get involved in industry associations. Spend time with people you admire or people who have done what you strive to do. The fact is we're all going to change careers several times, and when you find a new job, it is usually the result of knowing someone, not answering an ad in the paper.

Danielle Voorhies
Strategic Angle Marketing

You can find your biggest victories in your worst defeats. Failure allows you to see what type of people you need to surround yourself with to succeed. And, ultimately, in failure you have an end point. Many people pass through their lives being just okay. They never stop to think about what could be because they are comfortable. Failure is not comfortable; it forces you to change directions. If you play it safe, you will lead an average existence.

Stephanie Ratko,
Marketing Communications, FinancialAid.com

Always assume that your employer will never give you enough training, and much of what you learn will be "on the job" training. Also, assume that someone at work will be angry with you for not knowing what no one ever taught you. That's life.

Mistakes will be often forgiven, if you disclose them early enough. Rare is the mistake that can't be corrected, if you disclose it early enough.

The contemplation of an act is worse than its execution.

When it feels like the world is closing in on you, take time to do something mildly irresponsible. Go for a walk. Shut the door and take a catnap. Refuse to accept incoming calls.

Anonymous

Be prepared—never assume anything and be ready for everything. Good thought, but difficult to do!

Realize that you don't know everything. Find an older person to bounce ideas off of and listen, listen, listen to what they have to say.

Learn how to give to others—by helping others, volunteering, sharing what you have, mission trips to third world countries, etc. By giving, you receive much more in return than you ever gave.

I would expand my horizons a bit more, try new things more quickly, and not take myself so seriously at times. I would laugh more.

It is essential to help young people to recognize their strengths and help them utilize them. Not to settle, but excel. To hold out for what they want, and believe in achieving it.

Anonymous

Pay most attention to corporate culture. How you are treated will mean the most in whether you like your job.

Sherron Bienvenu, Ph.D.,
Professor Emerita, Emory University

Although I have been very blessed with my career, I believe pursuing a college degree would have been beneficial. I was married right out of high school and had to wait for my husband to finish college before we could afford for me to go. After four years of waiting, I was ready to settle down and college was the furthest thing from my mind. I wish I had pursued my passion of having a degree in business. Although my years of experience have helped me achieve my goals, I believe a college education would have given me more opportunities.

Anonymous Entrepreneur

I learned as a senior in high school that believing in something greater than yourself was the key to living in this world.

Steve Hall C.P.C.,
Senior Consultant, FGP International

I think the very most important thing to search for when choosing a career is to find something that you can enjoy doing, and then put all of your energy into it. If you can, at the end of the day, honestly say that you'd do whatever it is that you were doing for free as if you didn't need the money, then you have truly hit the jackpot.

Barry Witkow,
Vice President, Software Solutions, eSpeed, Inc.

Index

speech patterns 15, 56–60
spending. *See* money
Spielberg, Steven 237
Stallone, Sylvester 236
Streisand, Barbra 237
stress management 178–180
success
    believing in your 229–232
    celebrating 216
    commitment to 106
    drive toward 106–107
    meaning of 5
successful people
    learning from failure 236–238
    practices of 106–108
swearing 80–81

T

talking. *See* conversations
team players 92, 107, 118
technology precautions 156–159. *See also*
    computers
temporary work 28
tetanus shots 185–186
text messages 35, 54–56
thankfulness
    showing 150–152
    for what you have 5, 197–198
"thank you," saying 78–79
thank-you notes 151
time
    face vs. screen 147–148
    management of 171–175
    for yourself 160–161
timing
    of interviews 28
    of phone calls 27–28
toxic people 217–220

treatment of others 141–142, 201
truth, telling the 74–75
TV 147, 148
Twitter 119–120

U

understanding people 5
unemployment, dealing with 47–50
the unexpected
    making someone's day with 192
    planning for 173

V

values 5
vocabulary 79–81
voice
    improving 56–60
    in interviews 15
    in phone calls 64
voice mail 65–66, 173
volunteering 221–223

W

wants
    asking for 100–102
    vs. needs 155
Web. *See* Internet
willingness 5
words vs. actions 141
work. *See* job
work and play balance 114–117
work skills 1–50, 247–250
worry 211
writing
    daily plans 172, 174
    journal 161
    proofreading of 68–70